D1568472

Praise for 'The Complete Walt Disney Wo

> "It's so well done... If you are going to Walt Disney World and you don't have this book you're making a mistake."
—*Rudy Maxa, "Rudy Maxa's World," National Public Radio*

> "Seriously thorough." —*Family Circle*

> "Highly recommended." —*New York Daily News*

> "Leaves fans of Mickey smiling from ear to ear." —*Chicago Tribune*

> "A thorough overview, with inside tips." —*Boston Globe*

> "Far and away the best guide to Disney." —*St. Louis Post-Dispatch*

> "Unusual details that matter to families." —*Orlando Sentinel*

> "Our favorite Disney guidebook." —*Ft. Worth Star Telegram*

> "Endless tips and trivia." —*Knoxville News-Sentinel*

> "Very detailed descriptions." —*Florida Times Union (Jacksonville)*

> "Simply fun. Immerses you in the magic." —*Kirkus Reviews*

> "Definitely the book to purchase." —*Midwest Book Review*

> "The ultimate Walt Disney World guidebook." —*Writer's Digest*

> "Visually engaging." —*Library Journal*

Awards and honors

> **Outstanding Family Product.** *Disney's iParenting Media Awards.*

> **Travel Guide of the Year.** *2012 ForeWord Reviews Awards; 2012 Next Generation Indie Book Awards; 2010–2012 Int'l Book Awards; 2008–2011 Nat'l Independent Excellence Awards; 2010, 2012 Benjamin Franklin Awards (silver medal); 2009 ForeWord Reviews Awards (silver); 2009 Living Now Book Awards (silver); 2008 Nat'l Best Book Awards (finalist)*

> **Travel/Family Activity Book of the Year.** *2010 Living Now Book Awards; 2009 Living Now Book Awards (silver medal)*

> **Nonfiction Book of the Year.** *2009 National Independent Excellence Book Awards; 2008 Writer's Digest International Book Awards*

> **Book of the Year.** *2012 Eric Hoffer Book Awards (finalist)*

> **Best Interior Design.** *2010 International Book Awards (finalist)*

> **Reference Book of the Year.** *2009 Writer's Digest International Book Awards (silver medal)*

> **Best Southeast Nonfiction.** *2008 Independent Publisher Book Awards (silver medal)*

The Complete Walt Disney World Fun Finds & Hidden Mickeys
ISBN 978-0-9903716-2-5

Writing and research: Julie Neal
Photography: Mike Neal
Additional photography, writing and research: Micaela Neal

Produced by Coconut Press Media Inc.
Published by Keen Communications, LLC
Manufactured in the United States of America
Distributed by Publishers Group West

To Jeff and Dawn Riordan, and Jay and Jenn Wakelin. Our inspirations.

The Complete

Walt Disney World® Fun Finds & Hidden Mickeys

JULIE AND MIKE NEAL

Contents

6 What's a Fun Find?
And what's a Hidden Mickey?

8 Magic Kingdom
10 The Haunted Mansion
52 Jungle Cruise
68 Pirates of the Caribbean
82 Big Thunder Mountain Railroad
104 Also at Magic Kingdom

188 Epcot

196 Disney's Hollywood Studios
198 Star Tours
212 Also at Hollywood Studios

226 Disney's Animal Kingdom

244 Water Parks

254 Index

What's a Fun Find?

THE THEME PARKS AND WATER PARKS of Walt Disney World stand out from those run by other companies in that they're filled with little details—in-jokes, props, sight gags, story elements and tributes that appear right in front of you but that you're not really supposed to see. Perhaps they just blend together to form a landscape. Maybe at the time you're near one your attention is—by design—supposed to be on something else, like walking into the park or boarding a ride vehicle. Or you don't notice it simply because its environment is so detailed that you can't take it all in at once.

Some of these "Fun Finds" honor Disney imagineers and cast members; some recall Disney history,

others are disguised little tributes to movies and television shows, both Disney and non-Disney productions. Often, however, it's just something silly.

And what's a Hidden Mickey?

Camouflage shapes that most often form the silhouette of the head or figure of Mickey Mouse, Hidden Mickeys conceal themselves in every Walt Disney World park, in its landscape, attractions, shops and restaurants. For the most part this book only considers something a Hidden Mickey if it actually lives up to that phrase—in other words if it's not obvious at first glance, has nothing to do with its surroundings and forms the shape of Mickey Mouse, not some other character. Hidden Minnies, Donalds and the like are in our regular Fun Finds lists.

Magic Kingdom

The Haunted Mansion

Welcoming foolish mortals for more than four decades, this ghostly retirement home has more fun details than any other attraction at Walt Disney World.

RESEARCH BY **MICAELA NEAL**

GHOSTS DANCE, DUEL, SING, play music, sip tea, guzzle booze, even hitchhike in this dark indoor ride, one that's so tongue-in-cheek it's never truly scary. Sitting comfortably in an open "Doom Buggy," you creep through it room-by-room as you pass hundreds of ghosts, most of which are brought to life by age-old visual tricks. "The Complete Walt Disney World" travel guide awards it five stars and a checkmark, the book's highest rating.

The manor serves as a supernatural senior center, a nursing home for ghosts who by their nature have no need for nurses. Like similar places in the mortal world, it has a strong marketing effort focused on getting more residents.

Your tour is the sales pitch. An unseen "ghost host" leads it. "There are several prominent ghosts who have retired here from creepy old crypts from all over the world," he boasts. "Actually, we have 999 happy haunts… but there's room for a thousand. Any volunteers?" As you leave, an eerie doll-sized bride urges you to "be sure to bring your death certificate, should you decide to join us."

History

Walt Disney first pondered building a haunted house in the early 1950s as he was planning his first theme park, California's Disneyland. He imagined it as a walk-through tour, led by live butlers and maids. For a storyline, he considered Washington Irving's spooky 1820 tale "The Legend of Sleepy Hollow," which his company had just included in its 1949 compilation movie "The Adventures of Ichabod and Mr. Toad." But he also flirted with two other stories, one of a sea captain who kills his nosy bride and then hangs himself; another of a wedding party attended by villains such as Captain Hook, the bad guy of his then-current film project "Peter Pan." Distracted by more-finished Disneyland concepts such as Main Street U.S.A. and the Jungle Cruise, Disney didn't have time to flesh out his haunted house thoughts and the project stagnated.

Nevertheless, in 1961 Disneyland passed out handbills to guests announcing that it was about to build a haunted house. Two years later the exterior facade was done; a sign out front referred to it as a "haunted mansion" and promised that its interior would include a scary portrait gallery and a "Museum of the Supernatural."

Delays. The attraction, however, still wasn't built for years, as Walt Disney was again sidetracked by other projects. First he focused on the 1964 New York World's Fair, which would introduce his attractions Carousel of Progress and It's a Small World as well as his robotic Abraham Lincoln. When the fair closed, he obsessed on EPCOT, his planned Experimental Prototype Community of Tomorrow in Florida which he felt could solve the problems of America's inner cities.

Without Walt's leadership, the imagineers in charge of the

Walt Disney's proposed Experimental Prototype Community of Tomorrow (EPCOT) helped divert his focus from his haunted house project.

Haunted Mansion lacked a cohesive vision. They developed conflicting ideas for the ride, some scary, some silly, some strange. By the time they appeared with Walt on a 1965 episode of the television series "Walt Disney's Wonderful World of Color" to introduce the public to the attraction, no one was on the same page. Walt seemed unfamiliar with the ride, referring to it as "The House of Illusions." When an imagineer sheepishly corrected him with "The Haunted Mansion," Walt added "of the Supernatural." Later, when he again referred to the ride as "The House of Illusions," another imagineer corrected him

by calling it "The Museum of the Weird," and went on to explain how it would have man-eating plants.

Finally, a ride. After Walt Disney's death in 1966, imagineers decided the ride would be a hodge-podge of nearly all of their ideas— the scary ones, the silly ones, the strange. Everything but man-eating plants. Disneyland's Haunted Mansion opened in August, 1969, almost two decades after Walt Disney's first haunted-house thoughts. The mishmash of scenes left many riders less than thrilled. Even some of its imagineers openly disliked it; one summed it up as having "too many cooks."

MagicKingdom

Soon, though, a special quality of the mansion came to light: it had so many details that no matter how often someone rode it they always saw something new. A second version premiered at Walt Disney World's Magic Kingdom when that park opened in 1971.

It had so many details that no matter how often someone rode it they always saw something new.

Updates. Disney revamped the ride a few years ago. It expanded the standby queue, adding a side plaza filled with new busts, tombstones and interactive crypts. It enhanced the seance, upgrading the spiritualist's crystal ball so that instead of sitting on a table it floats in the air. The hitchhiking ghosts gained the power to pull pranks, such as removing your head and blowing it up like a balloon.

Disney replaced portraits that followed you with their eyes with ones that changed when flashed by lightning, swapped some huge rubber spiders for a roomful of odd staircases, and added a story of a murderous bride to the attic. It also overhauled the mansion's audio, including adding three-dimensional sounds to its stretching room.

Characters

Though the ride has no real story, it does have some key characters:

The Ghost Host. A disembodied voice, this gleeful pun-loving spirit introduces himself in the portrait gallery, reveals he hung himself to escape it, and then repeatedly tempts you to join him.

Madame Leota. The spirit of a psychic medium, this floating head appears halfway through the ride in a hovering crystal ball. She sends "sympathetic vibrations" to the mansion's ghosts, who materialize for you from then on.

The Bride. This menacing spirit and her dusty wedding memorabilia haunt the mansion's attic. Her name— Constance Hatchaway—tells her story: she *constantly* used her *hatchet* to do *away* with her husbands. She murdered them for their money, as she had an appreciation of fine jewelry.

Master Gracey. Supposedly the owner and main resident of the mansion, this character originated in fan fiction written by cast members which went viral online. The mansion has no character by this name; though a tombstone bears the inscription "Master Gracey" it refers to Disney imagineer Yale Gracey, who was known as a master of special effects. Despite all this, Disney created a Master Gracey character for its 2003 movie "The Haunted Mansion" and sells Master Gracey merchandise.

The Hitchhiking Ghosts. A hunchbacked top-hatted carpetbagger, a thin dapper skeleton in a long coat and a hairy little prisoner shackled to a ball and chain, these three ghosts hitch rides in the mansion's Doom Buggies near the end of the tour. Thanks to a mirror, you see yours travel with you; the Ghost Host claims he follows you home. Cast member fan fiction has given the hitchhikers names which Disney itself has embraced—the carpetbagger is Phineas, the skeleton Ezra, the prisoner Gus.

The Raven. This robotic black bird flaps its wings and glares at you throughout the ride. Originally it was to chide the Ghost Host for hanging himself (*"Caw... caw... he took the coward's way!"* it squawks on an unused 1960s audio track) and the conservatory's piano player for playing too loud (*"Caw... caw... you've disturbed another guest!"*).

The Hatbox Ghost. A fan favorite who doesn't even exist, this elderly cloaked figure with stringy hair and a gold tooth has gained a cult following among Haunted Mansion enthusiasts. He debuted in the original mansion at California's Disneyland in 1969, standing across from the bride in the attic. Decked out with a top hat and a huge grin, he clutched a cane with one hand and held a translucent hatbox in the other. Thanks to some lighting tricks, as riders passed him his head disappeared from his body and reappeared in the box in time with the bride's beating heart.

Or at least it was supposed to. Unfortunately, the tricks didn't work. Since the attic wasn't completely dark, ambient light in the room prevented the ghost's head from completely disappearing. So as riders passed him, he looked like he was simply standing there, holding—for some reason—a flashing box with his face in it. The gag was quickly removed. A year later, Disney built a second version of the ghost for its mansion at Walt Disney World, but never used it.

The Hatbox Ghost hasn't appeared anywhere since. Still, Disney has continually produced merchandise that features him, and has snuck images of him into the ride's corridor of doors.

Fun facts

As you might expect, the Haunted Mansion has more than its share of nonessential but interesting facts. Here are some of the best:

It holds two firsts. It was the first Disney attraction created after Walt Disney died. It debuted at California's Disneyland in 1969, three years after his death. It was also the first Walt Disney World attraction—the first one completed before the resort opened in 1971.

It held a world record. The Haunted Mansion was in The Guinness Book of World Records—for one year. Named the World's Largest Dark Ride in 1999, it lost that title in 2000 to Valhalla, an indoor log flume in England.

It has two antiques. The hearse outside the mansion was built during the Civil War. It was later used in Hollywood movies, including the 1965 John Wayne Western "The Sons of Katie Elder."

MagicKingdom

The piano in the conservatory was built by Philadelphia's Schomacker Piano Co. in the late 1800s.

It has two tunes. The music heard during nearly every moment of the ride is actually the same song—"Grim Grinning Ghosts (The Screaming Song)." It's performed in eight styles, everything from a sluggish instrumental dirge to a zippy barbershop harmony. Music buffs will note that its tension comes from sharps or flats that aren't part of its key signature. The ballroom version of the song sounds so strange because Disney sound engineers had an organist play it backward and then reversed the recording; they used the same technique to record the flute of the graveyard band. Gaylord Carter—who during the 1920s was the house organist at Grauman's Metropolitan Theatre, the largest movie palace in Hollywood—recorded the versions heard in the foyer and corridor of doors.

An off-key dirge of Wagner's Bridal Chorus ("Here comes the bride") adds ambience to the attic and its nefarious newlywed. It's the only mansion tune that is not "Grim Grinning Ghosts."

It's prepared for your cat. Kitty Litter is the main product made from fuller's earth, the substance used to create the mansion's dust and cobwebs. A light tan dust made from clay, it's also used by Hollywood set dressers to make scenes look dusty or dirty.

It's one of a kind. The Haunted Mansion is the only Disney ride that suggests its visitors kill themselves—which its Ghost Host does after he invites you to find a way out of the windowless, doorless gallery. "Well, there's always my way," he coos, as the room's lights go out to reveal his hanging, swinging corpse high above you.

It's sometimes flat. Only a few books are in the library, the ones that move. The rest are part of a painted backdrop. Also flat: the ballroom's rear wall, including its molding and woodwork.

There's plenty of pepper. The ballroom scene contains the largest implementation of Pepper's Ghost, a theatrical illusion from the Victorian era in which objects appear to fade in or out of existence or transform into other objects.

Employed at theme parks and museums throughout the world, the trick usually uses two rooms, only one of which its audience can see. Thanks to a large angled mirror, objects in the second room reflect into the first, appearing or disappearing as lights on them turn on and off. The mansion's robotic figures reflect into its 90-foot-long ballroom from multiple rooms above and below its passing Doom Buggy audience.

The effect is named after John Henry Pepper, a scientist who gained fame with it in 1862.

There's Sister Sunshine! Julia Lee appears as the attic bride, Constance Hatchaway. Lee played Anne Steele (also known as "Sister Sunshine") in the 1990s television series "Buffy the Vampire Slayer."

Madame Leota voice Eleanor Audley (lower right) co-starred in "Green Acres."

They're all heathens! None of the tombstones contain a cross or any other religious symbol.

You never go in the home. The entire ride takes place in a nondescript warehouse building behind the mansion's facade.

Voices

Tony the Tiger? Gumby? Ripper Roo? You'll hear them all, or at least their voice talents, as you travel through the mansion. Even Mickey Mouse shows up.

X Atencio. This famed Disney imagineer voiced the man trapped in the coffin ("let me outta here!").

Eleanor Audley. A well-known character actress in her day, she voiced spiritualist Madame Leota. Though famous among Disney fans as the woman who brought stepmother Lady Tremaine to life in the 1950 movie "Cinderella" as well as evil fairy Maleficent in 1959's "Sleeping Beauty," Audley was best known for her roles in dozens of 1960s sitcoms, including "The Beverly Hillbillies" (as private-school headmistress Mrs. Millicent Schuyler-Potts), "The Dick Van Dyke Show" (as Parents Council President Mrs. Billings), "Green Acres" (as Eunice Douglas, the disapproving mother of Oliver Douglas) and "My Three Sons" (as Mrs. Vincent, the disapproving mother-in-law of that show's Steve

MagicKingdom

Loulie Jean Norman

Louder! I can't hear you! Eh?").
McKennon worked in Hollywood
for five decades. He played the inn-
keeper on the 1950s television
series "Daniel Boone," voiced animated stars Archie Andrews and
Gumby, and late in life supplied the
insane laugh of Ripper Roo in the
video game series "Crash
Bandicoot." Disney fans will know
him as the voice of the safety spiel
at the Big Thunder Mountain
Railroad roller coaster ("...this
here's the wildest ride in the wilderness!"), banjo player Zeke in the
Country Bear Jamboree and Ben
Franklin in the Epcot theatrical
show The American Adventure.

The Mellomen. This harmoniz-
ing quartet contributed the voices
of the graveyard's singing busts. It
performed on many pop hits of the
1940s and 1950s, including
Rosemary Clooney's 1954 snappy
"Mambo Italiano" and appeared as
Elvis Presley's backup group in
four of his 1960s movies: "It
Happened at the World's Fair"
(1963), "Roustabout" (1964) and
"Paradise Hawaiian Style" (1966)
and, as the Bible Singers, "The
Trouble with Girls" (1969). The
Mellomen were heard in many
Disney animated movies of the
period, including 1951's "Alice in
Wonderland," 1953's "Peter Pan,"
1955's "Lady and the Tramp" and
1967's "The Jungle Book." Only one
of the group's faces appears on the
busts; that of bass singer Thurl
Ravenscroft (see next page).

Jimmy Macdonald. This
Disney sound-effects man provided

Douglas). She had a bit part in "The
Hitch-Hiker," a 1960 episode of the
mystery anthology "The Twilight
Zone" that helped inspire the creation of the Hitchhiking Ghosts.

Kat Cressida. The voice of attic
bride Constance Hatchaway,
Cressida voiced ditzy sister Dee
Dee in the 1990s Cartoon Network
series "Dexter's Laboratory."

Paul Frees. The Haunted
Mansion's Ghost Host, he also
voiced villain Boris Badenov in the
1959-1964 television series "The
Adventures of Rocky and
Bullwinkle." Other gigs included
being Disney character Professor
Ludwig Von Drake and, in falsetto,
Pillsbury Doughboy Poppin' Fresh.

Dallas McKennon. This
Hollywood fixture supplied the
voice of the bearded ghost in the
graveyard who struggles to under-
stand a mummy ("What's that?

the shrieks and screams heard in the mansion's corridor of doors. After World War II he took over the voice of Mickey Mouse from Walt Disney. He also barked for Pluto and voiced chipmunks Chip 'n' Dale and "Cinderella" mice Jaq and Gus.

Loulie Jean Norman. The voice of the graveyard's female opera singer, Norman sang the high background melody of the 1961 No. 1 hit by the Tokens, "The Lion Sleeps Tonight" (*"Ah...ah... ah... AHHH!"*) as well as the signature background accompaniment to the theme song of the 1960s television series "Star Trek" (*ooh-OOH... oh-oh-oh-oh ooh..."*). For her Haunted Mansion recording Disney asked her to sing as if she was possessed.

Thurl Ravenscroft. The founder and bass singer of the Mellomen, he leads the graveyard's singing busts, his head broken off from its pedestal. Ravenscroft also sang "You're A Mean One, Mr. Grinch" in the 1966 Dr. Seuss television special "How the Grinch Stole Christmas!" and was the longtime voice of Kellogg's Frosted Flakes mascot Tony the Tiger. At Walt Disney World he can also be heard as buffalo head Buff at the Country Bear Jamboree and German macaw Fritz at the Enchanted Tiki Room. In the Haunted Mansion his smiling, mustachioed mug is often mistaken as that of Walt Disney.

In pop culture

The mansion has been featured a few times in movies, television and rock music, often in unique ways.

"Hercules." Greek muses appear as the graveyard's singing busts in Disney's 1997 movie "Hercules," during the song "I Won't Say (I'm in Love)."

"The Haunted Mansion." Scoring just a 13 percent audience rating on the website Rotten Tomatoes, the 2003 Disney live-action movie "The Haunted Mansion" was also blasted by critics. Richard Roeper of the Chicago Sun-Times called it "dreadful." It starred comedian Eddie Murphy.

"Clerks: The Animated Series." Doom Buggies are used to scare people into buying needless snacks and drinks in the debut episode of this short-lived ABC sitcom. As entrepreneur Alec Baldwin leads his townsfolk on a Doom Buggy trip through his new convenience store Quicker Stop, his reflected image hops in and rides with them, which scares them so they panic, and buy everything in sight. Debuting in 2000, the series met with horrible reviews, and was cancelled after just two weeks.

Buckethead. A Doom Buggy is the vehicle of choice for this acclaimed speed guitarist on the cover of his 2007 album "Pepper's Ghost." Known for wearing a white mask and an upside-down Kentucky Fried Chicken bucket on his head during his shows, the eclectic performer has improvised "Grim Grinning Ghosts" during his live performances. A member of the band Guns N' Roses from 2000 to 2004, he grew up just down the street from California's Disneyland.

MagicKingdom

© Walt Disney Studios Home Entertainment

"The Adventures of Ichabod and Mr. Toad" (above), a 1949 Disney movie, was once planned to be the starting point of the mansion's story, in particular the film's take on Washington Irving's 1820 tale "The Legend of Sleepy Hollow." Disney scrapped that idea early on, but kept its New England setting for its Florida mansion, which recalls 19th-century Gothic homes seen often in New York's Hudson River Valley.

The Winchester Mystery House in San Jose, Calif. (above), influenced the mansion's interior. Built in 1884 by Winchester rifle heir Sarah Winchester, it was continually expanded and contracted for 50 years, as she believed the ghosts of those killed by the revolutionary gun were out to take her as payback, and couldn't if they kept getting lost. Today

The Harry Packer Mansion (shown at left) greatly inspired the look. Located in rural Jim Thorpe, Penn., its an epitome of Gothic Victorian architecture and design. The home was built in 1874 by coal and railroad magnate Asa Packer, who gave it to son Harry as a wedding present. Today it's a bed and breakfast.

a tourist attaction, the 160-room estate has doors that open to walls, stairs that lead nowhere and many secret passageways.

Grim Grinning Copyright! Though credited to Disney's Xavier ("X") Atencio and Buddy Baker, the lyrics and music of "Grim Grinning Ghosts" ("When the crypt doors creak and the tombstones quake, spooks come out for a swinging wake...") are eerily similar to those of "Haunted House," a 1931 novelty tune by Englishman Ray Noble and his New Mayfield Orchestra ("When the doors all squeak and the windows creak, and the ceilings leak 'cause the roof's antique..."). Noble is best known for his pop standard, "The Very Thought of You."

Packer Mansion, Winchester Mystery House: National Park Service

graveyard, of a human arm troweling itself into its brick crypt. In it a bricklayer trowels an enemy into a similar crypt, leaving him to die with his arm sticking out in the same manner. The gag is the second of two Haunted Mansion jokes based on immurement, an ancient form of imprisonment and eventual death in which a person is locked within a space and all possible exits are turned into walls. The first: its portrait gallery, which once you enter the Ghost Host tells you "has no windows and no doors" and "offers this chilling challenge: to find a way out!"

The dune buggy (shown above), a 1960s homemade open sand vehicle built on the chassis of a VW "bug," gave rise to the name Doom Buggy.

A flattened candy apple sparked the shape of the mansion's Doom Buggies.

life. Its walls stretched, and its doors breathed, tapped and thumped.

A white Styrofoam wig holder inspired the head of the spiritualist. The original animator of Mickey Mouse, longtime Disney collaborator Ub Iwerks also created its first projection system and the one used for the singing busts.

"The Haunting" a 1963 British horror movie starring Julie Harris (above), inspired the mansion's stretching room and corridor of doors. It portrayed a haunted house in New England that came to

"The Cask of Amontillado," a 1846 novel by American writer Edgar Allen Poe (above), led to the final gag in the mansion's

"The Raven," an 1845 poem by Poe, inspired Disney's recurring use of the black birds in the attraction. In Poe's verse, the narrator accuses the bird of stealing people's souls.

MagicKingdom

Two scenes from "Nosferatu," a 1922 German silent film, spawned a moment in the corridor of doors when the shadow of a grasping claw passes over a demonic grand-father clock. In one scene, a death clock so startles a young man he cuts himself with a knife. In another, a shadowy clawed figure (above) reaches out to seize a young woman's heart. "Nosferatu" was the first film adaptation of Bram Stoker's 1897 novel "Dracula."

"The Picture of Dorian Gray," an 1890 novel by Oscar Wilde (right), sparked the foyer's por-trait of a young man who transforms into an old skeleton. In Wilde's story, Gray sells his soul to the devil in exchange for a future where a portrait of him ages but he does not, leaving him carefree forever.

"Relativity," a 1953 illustration by Dutch artist M.C. Escher, is the basis of the ride's inter-locking staircases. The sketch depicts three such stairways, each with its own plane and source of gravity.

"The Drummer of Tedworth," a 1668 tale by Joseph Glanvill, inspired the look of the graveyard drummer. It's about a man who con-fiscates the drum of an enemy but then still hears its rhythmic raps.

"The Hitch-Hiker" (above), an episode of the 1960s television series "The Twilight Zone," may have inspired the hitchhiking ghosts. In the episode, a woman is followed by a ghostly hitchhiker, and at one point gets into her car only to dis-cover him in her back seat. "I believe you're going...my way?" he asks. Eventually she learns that she herself has died, and that the hitchhiker is an angel who has been sent to escort her to heaven.

William Shakespeare (above) coined the phrase "grim grinning ghost." In his 1592 poem "Venus and Adonis," Venus refers to Death by the term after Death kills her lover Adonis. "Grim-grinning ghost, earth's worm, what dost thou mean?" she complains. "To stifle beauty and to steal his breath?" In Greek mythology Venus is the goddess of love, Adonis the god of beauty.

Joan Crawford (above), a legendary movie star during Hollywood's Golden Age, influenced one of the portraits in the stretching room. A Life Magazine photo for the 1964 film "Hush Hush, Sweet Charlotte" showed her sitting on a tombstone in a pose similar to that later used for the portrait of the widow. In the movie, a wealthy spinster is driven to madness after local townfolk suspect her of beheading her lover with an axe in their large estate.

"The Phantom of the Opera," a 1910 novel that led to a 1925 silent movie starring Lon Chaney Sr. (above) and later films and stage shows, helped inspire the ballroom ghost playing the organ and the graveyard's opera singers. In "Phantom" a troubled ghost plays the organ of an opera house he haunts.

"An Assembly of Witches," a 17th-century painting by French artist Frans Francken, lends much of its detail to a Haunted Mansion loading-area portrait, "The Witch of Walpurgis." Both show a bat with outstretched wings, a dagger stabbed into a skull, and a skeletal Hand of Glory with its fingers lit like candles. In European folklore, a Hand of Glory came from a hanged murderer, and was dried and coated with wax. It supposedly allowed a thief to break into a home without being detected, as the inhabitants would stay asleep as long as the hand was lit.

"La Belle et la Bête," an artsy 1946 French version of Beauty and the Beast (and titled that for Western audiences, above), inspired the library busts that follow you with their eyes; its busts track Belle that way. The film's dining hall has wall torches held by human arms, just like those in the ride's de-boarding area.

Fun finds: Grounds

>1 A bronze bat peers down on you from the Haunted Mansion's wrought-iron gate, above the clock of its Fastpass+ entrance. The bat's tail is forked. **>2** The horned head of Satan decorates the top of two oval signs on either side of the entrance gate. Snakes slither around his neck. **>3** The howl of a wolf wafts through the air. **>4** The mansion's weathervane is a bat, its wings outstretched. **>5** Though chess-piece-like chimneys and trim details were common on 19th-century Gothic rooftops, Disney says those atop the mansion were intentionally designed to resemble pieces of the game. Every piece is represented except the knight, "because it's always night at the Haunted Mansion." **>6** Columns alongside its front door resemble coffins. **>7** A black wreath decorates the door. **>8** Human figures top some metal railings and stand within others. **>9** Stone-faced cast members dress as butlers and maids. They often speak in a glum monotone. **>10** At night the lights around the Haunted Mansion flicker. **>11** Lightning flashes on it at night, accompanied by cracks of thunder. **>12** Holding a lantern, a shadowy figure wanders behind the mansion's windows at night. **>13** Out front, dead roses lay in a horse-drawn hearse. **>14** A bridle and tack hang in front of the hearse, but hold no visible horse. **>15** Lanterns on the hearse glow at night. **>16** Horseshoe and wheel tracks lead to the hearse from a nearby barn. **>17** Next to the barn is a boathouse. Oars are stored inside. **>18** Children under the age

Julie Neal

MagicKingdom

Children under seven years old must ride with a mortal that is fourteen years or older

18

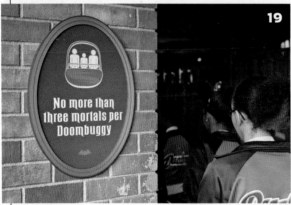

No more than three mortals per Doombuggy

19

Julie Neal

14

8

20

of 7 must ride with a "mortal" who is at least 14 years old. >**19** Mortals are restricted to three per Doom Buggy. >**20** Near the end of the Fastpass+ queue, the second touchpoint makes a spooky theremin sound as it reads your MagicBand or park ticket. >**21** During Mickey's Not-So-Scary Halloween Party events a ghostly storyteller often sits on the mansion's front lawn telling jokes and chatting up guests in line, >**22** and cast members wear ghoulish makeup, with cobwebs.

MagicKingdom

Julie Neal

38

Dread family busts

In the standby queue, a murder mystery similar to those in the game of Clue hides on a collection of busts that arc around a small enclave. Dread family members **>23** Bertie, **>24** twins Forsythia and Wellington, **>25** Aunt Florence, **>26** Uncle Jacob and **>27** Cousin Maude have, for most the part, killed each other (though one killed no one, and one accidentally killed herself) and its your job to figure out who did who in. Hints appear on the busts and on tarnished plaques beneath them. **>28** A snake around Bertie's neck hints how he killed his victim. **>29** A vial of poison on his plaque offers you another clue. **>30** His victim is revealed on a nearby inscription which includes the phrase "...the poison he had swallowed." **>31** A pistol on the plaque of Florence divulges her weapon of choice. **>32** Her victim's inscription describes its subject as an "expert shot" and closes with "in the end that's what he got." **>33** A dead bird on the plaque of the twins hints how they murdered their victim. **>34** A small bag of bird seed between them provides a further clue. **>35** Their victim "was found face down in canary seed." **>36** A tiny hammer on Maude's plaque makes known her weapon. **>37** Her victims' inscription reveals they died from "bumps." **>38** Matchsticks in Maude's hair foretell her fate. **>39** Her inscription reveals that her "dreams went up in smoke." The solution to the murder mystery appears in this guide on the page after the next one, upside down.

MagicKingdom

40

Interactive crypts

Musical crypt: >40 The Haunted
Mansion's theme song "Grim
Grinning Ghosts" plays when
embossed images of musical instruments on the side of this crypt are
touched. Each instrument plays the
tune separately. A band plays these
same instruments in the ride's
graveyard scene. **>41** "He's gone
from this world of trouble and
strife," reads an inscription above.
"But a touch of your hand brings
his music to life." **>42** "Grim
Grinning Ghosts" also plays when
you touch the keys of a pipe organ,
itself an homage to the organ in the

mansion's ballroom. **>43** Sculpted
banshees fly from the organ's pipes.
>44 Play the keys dramatically for
a dramatic rendition. **>45** Play too
long and the banshees blow air and
spit water at you. **>46** A huge red-
eyed raven peers down from atop
the pipes with its wings spread
open. **>47** The brand of the
organ—"Ravenscroft"—is a shout-
out to Thurl Ravenscroft, the voice
and face of the baritone singing bust
in the ride's graveyard. **>48** A horn
with tentacles is among the supernatural instruments on the right
side of the crypt, which also play
when you touch them. **>49** A
nearby one-eyed cat meows angrily
when touched. **>50** "A composer of
note and renown here reposes," the
inscription on this side of the crypt
reads. "His melodies fade as he now
decomposes." **Sea captain's**

*Who killed who? Bertie Dread killed
Uncle Jacob, Aunt Florence killed
Bertie. The twins killed Aunt Florence.
Cousin Maude killed the twins, and
accidentally herself.*

59

crypt: **>51** "Here floats Captain Culpepper Clyne, allergic to dirt so he's pickled in brine," reads the inscription on this crypt. "He braved the sea and all her wrath, but drowned on land while taking a bath." **>52** Bubbles billow over the sides of an open bathtub atop the crypt. It holds Clyne's body. **>53** His waterlogged fingers grip the tub's edge. **>54** Clyne often sneezes, which sprays water onto those nearby. **>55** He sometimes slurs the ancient sea shanty "Drunken Sailor"—*"What shall we do with a drunken sailor, early in the morning?"* **>56** Water often squirts from barnacles attached to Clyne's crypt. **>57** If you cover the barnacles with your hands, sculpted green fish on the crypt

spit water at you. **>58** Two foggy portholes dot the back of the crypt. **>59** Far to the right of Clyne's crypt, the silver wedding ring of the bride who haunts the mansion's attic is embedded in the concrete walkway. **Writer's crypt: >60** Books pop in and out by themselves on this crypt, the resting place of poetess Prudence Pock; **>61** but if you push in one book another will pop out. **>62** The books are in groups of 13. **>63** A secret coded message—a cryptogram, get it?— hides in symbols on their spines. Each symbol represents a letter of the alphabet. (The decoded message appears upside down on the page after the next one.) **>64** Monstrous faces decorate the crypt. **>65** The nibs of ink pens border the top of it. **>66** "Writer's block" killed the poetess, according to the epitaph on the back of Prudence's crypt. **>67** Speaking from within it, she repeatedly asks passersby for help with her writing efforts. "In the swamp, poor Sally Slater was eaten by an… what rhymes with 'Slater'?" **>68** She can hear you if you answer her question in front of the Spectrecom, a small microphone gadget on the front of her tomb. **>69** Answer her question correctly and she responds with delight. **>70** The Spectrecom's small print shows it was patented by "R.H. Goff." That's a shout-out to Ralph Harper Goff, a key mansion concept artist. He also designed the layout of Epcot's World Showcase and created concepts of its Japan, Italy and United

57

Kingdom pavilions. Outside of Disney, Goff designed the sets for the seminal 1942 Warner Brothers movie "Casablanca" and was the art director of the 1971 Paramount film "Willy Wonka and the Chocolate Factory." **>71** As the

The writer's crypt message reads: "Welcome home you foolish mortal, this mansion is your mystic portal. Where eerie sights and spooky sounds fill these happy haunting grounds."

poetess composes her poems, they appear in a book behind the Spectrecom in her handwriting.

Back wall crypt: >72 Easy to miss on your left as you pass by it, a non-interactive four-person crypt pays homage to more Haunted Mansion creators: Paul Frees, the voice of the Ghost Host (*"Farewell forever, Mister Frees; Your voice will carry on the breeze."*) (for more information on Frees, see the earlier "Voices" segment of this

FAREWELL FOREVER,
Mister Freeo
YOUR VOICE WILL CARRY
ON THE BREEZE

DRINK A TOAST TO
OUR FRIEND
Ken
FILL YOUR GLASS
AND DON'T SAY
"WHEN"

WHILE
BROTHER ROLAND
HERE REPOSES

HIS SOUL'S ABOVE,
ONE SUPPOSES

A TRAIN
MADE A STAIN
OF ABSENT-MINDED

UNCLE BLAINE

REST IN PIECES

72

69

73

article); concept artist Ken Anderson *("Drink a toast to our friend Ken. Fill your glass and don't say 'when.'")*; key developer Rolly Crump *("While Brother Roland here reposes, his soul's above, one supposes.")*; and character sculptor Blaine Gibson *("A train made a stain of absent-minded Uncle Blaine. Rest in pieces.").*

>73 A metal gate in front of that crypt (for use by cast members only) stands ready for use by the mansion's graveyard caretaker—the character seen on the ride who cowers with his dog at the gate of the graveyard behind the mansion.

>74 A dog door in the gate's bottom right corner is designed for his pet.

>75 The caretaker's shoe prints lead to and away from the gate.

>76 So do his dog's paw prints.

Outdoor tombstones

A graveyard sits to the left of the Haunted Mansion entraceway, filled with tombstones that often have witty epitaphs. Many are sly tributes to Disney imagineers who played key roles in designing and building the attraction. Most of the markers can only be seen from the Standby queue. **>77** Xavier ("X") Atencio's headstone stands in a sliver of land within the standby queue. Atencio wrote the mansion's script, created the lyrics to "Grim Grinning Ghosts" (see Inspirations) and coined the term "Doom Buggy." He also wrote the script of the original Pirates of the Caribbean attraction, the lyrics to its theme song "Yo Ho (A Pirate's Life for Me)" and the lyrics to "The Bear Band Serenade" at the Country Bear Jamboree. A key Disney staffer for decades, Atencio also helped animate the 1940 movie "Fantasia." (His inscription reads *"Requeisat Francis Xavier. No time off for good behavior."*) **>78** Dave

Burkhart built mansion architecture and show models. The Haunted Mansion was one of his biggest projects. *("Dear departed Brother Dave. He chased a bear into a cave.")* **>79** Harriet Burns, Disney's first female imagineer, built mansion models, finished figure models and designed sets for the attraction. Her tall obelisk is themed to the opera, and includes a tiny horned Viking helmet near its top. *("First Lady of the opera, our haunting Harriet. Searched for a tune but could never carry it.")* **>80** Collin Campbell created concept art for all of Walt Disney World. Ironically, he died just a few days after his obelisk debuted in 2011. It stands in a paved portion of the standby queue. **>81** Claude Coats championed the mansion's scary elements. *("At peaceful rest lies Brother Claude. Planted here beneath this sod.")* **>82** Marc Davis masterminded the ride's silly elements, including its cartoonish faces and sight gags. One of

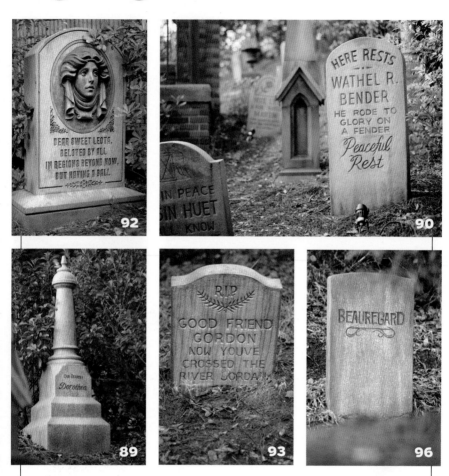

Disney's legendary "Nine Old Men," he was a key company artist. His characters included Cruella De Vil, Maleficent and Tinker Bell. His tombstone stands in a sliver of land within the standby queue. *("In memory of our patriarch. Dear departed Grandpa Marc.")* **>83** Yale Gracey developed nearly all of the mansion's special effects. His tombstone—which is in its own small plot in the standby queue, surrounded by crypts—refers to him as "master" as a tribute to his

mastery of his craft, though many fans mistake the word to mean that "Gracey" is a fictional Disney character, the head of the mansion household. *("Master Gracey, laid to rest. No mourning please at his request.")* **>84** Placed there by cast members playfully paying their respects to both the character and the person, a real red rose often rests atop Gracey's tombstone. It's picked from roses that grow on the grounds. **>85** Cliff Huet designed the building's interior. *("Rest in*

peace Cousin Huet. We all know you didn't do it.") **>86** Fred Joerger designed all the original rock work at Disney World, including that of the mansion's exit crypts. (*"Here lies good old Fred. A great big rock fell on his head."*) **>87** Bud Martin designed the mansion's lighting. (*"Here lies a man named Martin. The lights went out on this old spartan."*) **>88** Chuck Myall was a Walt Disney World master planner. (*"In memoriam Uncle Myall. Here you'll lie for*

quite a while.") **>89** Dorothea Redmond painted mansion concept art. The first female production designer in Hollywood, she designed the sets for more than 30 movies, including 1939's "Gone With the Wind" and many classic Alfred Hitchcock films. She also created the model paintings for the mosaic murals inside Cinderella Castle. Her obelisk has no epitaph. **>90** Wathel Rogers helped pioneer Disney's Audio-Animatronics technology, which is used throughout

MagicKingdom

the mansion. His earlier work included Disney's robotic Abraham Lincoln figure and Carousel of Progress family seen at the 1964 New York World's Fair. He later became the art director of the Magic Kingdom. *("Here rests Wathel R. Bender. He rode to glory on a fender.")* **>91** Robert Sewell led Disney's model makers. *("R.I.P. Mister Sewell. The victim of a dirty duel.")* **>92** Disney artist Leota ("Lee") Toombs posed for the ride's disembodied head that speaks from inside a crystal ball, a spiritualist who came to be known as "Madame Leota." Chosen for the part only because her eyes were the right distance apart to fit a test model, she also provided the face and voice of "Little Leota," the eerie bride at the end of the ride. Toombs' stone (cute, huh?) is the only one with an embossed face, and the only one that's animated. Its face tilts forward and back, its closed eyelids open and its green eyes shift from side to side. The movements are tough to catch, as they only occur about once a minute. Children often notice them first. Born Leota Wharton, Toombs married Disney animator Harvey Toombs in 1947. Her daughter, current imagineer Kim Irvine, animated the face of the bride in the attic. The marker is easy to find; it's the one closest to the mansion's entrance doors. Its epitaph *("Dear sweet Leota, beloved by all. In regions beyond now, but having a ball.")* recalls one of Madame Leota's incantations *("Creepies and crawlies, toads in a pond; let there be music, from regions beyond.")*.

>93 Audio engineer Gordon Williams created the mansion's sound effects. *("R.I.P. Good friend Gordon. Now you've crossed the river Jordan.")* **>94** A collection of tough-to-see tombstones sits farther up the hill under trees and often behind overgrown greenery. These honor fictional characters of the mansion, some of which existed only in concepts for it. One marks the grave of Bartholomew Gore, a ghostly pirate captain featured in the very first story treatment for The Haunted Mansion, written in 1957. **>95** Another honors Gore's bride Priscilla, whom he murdered in that tale. **>96** A third is for Beauregard, a live butler who would have guided guests through the Gore mansion. **>97** Five markers up high on the hill mark the graves of the singing bust characters in the ride's graveyard: Cousin Algernon (a moniker that comes from the 1895 Oscar Wilde play, "The Importance of Being Earnest"), **>98** Ned Nub, **>99** Phineas Pock, **>100** Rollo Rumkin, **>101** and Uncle Theodore (the broken bust). Disney used the names in 1960s concept art but not on the ride. **>102** Hidden under trees on the hill in overgrowth, two tombstones honor two of the ride's hitchhiking ghosts: Gus, the short bearded prisoner; **>103** and Ezra, the lanky, bug-eyed skeleton. **>104** Two gravedigger shovels are thrust into the bottom of the hill. Vines curl up their shafts.

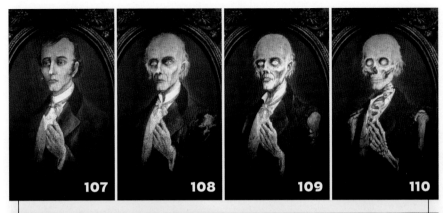

107 108 109 110

149

Inside the mansion

Foyer: >105 As you enter an unseen owl hoots and flaps away. **>106** A cross-eyed, arrow-tongued face appears in the pattern of the fireplace grate. **>107** In a portrait above the fireplace, a young debonair man **>108** morphs into an old man **>109** who turns bug-eyed and bony **>110** as he transforms into a skeleton. **Portrait gallery: >111** Monstrous faces appear in the patterns of the floor grates. **>112** Bat-eared gargoyles on the walls hold flickering candles. **>113** The voice of the Ghost Host circles the gallery. **>114** Creaks fill the air as the chamber begins to stretch. **>115** In one of the portraits, a widow who sits on the tombstone of her husband is

MagicKingdom

144

Constance Hatchaway—the bride in the attic. **>116** Unseen bones clatter to the floor after the Ghost Host reveals his hanging corpse. **>117** Unseen bats flap away after the exit door opens. **>118** Gargoyles whisper "stay together" after the Ghost Host urges groups to "all stay together, please." **>119** The gargoyles giggle. **>120** Linger too long in the gallery and they hiss "Get out!" **Boarding area: >121** A distant wolf howls. **>122** Grinning skulls frame doors. **>123** Screaming skulls top woodwork. **>124** Toothy brass bats top chain stanchions. **>125** A bat-shaped lamp to the left of the Doom Buggy track illuminates the ride's safety warnings. **>126** Hung on the walls are seven portraits that have appeared in the mansion since it opened. Among the subjects are an arsonist in front of a burning building; **>127** Capt. Culpepper Clyne, a ghostly seafarer who holds a harpoon; **>128** the mansion's Ghost Host, a tall, ghoulish man who clutches a hatchet and has a severed noose hanging from his neck; **>129** Rasputin, an ominous, bearded man with clasped hands; **>130** Jack the Ripper, a mustachioed man with a top hat and a disturbing grin, who grips a knife; **>131** Dracula, a smiling pale man who wears a cape and holds a lantern aloft; **>132** and the Witch of Walpurgis, a black-haired woman who holds a black cat.

On the ride

>133 Half eagle and half lion, a rearing griffin appears on your left, at the base of a candelabrum. **>134** A second candelabrum floats above your head. **>135** The subjects of wall portraits include a wrinkled crone **>136** and a stern upper-class couple, who stand in front of a painting of the Haunted Mansion.

Portrait hall: >137 Everyday subjects transform into extraordinary ones when flashes of lightning illuminate a line of paintings on the wall. A reclining young woman holding a rose turns into a snarling white tiger holding a bone; **>138** a knight and rearing horse turn skeletal; **>139** a stately sailing ship changes into a ghost ship; and **>140** as a woman's hair turns into snakes, her body gets covered by snake bites as she morphs into Medusa. Her necklace turns into a serpent. **Library: >141** Glowing marble busts between the bookshelves seem to turn their heads and follow you with their eyes. **>142** Carved bats leer at you from the paneling. **>143** A ladder teeters as an unseen ghost atop it shuffles between the shelves. **>144** An abstract image of Donald Duck appears in a rope-like pattern on a red velvet chair (similar chairs appear later in the ride). **>145** The chair rocks by itself. **>146** Snarling beast heads extend from columns (similar columns appear in themansion's corridor of doors and ballroom). **>147** "The Nightmare Before Christmas" lays on a table with a lamp that's near your passing Doom Buggy. Its spine shows the face of Jack Skellington. **>148** A red book on the floor below that table has Jack's image on its cover. **Music room: >149** Sheet music on the floor has staff lines but no notes, implying the composer died before completing his work. **>150** Behind the piano, a storm brews outside a window. **>151** Upright coffins top the sides of the window frame. **>152** Other instruments in the room include a violin on a settee to the left of the piano, and an ornate cello to the right. **>153** Sheet music for a "Vocal Concert in the Open Air" foreshadows the ride's graveyard scene. It's on a music stand. **>154** A large griffin forms the base of a banister. **Staircases: >155** Ghostly glowing footprints climb the stairs. **Endless hallway: >156** Demons hiss at you from the wallpaper. **>157** Their eyes blink and glow. **>158** A suit of armor subtly moves. It holds a shield and an elaborate axe. **>159** Carved fang-baring serpents hang from crown molding. **Conservatory: >160** The coffin's handles resemble bats. **>161** Withered plants and rotting flowers remain from a funeral. **>162** Perched on a wilted wreath, the mansion's raven glares at you with glowing red eyes. **Corridor of doors: >163** The Hatbox Ghost appears in framed sketches on the walls. In one, a crown tops his head. **>164** A cut noose hangs from the Ghost Host in another sketch. His shadow raises an axe. **>165** Clangs, knocks, moans and laughter fill the air. **>166** Doorknobs turn, their knobs snarling serpents. **>167** Mace knockers bang. **>168** Doors appear to breathe. **>169** Menacing faces hide in the patterns of the doors' transoms. **>170** Green light leaks out from the last door on each side of the corridor. **>171** "Tomb Sweet Tomb" reads a sampler. **>172** A grandfather clock channels a demon. Its casing forms hair and eyes, its face a fanged mouth, its pendulum a tail. **>173** Spinning backward, the clock's glowing dial marks the hour of "13." **>174** The shadow of a giant clawed hand passes in front of the clock. **Seance room: >175** Lit candles and tarot cards top Madame Leota's table. **>176** The ride's raven settles on her velvet chair. **>177** A harp, tambourine and trumpet are among the instruments that float around the room. **>178** Other flying objects include a bullfighter's red cape and a flickering Tiffany lamp with its table. **>179** A green orb leaves a glowing trail as it wanders along a back wall. **Ballroom: >180** Ripped drapes flutter in a breeze. **>181** An old woman knits in a rocking chair in front of a fireplace. She's seen in the same pose at the Tomorrowland attraction Walt Disney's Carousel of Progress. **>182** The ballroom's blazing fire is a ghostly green. **>183** A ghost on the mantle wears a top hat, and has his arm around a bust of a stern old woman (a bust once planned to sing along with the five male busts in the graveyard). **>184** The fireplace grate forms black-cat silhouettes. **>185** A hearse is backed up to an opened door. A coffin has fallen out of it. **>186** Five ghosts float out of the coffin. **>187** The female ballroom dancers lead the males, due to a oversight in Disney's Pepper's Ghost design.

Since the figures are actually in a hidden room and reflected on glass, their images are reversed. **>188** At the banquet table, a female ghost has been presented a "death-day" cake, topped by 13 candles. **>189** Each time she blows them out, she also blows out the apparitions of the ghosts around her. **>190** One of the ghosts is also a Pirate of the Caribbean: the sprawled-out buccaneer who blathers on about his treasure map. **>191** A drunken ghost has slid under the table and passed out. **>192** Julius Caesar ("Great Caesar's ghost!") sits at the end of the table. **>193** His lover Cleopatra perches above him on the chandelier. **>194** She's with her later conquest, Marc Antony. **>195** Mr. Pickwick, from the Charles Dickens 1836 novel "The Pickwick Papers," swings from the chandelier. **>196** Banshees rise out of the pipes of the ballroom organ. **>197** Its music stand forms a leering bat. **>198** Appearing in separate portraits on the ballroom's back wall, two ghosts duel above a balcony. Painted with their backs to each other, they emerge from their paintings to turn and fire pistols. **>199** In another portrait, a blonde's opera glasses have eyes of their own. It's to the left of the balcony, obscured by shadows. **Attic: >200** "Here Comes the Bride" (Wagner's "Bridal Chorus") wafts through the air, its chords melancholy and off-key. **>201** A heart thumps in the background. **>202** A Jack Skellington doll sits on a far-right shelf. **>203** Props from earlier versions of the

192

196

267

221

ride hide in the bric-a-brac. These include (in the order you come upon them): the red carpet which lay under the previous bride (beneath the first wedding portrait); **>204** a candelabrum that once sat atop the music room piano (near the third wedding portrait); **>205** a carpet bag that previously held a pop-up ghost in the attic (to the right of Constance); **>206** and an old lamp that originally hung over Leota's crystal ball (across from Constance). **>207** The bride's marriage certificates are scattered throughout the attic. **>208** The heads of her grooms fade and disappear from her wedding portraits. **>209** The bride's expression changes from portrait to portrait. At first she's grimacing, as she poses with a short humble country boy, Ambrose Harper, who wears an ill-fitting suit. **>210** A nearby wedding album reads "Our Wedding Day." **>211** After her second marriage—to banker Frank Banks—she looks bored. **>212** A hanging banner reads "True Love Forever." **>213** In her third portrait, after hooking Chinese diplomat Marquis de Doome, she appears to be hiding a smile. Her husband wears military regalia, including a sash, medals and a plumed hat. **>214** For her fourth wedding portrait she's pleased, after marrying spiffy if stocky Reginald Caine, a gambling railroad tycoon who sports a gem in his lapel and a ring on his little finger. **>215** The spoils of his globetrotting adventures litter the floor. **>216** By her fifth wedding, she's smiling and satisfied, having snagged wealthy George Hightower. **>217** A suit of armor and a harp are among the couple's many wedding gifts, which surround the portrait's ornate frame. **>218** The bride wears the same dress in each photograph, but always has another string of pearls. **>219** She holds a rose in her final portrait, just like she does in her stretching-room portrait. **>220** The hatchet she used to behead her grooms rests on the floor to the right of a wedding cake. **>221** Her ghost brandishes a glowing version of the weapon, and giggles sinister variations on classic wedding vows—"In sickness and in wealth!" **>222** The hats of her grooms hang on a rack across from her. **>223** Hatboxes behind it allude to the Hatbox Ghost, the character originally intended for that spot. **>224** Disney's 1993 movie

"The Nightmare Before Christmas" is represented in the attic by four props. The face of Jack Skellington appears on the cover of a red book near the bride's second wedding portrait, on the floor; **>225** a Jack snowglobe sits on a shelf in the back right corner; **>226** the black-and-white-striped limbs of a Jack plush stick out from behind the hatboxes; and **>227** a doll that looks like Sally hides on a shelf, under a table.

Graveyard: >228 The ride's raven caws from a branch to your right. **>229** The archway of the graveyard gate forms a monstrous face. **>230** Ghouls pop out from behind tombstones after each chorus of "Grim Grinning Ghosts." **>231** One wears a golden hoop earring. **>232** Some tombstones "quake," just as the lyrics of "Grim Grinning Ghosts" say they do. **>233** A medieval minstrel band consists of a flutist emerging from his crypt, **>234** a drummer beating bones against it, **>235** a kilt-wearing bagpiper, **>236** a soldier playing a small harp **>237** and a trumpeter who's wearing pajamas. **>238** When the trumpeter rears up with a flourish, so do two owls above him. **>239** Sitting on tombs to the right of the group, cats hiss and yowl to its beat. **>240** A skeletal dog howls on a hill. **>241** A king and queen ride a makeshift seesaw—a board balanced on a tombstone. **>242** Their princess daughter sips tea as she swings from a tree branch. **>243** A British duke and duchess toast at a candle-lit table. **>244** Bicycling ghosts circle behind them. **>245** A skeletal corpse raises a teacup behind a grave. **>246** Sometimes he raises his head. **>247** A floating teapot pours tea into a cup. **>248** Tracks veer off your path, leading to a hearse stuck in mud. **>249** Its driver chats with a duchess, who sits atop the hearse sipping tea. **>250** A ghost sits up from a coffin, which has fallen out of the back of the hearse. **>251** He's talking with a sea captain. **>252** A skinny dog sniffs an Egyptian sarcophagus. **>253** Its mummy mumbles through its bandages as it stirs its tea. **>254** "What's that? Louder! I can't hear you! Eh?" cries an old bearded man leaning toward the mummy, holding a horn to his ear. **>255** The Grim Reaper hovers in a tomb, his beady eyes staring at you from inside a dark hood. **>256** Opera-singing ghosts in Viking gear belt out solos. **>257** Holding his severed head, a decapitated knight stands alongside his executioner. **>258** The executioner cheerfully sings a duet with a pint-sized prisoner, **>259** who around the corner reappears as a hitchhiking ghost. **>260** The ride's raven appears above you as you leave the graveyard. **Mausoleum: >261** A portrait of Cousin Maude Sweeny lays next to the hitchhiking ghosts. A member of the Dread family, Maude appears on a bust in the standby queue. **>262** In the reflection of your Doom Buggy, your hitchhiker may stretch your face, place a hat on your head, blow your head up like a balloon, or switch heads with you.

>263 "Hurry back... hurry back..." a miniature bride beckons from above, in what strikes the author as the attraction's creepiest moment. "Be sure to bring your death certificate if you decide to join us." **>264** The little bride clutches a dead bouquet. **>265** Her veil flutters in a breeze. **Exitway: >266** A green left-facing arrow floats across the back of the Doom Buggy in front of you, telling which way to step out. **>267** Yellow bat silhouettes replace the typical safety shoe prints on the moving walkway. **>268** Human arms hold up wall sconces. **>269** The ghosts make one final pitch for you to join them by faintly singing an a cappella dirge of "Grim Grinning Ghosts": *"If you would like to join our jamboree, there's a simple rule that's compulsory. Mortals pay a token fee. Rest in peace, the haunting's free. So hurry back, we would like your company."* **>270** Valet bells hang in one of the exitway's "Servant's Quarters," an area that's closed to most visitors. Again honoring imagineers, each is for a mythical room: Ambassador Xavier's Lounging Lodge (Xavier Atencio), **>271** Colonel Coats' Breakfast Berth (Claude Coats), **>272** Uncle Davis' Sleeping Salon (Marc Davis), **>273** Master Gracey's Bedchamber (Yale Gracey), **>274** Grandfather McKim's Resting Room (a tribute to Sam McKim, a mansion concept artist), **>275** Professor Wathel's Reposing Lounge (Wathel Rogers), **>276** and Madame Leota's Boudoir (Leota Toombs).

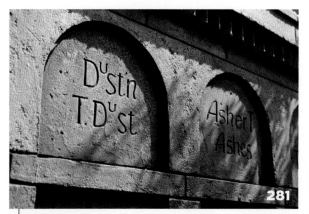

Outdoor exitway

Wall crypts: Occupants of crypts just outside the building have puns for names: **>277** Asher T. Ashes, **>278** Bea Witch, **>279** C. U. Later, **>280** Clare Voince, **>281** Dustin T. Dust, **>282** Hail N. Hardy, **>283** Hal Lusinashun, **>284** Hap A. Rition, **>285** I. Emma Spook, **>286** I. M. Ready, **>287** I. Trudy Dew, **>288** Love U. Trudy, **>289** M. T. Tomb, **>290** Manny Festation, **>291** Metta Fisiks, **>292** Paul Tergyst, **>293** Pearl E. Gates, **>294** Rustin Peece, **>295** Rusty Gates and **>296** Wee G. Bord. **>297** "The seventh did him in" explains the inscription on a large crypt that holds French aristocrat Bluebeard and six of his seven wives. In the folktale, after his seventh spouse Lucretia discovers that he had murdered each of his previous wives, she had her brothers murder him.

Pet cemetery

>298 Mr. Toad is the most famous inhabitant of this small wooded hillside. He rests at the far back left corner. Toad's grave is an inside joke, Disney toying with the idea that it "killed" the character in 1997 when it converted its raucous Mr. Toad's Wild Ride to the Many Adventures of Winnie the Pooh. The move led to in-park protests. On the Wild Ride's final day, one

297

303

305

upset fan held a sign in front of the attraction that read "Here lies dear old J.T. Toad. He hit some Pooh upon the road." Other pet cemetery residents are: **>299** Eric, a snake named for Disney Imagineer Eric Jacobson, who led the mansion's 2007–2012 refurbishment (the snake *"met his fate at the hands of a garden rake"*); **>300** Little Maisy, a poodle (*"So prim and proper and never lazy. All you do now is push up daisies."*); **>301** Rover, a dog (*"Every dog has his day. Too bad today was your last."*); **>302** a duck (*"Little Waddle saw the truck. But Little Waddle didn't duck."*) **>303** and a cat (*"Nine lives always go so fast. Poor Whiskers couldn't make them last."*). A small circular plaque lists the cat's lives and how he lost them—"bad catnip," "a shoe at two," "sour milk," "hairball," "one bad year," "same year," "local dog," and "fell off limb." **>304** Faux bird chatter comes from trees behind the graves. **Benches: >305** Red-eyed dogs and grape-eating snakes appear in the wrought-iron frames of benches that sit near the pet cemetery, often behind the hearse.

Julie Neal

306

307

Memento Mori gift shop

>306 The eye on the store's main sign follows you as you pass it. **>307** Madame Leota's face hides in the pupil on the shop's sign that faces Fantasyland. **>308** Inside the shop, Leota's face often materializes in a wall mirror, accompanied by a snippet of "Grim Grinning Ghosts." **>309** Roses and a raven trim the mirror's frame. **>310** The mortal Leota appears in a wall portrait holding a skull. Her tarot cards and crystal ball sit on a table behind her. **>311** The portrait changes when her spirit visits the shop. The skull's eye sockets shine orange, a green-eyed black cat appears at her feet, and a red-eyed raven spreads its wings behind her. **>312** Also at that time, eyes of demons appear in the shop's wallpaper. **>313** "The Old Curiosity Shop," an 1841 Charles Dickens novel about how death transforms living angels into heavenly ones, lays on a bottom shelf to the right of Leota's portrait. **>314** Her face appears on brooches worn by female sales clerks. **>315** Atop merchandise shelves are potion ingredients, **>316** flickering candles and **>317** raven-adorned candelabra. **>318** Spiderwebs decorate the woodwork of merchandise racks. **>319** A flaming red ghost light hovers in a jar on the far left of

326

a shelf on the wall with Leota's portrait. **>320** A sparkly blue ghost light floats in a jar on a shelf on the right side of the store, near a small window. **>321** A fiery blue ghost light appears to the left of the shop's small Spirit Photography image studio, in a jar on a high shelf. **>322** Complete with a wooden frame and a crank, the studio's huge camera resembles a 19th-century antique. **>323** Skeletons wear Victorian attire on the studio's linen wallpaper. **>324** Have your ghostly picture taken and a cast member will inform you that your impression will be ready when "the spirits ring the bell"—a sly allusion to Madame Leota's incantation in the ride's seance room, "Wizards and witches, wherever you dwell… give us a hint by ringing a bell!" **>325** A bell eventually rings.

Hidden Mickeys

>326 Three barnacles form a cockeyed Mickey on the crypt of Capt. Culpepper Clyne, just under and between the "R" in "Culpepper" and the "C" in "Clyne." **>327** The mansion's circular foyer and two stretching rooms form the three circles. **>328** Mickey appears twice in the music room, in the metal loops of the music stand. **>329** In the ballroom he's formed by the left-most place setting on the near side of the banquet table. **>330** In the attic he's created by plates on the floor near the third wedding portrait. **>331** In the graveyard he's held aloft by the silhouette of the Grim Reaper.

Jungle Cruise

Disney goes overboard with silly jokes and puns at this attraction, and not just on the ride.

Paramount Pictures / Viacom

Woody Strode

LAMPOONING BRITISH EFFORTS to colonize other areas of the world in the early 1900s, this tongue-in-cheek outdoor boat ride threatens you with peril at every turn. Snakes, cannibals, head-headers, hungry hungry hippos—none of them are scary, but they're all fodder for corny puns and jokes, thanks to a crazed Jungle Cruise skipper who is only worried about one thing: her destiny of never being anything more than a crazed Jungle Cruise skipper. "I think I'll go again," she (or he) will probably announce at the end of your trip. "And again. And again. Every 10 minutes. For the rest of my life."

You start your trip at a tropical jungle outpost, a remote boat dock that is somehow stuck in the 1930s. From there you board a canopied tramp steamer for a trip down some of the world's most treacherous rivers—the Amazon, Congo, Nile and Mekong. Though your guide speaks from a script, it changes often and includes far more jokes than he or she needs. The result is a routine that may appear to be improvised, and is often totally hilarious. Some skippers slyly toss in jokes of their own.

History

The Jungle Cruise is Disney's oldest major attraction, debuting in 1955 with the opening of California's Disneyland. For its first seven years it was a serious ride, an educational experience designed to give Americans a sense of exotic areas of the world most of them had never before seen, even in photographs. Inspired by the 1951 movie "The African Queen" and created at the same time as one of Disney's "True-Life Adventure" nature films (1955's "The African Lion"), the Jungle Cruise was the signature attraction of Disneyland, Walt Disney's pride and joy.

Serious it stayed for years, until Walt Disney began to hear of returning park guests not wanting to go on it anymore, since it was always the same old serious thing. So, starting in 1962, its skippers became slightly sarcastic, and a new scene showed playful bathing elephants using their trunks to almost-but-not-quite squirt the boats with water. Two years later, another new scene showed a rhino poking a cartoonish safari party up a pole. By 1971, when Disney debuted a second version of the

Jungle Cruise in Florida as part of the new Walt Disney World, the entire ride was played for laughs. Later, humorous props (1991) and a silly radio broadcast (1994) were added to the waiting area, and the boats were redone with details such as cooking gear that hangs from roof nets (1998). Disney has added more gags in recent years.

Fun facts

So definitively Disney, the ride has a boatload of fun facts. The best:

It was a manly cruise. Jungle Cruise skippers were exclusively male until May, 1995. A year later, half were female.

It changed its pole climbers. For the ride's first 25 years, the safari party being chased up a pole consisted of four black porters in khaki uniforms and red hats—the implied guides of a hunting expedition. In 1996 they were changed to Caucasians, their outfits and gear switched to that of a film crew.

One native is famous. The ride's dancing natives were formed using molds of Woody Strode. One of the first non-white college (U.C.L.A.) and professional (Los Angeles Rams) football stars and later an accomplished actor, Strode posed for a nude painting that was displayed briefly at the 1936 Berlin Olympics until Germany's ruling Nazi party discovered it. Known for his stunning good looks, Strode came from parents who both had black and American Indian ancestors. "Toy Story" character Sheriff Woody is named after him.

Former skippers are famous. Comedian Steve Martin once worked as a Jungle Cruise skipper, as did Disney-Pixar animation guru John Lasseter, actor Kevin Costner and Ron Ziegler, the humor-free press secretary who became the public face of President Richard Nixon's embattled administration during the Watergate scandal. He became famous for his non-denial-denial, "This is the operative statement. The others are inoperative."

One of its boats sank. It happenned in 2004, directly in front of the dock as guests waited to board it. The only person aboard was its skipper—on his first day on the job.

There's a song about it. Comedic songwriter "Weird Al" Yankovic parodied the ride in a 2009 tune, "Skipper Dan," which tells the tale of a failed actor who is stuck working as a Jungle Cruise skipper. *"Look at those hippos! They're wigglin' their ears! Just like they've done for the last 50 years!"* The song was inspired by a popular self-deprecating tune from 2008, Weezer's "Pork and Beans."

Walt wanted live animals. During the ride's initial planning stages Walt Disney wanted it to use live animals until he learned that they'd often be asleep during operating hours. The Disney Co. fulfilled his dream in 1998, with the opening of the Kilimanjaro Safaris attraction at the nearby Animal Kingdom theme park. Many of its creatures also nap during the day, but it includes such a wide variety of species that no one notices.

Magic**Kingdom**

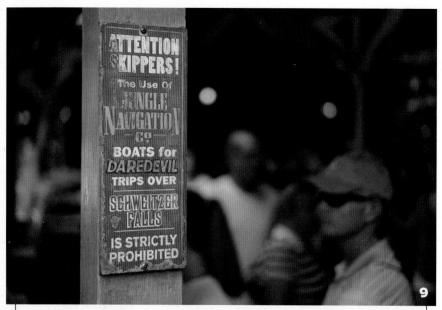

Fun finds

>1 Behind the Fastpass+ kiosks, a missing search party sent to find a previous Jungle Cruise boat is identified by six skulls on a poster tucked. **>2** "Danger! Please contact Wathel Rogers, animal handler, to enter live cargo holding area" reads a sign on a cage as you enter the attraction. One of the original Disney imagineers, Rogers designed the mechanical systems used to make the Jungle Cruise animals move. **>3** The Adventurers Club—an innovative longtime comedy spot at Downtown Disney (today's Disney Springs) that has been closed for years—is the destination of a few items in a large wire cage between the two queue lines.

OPPORTUNITIES
FOR
IMMEDIATE ADVANCEMENT
AT OUR
AMAZON RIVER BASE

RECENT EVENTS
HAVE CREATED
A NUMBER OF
OPENINGS AT
WHAT IS SURELY
OUR MOST
EXCITING
OUTPOST

IF INTERESTED PLEASE CONTACT
THE PERSONNEL OFFICE

11

A bike frame and cameras are addressed to the club's Fanny Bullock Workman Collection; a coffee mug to the Sir Henry H. Johnston Collection. Real people, Workman bicycled across Europe and Asia in the 1800s, while Johnston helped lead the colonization of Africa. The Adventurers Club address is listed as 5189 Hill Street, a nod to the club's opening date of May 1, 1989. **>4** The office of Albert Awol, the disc jockey for the Jungle Cruise company's radio network, sits alongside the standby queue. The "Voice of the Jungle" broadcasts period news, bulletins, music and quizzes on the DBC (Disney Broadcasting Company). **>5** "Fishing in the Jungle Cruise waters is prohibited," he warns, "unless you're fishing a relative out of the water." **>6** Later he asks,

"Would the Jungle Cruise skipper working on the dock wearing khaki fatigues please report to the boat storage area... I'm sorry, let me clarify that. Would the Jungle Cruise skipper in khaki fatigues working on the dock wearing the big floppy hat and black walking shoes answering to 'HEY YOU!' please report to the boat storage area." **>7** Dr. Winston Hibler, the narrator of Disney's "True-Life Adventure" movies, is the intended recipient of a barrel in the queue. His address is Outpost 71755, a belated acknowledgement that Hibler wrote the speech Walt Disney gave at the dedication of California's Disneyland on July 17, 1955. **>8** Near the end of the queue, a crate of Goff-brand "crocodile-resistant pants" is a reference to Harper Goff, one of the original

CRew Mess
LUNCH MeNU

MONDAY
Fricasse of
Giant Stag Beetle
(taste a bit like chicken)

TUESDAY
Barbecued
Three-Toed Skink
(has a chickeny flavor)

WEDNESDAY
Consomme of
River Basin Slug
(poultry like)

THURSDAY
Fillet of Rock Python
(chicken-esque)

FRIDAY
CHICKEN (REALLY!!)

13

Disney imagineers. He helped Walt Disney plan the Jungle Cruise ride at Disneyland as well that park's Main Street U.S.A. The crate lists the Goff company address as 1911 Main Street, Fort Collins, Colorado. Goff was born in 1911, and used the historic buildings of his Fort Collins hometown as the basis of his Main Street work. Goff was also the set designer for the classic 1942 movie "Casablanca," and the art director for the 1971 film "Willy Wonka and the Chocolate Factory." **>9** The use of the ride's boats for "daredevil trips over Schweitzer Falls is strictly prohibited," warns a poster in the queue. **>10** A giant black tarantula periodically jerks and rears up in a small cage near the dock. **>11** "Recent events have created a number of openings" at the company, announces an ominous poster at the loading area. **>12** E.L. O'Fevre is the Jungle Navigation Co.'s latest employee of the month, a sign announces over the boarding area. **>13** Every exotic dish the crew mess serves for lunch tastes like chicken, reports a menu board. **>14** Boat names include Amazon Annie, Congo Connie, Wamba Wanda and Zambesi Zelda. **>15** On the ride, signs of your impending doom include what your skipper may refer to as "the remains of my last Jungle Cruise crew"—some painted skulls mounted on trophy poles in the Congo. **>16** A nearby crate is labeled Ammo 717, a reference to the July 17, 1955 opening date of California's Disneyland. **>17** As the rhino chases the lost safari party up a pole, does the man on the bottom look familiar, foolish mortal? He's a dead ringer for the

15

WAMBA WANDA

14

19

caretaker of the graveyard at the Haunted Mansion. **>18** In a nod to how one recent princess movie seems to be taking over Walt Disney World, your skipper may introduce Schweitzer Falls as "one of the few things at Disney that isn't 'Frozen.'" **>19** The ears of the hippos often wiggle. **>20** "I know! I'll scare them away like I did my last boyfriend," some young female skippers confide when hippos pop out of the water, before facing the creatures to yell "Marry me! I want to take you home to meet my parents!" **>21** "I love disco!" secretly shouts one of the ride's headhunters just after the start of his chant, though the panicked patter of your skipper may drown it out. The

17

21

phrase was secretly added by a mischievous Disney audio engineer in the late 1970s. **>22** The monkeys in the temple will look familiar to fans of Epcot's Living With The Land attraction. The creatures also appear in that boat ride's tropical rainforest. **>23** The cobras in the temple also appear in the "Raiders of the Lost Ark" scene of The Great Movie Ride at Disney's Hollywood Studios. **>24** Your skipper transforms into Captain Obvious near the end of the ride. "And now I'd like to point out some of my favorite plants," she says, before silently gesturing toward random bits of greenery. Later, she may bid you farewell with "Of all the crews I've had today, you have certainly been the most... recent." **>25** Trader

Sam's red-and-white striped skirt is an homage to the ride's original candy-striped boat canopies from the 1970s, which are still seen in Jungle Cruise posters and some promotional photos. **>26** One of Sam's shrunken heads bears a resemblance to Katharine Hepburn, the co-star of "The African Queen." **>27** "Ilene Dover" and "Ann Fellen" (say them slowly, without the "and") are among previous Jungle Cruise passengers who have gone missing, according to a chalkboard in the exitway. **>28** "This end up... or was it this end up... or maybe this end up" read the sides of a square box below the chalkboard. **>29** "Quicksand! Rush!" is stamped on a second box. **>30** A third one warns "Fragile! Handle

31

32

Al Belaite
B.N. Eaton
Emma Boylen
C.M. Cooken

Ilene Dover
Ann Fellen

Seaum Yett
Albert Knot
Betty Dont

27

33

with care!" but then in small print acknowledges "Who's kidding who? Contents probably already broken." **>31** "Danger! Wild orangutan!" a sign warns on a nearby cage. Its bars forced open, the cage is empty, its gap lashed by rope. **>32** Poison darts bristle from a suitcase. **>33** Two roped crates pay homage to the 1960 Disney movie "Swiss Family Robinson." One, addressed to the film's director Kenneth Annakin, lists his address as "W\SS Supply Company, Colony of New Guinea"—a reference to "Swiss Family Robinson"

MagicKingdom

book author Johann Wyss and the intended destination of the Robinson family before its ship broke up. **>34** A second crate is headed to "Thomas Kirk Esq." at the Field Office of "M. Jones Cartographers Ltd." on the island of "Bora Danno." Thomas Kirk

played middle son Ernst in "Swiss Family Robinson" and was the lead character in Disney's 1964 film "The Misadventures of Merlin Jones." James McArthur was oldest son Fritz in "Swiss" and later Danny "Danno" Williams in the 1968–1980 television series "Hawaii Five-O."

MagicKingdom

51

The two crates originally sat alongside the entrance to the Swiss Family Treehouse. **Jingle Cruise:** >**35** Reindeer heads hide in tropical wreaths during November and December, as the ride transforms itself into the "Jingle Cruise." Other holiday finds include: >**36** gift tags on items inside crates that indicate that the skippers are giving passenger possessions to each other as presents (just inside the entrance), >**37** a can of Ethanol that's been turned into eggnog (on the boarding dock) and >**38** a squat makeshift snowman who has a banana for a nose (on the dock's skinny outside guide strip). >**39** Jingle Cruise boat names include Candy Cane Connie, >**40** Eggnog Annie, >**41** Icicle Irma, >**42** Mistletoe Millie, >**43** Orino-Cocoa Ida, >**44** Reindeer Ruby >**45** and Fruitcake Zelda. >**46** Trader Sam has become "Trader Sam-ta," with a sign that urges you to "get a head start on your holiday shopping." >**47** Skippers wear coats and tropical stocking caps. >**48** "75% passenger return rate" and "Overcome fear of passengers" are among the skippers' New Year's resolutions written on a chalk board along the exitway.

Hidden Mickeys

>**49** *"You're a Bendel bonnet, a Shakespeare sonnet, you're Mickey Mouse!"* croons singer John Hauser over the Jungle Cruise radio heard in the queue, as he and the Paul Whiteman Orchestra perform their 1934 version of the Cole Porter standard "You're the Top." >**50** Lichen patches form Mickey's three-circle shape on a tree across the river from the boarding dock. Look for it on a trunk that rises and splits to the right, above and behind the crew's shack. >**51** Formed by stamped circles surrounded by rivets, the three circles appear on the ride between and below the windows of the back end of a crashed aiplane, which rests in overgrowth on your right just after you pass Schweitzer Falls. The front of the plane, a period-correct Lockheed Model 12 Electra Junior, is also at Walt Disney World. Robotic versions of Humphrey Bogart and Ingrid Bergman stand in front of it in the "Casablanca" set on The Great Movie Ride at Disney's Hollywood Studios. >**52** Three gray stones form Mickey's shape on the ground in front of the rhino poking the safari party. >**53** Mickey's also hiding in the temple, on your right as three yellow dots on the back of a large spider.

50

Pirates of the Caribbean

Honest Abe wants the redhead.

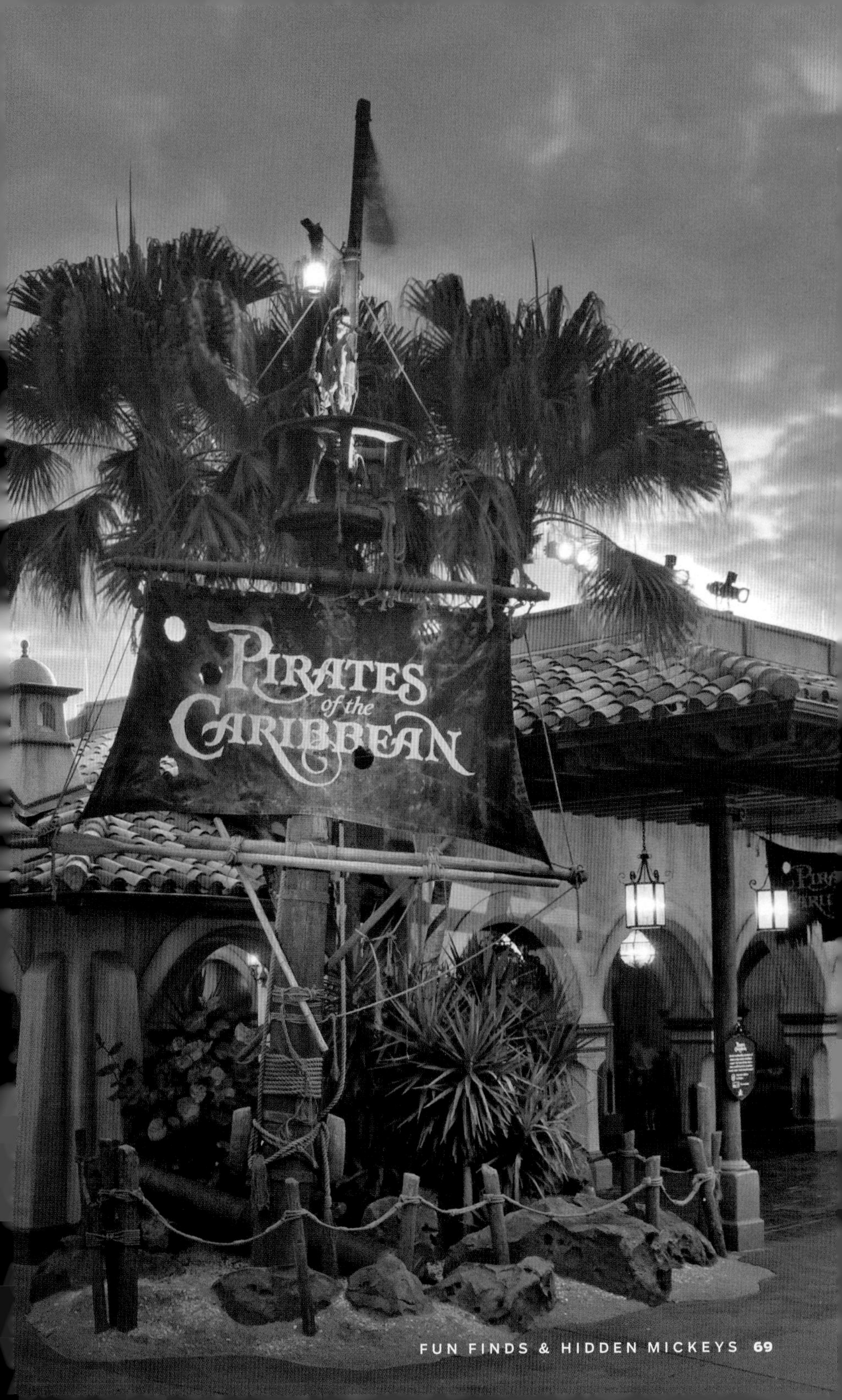
Pirates
of the
Caribbean

MagicKingdom

DRUNKEN PIRATES "pillage and plunder... rifle and loot... kidnap and ravage and don't give a hoot" in this rowdy, rum-soaked attraction, a dark indoor boat ride which takes you through the robotic ransacking of a Spanish port. There's plenty to look at, as you pass dozens of vignettes filled with sight gags and

"There's nothing politically correct about Pirates of the Caribbean," says one Disney imagineer. "In fact much of it is patently offensive."

details. Special effects simulate fire, lightning, wind and, best of all, splashing cannonballs. Designed in part by the same artists who created the goofy Country Bear Jamboree, the ride keeps a lightweight tone; its pirates have such caricatured features they seem straight out of a cartoon. The attraction later became the inspiration for Disney's "Pirates of the Caribbean" film series, and has since been updated to include Capt. Jack Sparrow and other characters from those movies. Its cool, dim queue winds through a stone fort.

Storied it be

Pirates of the Caribbean tells two distinct stories, which somewhat contradict each other. The first is a morality tale, told in flashback

form. It begins in the present day, as your boat passes through a watery grotto lined with skeletons of pirates, many of whom met their fate by being stabbed and left to die. Then, as your boat drops down a short waterfall, you travel back in time to see what led those pirates to their doom—an irresponsible life of debauchery.

The scenes after the waterfall also tell their own story, one added to the ride after the success of the "Pirates" movies. In it, Capt. Hector Barbossa has tracked Capt. Jack to the port. Barbossa's crew searches for Jack but never finds him, and he claims all of the town's riches for himself.

Scenes include the pirate ships' attack on the port, an interrogation of port officials, an auctioning of the port's women and the burning of its buildings—all of which is celebrated and set to music. Toward the end, prisoners in a dungeon are desperate to escape, though they can't get a dog to bring them the key to their cell. Meanwhile, draped over an ornate throne in the town's vault, Capt. Jack sings to a parrot.

Historic it be

The last attraction that Walt Disney helped design, Pirates of the Caribbean combines a Missouri farm boy's view of adventure with a Hollywood showman's use of theatrics. Though they first planned to make it a wax-museum-like walk-through exhibit, Walt and his assistants switched it to an Audio-Animatronics boat ride after the success of two company efforts at the 1964 New York World's Fair—General Electric's Carousel of Progress, with its life-like robotic characters, and United Way's It's a Small World, with its high-tech water jets that propelled boats of guests through its scenes. It debuted at California's Disneyland on March 18, 1967, three months after Walt Disney's death.

Expanding it be

Over the years Disney has filled the area around the ride with other Pirates-themed offerings.

Tortuga Tavern. Across the Adventureland walkway from the ride's exit, Tortuga Tavern is based on the young-adult book series "Pirates of the Caribbean: Jack Sparrow." Set in a time before the first "Pirates of the Caribbean" movie, its story includes the character Arabella Smith, an adolescent barmaid who takes over the Tavern after her drunken dad and pirate mom disappear. Living above the tavern, Arabella flirts with fellow teenager Jack Sparrow and dates young Bootstrap Billy Turner.

A Pirates Adventure. Players of this interactive scavenger hunt help Capt. Sparrow lift a curse by using a treasure map to find hidden objects throughout Adventureland, many of which come to life.

Pirates League. This makeover salon transforms adults and children into swashbucklers, swashbucklerettes and mermaids.

Captain Jack Sparrow's Pirate Tutorial. In this intimate live stage show, Capt. Jack teaches kids how to be rescued from a desert island, use swordplay to flee an enemy, and sing the ride's theme song.

PC it be not

The ride's scenes are all in good fun, of course, but parents may wonder if those showing torture, heavy drinking and the selling of women send the best messages to a wide-eyed young child. "There is nothing politically correct about Pirates of the Caribbean," admits Disney Imagineer Eric Jacobson. "In fact, much of it is patently offensive."

In fairness, the ride does imply the consequences of such behavior. Its first scene has always shown that its pirates end up murdered, and over the years its caveman view of women has been toned down. A barrel that today hides Capt. Jack once hid a scared female captive who appeared to be naked. Holding her lacy petticoat, a drunken pirate in front of her asked passersby, "Say, have you set your eyes on the bewitched maiden in your travels? Oh a lively lassie she be."

Disney replaced the petticoat with a treasure map in 1997, and changed out the pirate's dialogue so that he complained that "this map says X marks the spot, but I be seein' no X's afore me." As for the girl, Disney dressed her and gave her a small treasure chest to hold, hoping to convey that she was hiding not to protect her virtue, but rather her valuables. In California, the woman was replaced with a cat and the pirate's lust with gluttony, as he then told passersby "I be looking for a fine pork loin, I be!"

Disney changed the scene again in 2006, replacing the woman (in California, the cat) with a spying Capt. Jack Sparrow and giving the pirate yet another monologue and prop. Now he can read his map and lusts for only the riches it leads to.

The company redid another scene that year too. In it, a group of pirates continually chased young women in circles, the cute conquests-to-be giggling as they barely escaped. Then came the joke—an older, overweight woman chasing a pirate. The new version switches things up so that instead of showing amorous pirates chasing playful women, it shows angry women chasing pillaging pirates.

Though the complaints died down, the changes didn't please everyone. In an interview after they were made, an imagineer who helped create the original ride bitterly referred to the updated one as "Boy Scouts of the Caribbean."

Fun facts

Aye, there be a treasure trove of trivia at this attraction. Such as:

It was fashionably late. When Walt Disney World opened in 1971 it didn't include a Pirates of the Caribbean ride, as Disney bigwigs reasoned that since there were so many real pirate attractions in Florida nobody would be interested in a pretend one. The ride debuted at the Magic Kingdom in 1973.

It holds a Disney 'first'. Pirates of the Caribbean was the first Disney ride to exit through a gift shop. Most still don't do it today.

It had bona fide bones. The ride's skeletons were real—actual human remains from the UCLA Medical Center—when it first opened at California's Disneyland.

It has a famous ghost. The voice of the cryptic warning "dead men tell no tales" and that of its pirate auctioneer come from the Haunted Mansion's Ghost Host, voice talent Paul Frees.

Some of it's gone Hollywood. Many of the attraction characters appear in the "Pirates" movies, among them the magistrate, the redhead, the snoring pirate with the pigs and the jailed prisoners with their dog. In 2011 the bridal auction was expanded into a live-action short, "Tales of the Code: Wedlocked." In it, after a feisty blonde and a flirty redhead have both been left at the altar by Jack Sparrow, the two suddenly find themselves in an auction competing against each other. Angered by the higher bids for the redhead, the blonde accuses her of not only coloring her hair, but also enhancing her breasts. Still, the pirates shout "We wants the redhead!"

That really is Johnny Depp. The faces of the Jack Sparrow Audio-Animatronic characters were created using molds of Johnny Depp's face. The actor voiced the dialogue of the robots, too.

Fun finds

>1 Cannonball holes mar the attraction's sign, which is a sail on a mast. **>2** Broken oars support the sail. **>3** Pressing a telescope to an eye socket, the skeleton of a pirate peers down at park guests from a crow's nest atop the mast. **>4** Unseen Spanish guards shout commands amid cannon fire along the left entrance line, though both are nearly drowned out by the ride's theme music. **>5** Shackled in chains, two pirate skeletons play chess along the right entrance line, in a dungeon cell behind some wall slits and jail bars. Remnants of their clothes hang from their bones, as if they started their game when they were alive. Chess

16

22

players will note that the skeletons have reached a stalemate. During busy periods an extension of the left entrance line also passes by them. **>6** At the ride's boarding dock, a pirate ship appears off in the distance through an archway on your right. Cannons are aimed at it. **>7** A huge human skull hides in the rocky wall in front of you as you near a small beach. Obvious once you see it, it's formed by large rocks in the wall just to the left of the beach, and has no lower jaw. **>8** Mermaids swim next to your boat, appearing on both sides as faint glimmers of light. **>9** Their tails sometimes break the surface, creating small ripples. **>10** Their siren songs waft through the air. **>11** The skeleton of a mermaid lies in a fishing net of a small boat on the beach, next to some pirate skeletons. **>12** Still gripping its own sword, one skeleton is standing, pressed against a wall. **>13** A seagull nests in its hat. **>14** Just past the beach, a crazed pirate skeleton stands at the remains of a wooden helm, steering its ship's wheel during a violent storm, unaware that the wheel is not attached to a ship. **>15** The Wicked Wench is the name of the attacking pirate ship to your left in the battle scene, identified by a nameplate on its stern that's barely visible in the darkness. **>16** "Strike your colors you bloomin' cockroaches," Capt. Barbossa commands his crew, repeating a order yelled by the boat's original captain for 35 years

© Disney

© Disney

26

(1971 to 2006). **>17** Speaking Spanish, the fort's soldiers bark orders to each other and shout threats at the pirates. **>18** The pirate interrogating officials at the village well has a hook for a hand. **>19** When he commands that the magistrate tell him "Where be Capt. Jack Sparrow?" the magistrate's wife pleads from a window: "Don't tell him Carlos! Don't be chicken!" **>20** "I am no chicken! I will not talk!" Carlos calls back to her, just before getting dunked. **>21** Waiting to be questioned, a second town official shivers in fear. **>22** Near the well, Capt. Jack hides among some female dressmaking forms, his fingers pinching a derriere. **>23** At the bridal auction, the first woman in line is beaming, happy to be sold. **>24** Referring to her as "stout-hearted and corn-fed" the auctioneer gently orders the portly woman to "shift yer cargo, dearie. Show 'em yer larboard side." **>25** "Are you selling her by the pound?" a pirate jokes. **>26** Second in line, an impatient redhead lifts the hem of her dress to flash her leg, petticoat and heels. **>27** "Strike yer colors you brazen wench!" the auctioneer barks. "No need to expose yer superstructure!" **>28** When a pirate on your left fires his pistol, a sign on your right "pings" then sways in the air. **>29** Dressed in a bridal gown and veil, another women in line clasps her hands. **>30** A crying woman is consoled by a large-nosed spinster, who also wears a bridal veil. **>31** One of the pirates is Abraham Lincoln—or at least his scruffier identical twin. Appearing in plain sight near the right side of your

MagicKingdom

boat, he joins with the others to shout "We wants the redhead! We wants the redhead!" Rumors say the figure—who unlike his fellow buccaneers has no caricatured features and slow, graceful arm movements—is the same Audio-Animatronics character seen for decades at the nearby Hall of Presidents. Begging you to notice him, Disney has topped off its Pirate Abe with a tall stovepipe-like hat. **>32** The women chasing the pirates in circles still giggle, just as they did when the pirates chased them. **>33** Holding a map and key to the town's treasure, the pirate in front of the barrel gloats "What I wouldn't give to see the look on Capt. Jack's face when he hears tell 'tis only me that gots the goods"— unaware Jack is spying on him from behind. **>34** One pirate tries to get a cat to drink with him. "Here kitty, kitty, kitty," he slurs. "Have a little 'ol tot of rum with ol' Bill, aye?" **>35** A dog and a donkey bark and bray in rhythm as a cantina band performs the "Yo-Ho" theme song. **>36** A pirate nearly topples over as he steps into a boat, struggling to steal a towering amount of loot. **>37** A pirate snores as he sleeps in a puddle of mud, with pigs oinking behind him. **>38** As you reach a small bridge, a very hairy leg of a pirate dangles above your head. **>39** "A parrot's life for me!" sings the parrot next to that pirate. **>40** Frustrated that the dog in front of them won't bring them the key to their cell, one jailed prisoner suggests to another, "Hit

him with the soup bone!" **>41** As the dog glances at your boat, a captive calls "Rover, it's us what needs yer ruddy help, not them blasted lubbers!" **>42** Actually the prisoners could easily escape the cell, as its bars are widely spaced. **>43** In the treasure room, the key from the earlier pirate pokes out from the unlocked door. **>44** "I shall take this paltry sum as a stipend to cover my expenses," Capt. Jack drunkenly declares as he basks among the riches, "my reward for a life of villainy, larceny, skullduggery and persnickety." **>45** As Jack sings the ride's "Yo Ho (A Pirate's Life for Me)" theme song, a parrot interrupts him after *"maraud and embezzle and even hijack"* to squawk "Hi Jack! Hi Jack!" **>46** Jack refers to the colorful bird as "my chromatic winged beast." **>47** A peg-leg mark appears repeatedly on the ride's exit ramp, as part of some safety graphics that show you where to step. **Pirates Bazaar gift shop: >48** The stolen loot the pirates are selling includes wall decor from Kona Cafe, a restaurant at Disney's Polynesian Village Resort hotel. A hanging ceiling net holds the pieces. **>49** The cursed Aztec medallion that drove the plot of 2003's "Pirates of the Caribbean: The Curse of the Black Pearl" is affixed to a red vase in the gift shop. The vase sits high on a shelf, to the left of an open view of the Pirates League makeup salon. **>50** The key to Davy Jones' chest seen in 2007's "Pirates of the Caribbean:

At World's End" hides among other things in a caged shelf in an open room to the right of the gift shop, next to a restroom entrance.

Pirates League makeup salon: **>51** Out front, child mannequins model makeup options. **>52** Three "At World's End" props are inside— a rolled-up map of World's End, on a shelf behind a silver helmet; **>53** a chest that held the hearts of Davy Jones and Will Turner, nearby; **>54** an elaborate cannon from the Empress, a Chinese junk captained by Elizabeth Turner, in a corner. **A Pirates Adventure game: >55**

Pirate skulls stand on poles in a small garden along the left side of the Pirates of the Caribbean entrance, a nod to a key scene in the 2003 movie, "Pirates of the Caribbean: The Curse of the Black Pearl." The skulls speak and their eyes glow red for game players. **>56** A huge pearl hides inside a giant clam in front of Walt Disney's Enchanted Tiki Room. **>57** Alongside the Magic Carpets of Aladdin ride, the eyes of an ancient statue glow green just before its mouth reveals a golden idol. **>58** A glowing-eyed pirate skeleton

58

57

56

rises out of the water next to the Jungle Cruise entrance plaza. **>59** Secret agent Perry the Platypus (from the Disney Channel series "Phineas and Ferb") appears in the same small room as the key to Davy Jones' chest, on a shelf on the back wall. Perry's likeness is formed by an actual skull of a platypus that's been topped with a tiny fedora. **>60** Next to Perry, a belt buckle with the "KP" logo of the Disney Channel series "Kim

Possible" and a vintage ribbon and medal combine with the platypus skull to form an homage to the Disney World interactive games that preceded A Pirates Adventure: Agent P's World Showcase Adventure at Epcot, Kim Possible's World Showcase Adventure, and Sorcerers of the Magic Kingdom.
Tortuga Tavern: >61 Angry at her parents for abandoning her and the place, teenage proprietor Arabella Smith has tossed their sign for the

TORTUGA TAVERN

Code of Conduct

Every Man has Equal Title to
Fresh Provisions
iffin he has the gold

Ye fair ladies shall be treated in a
favorable manner
*Wenches be not
Fair Ladies*

A witness shall be present for
gaming at cards or dice
*Short Drop and Sudden Stop for
Cheatin Scallywags*

Duels by cutlass or pistol shall be
taken outside with witness
*Ye witness must have
one good eye*

Damages unto an establishment
shall be paid in gold, doubloons or
pieces of eight
*Parrots be not legal tender!
Ye be warned
No Monkeys*

67

64

Gentlemen you are
welcome to sit down
at your table.
Pay what you call for
& drink what you
please
**A. SMITH,
PROPRIETOR**

66

73

59

75

tavern—which they ran as "The Faithful Bride"—into a nearby cart. **>62** To attract customers, the shy girl has posed for a bold portrait on a new sign. **>63** "Est. 1673" is a sly reference to the 1973 opening of the nearby Pirates of the Caribbean. **>64** Figureheads of Arabella's mom —the notorious Laura Smith—hang off a sign above the entrance. **>65** Arabella has hung her coat and hat outside of her second-floor living quarters. **>66** Inside the tavern, she politely asks "gentlemen" to "pay what you call for" via a poster on the wall. **>67** "Ye Fair Ladies Be Treated in a Favorable Manner" she promises in her posted Code of Conduct, to which she has scribbled "Wenches be *not* Fair Ladies," **>68** "Parrots be not legal tender!" and **>69** "No Monkeys!" **>70** Lit candles and fuses in the hair of Blackbeard in a nearby mural show how that real-life pirate (and supposed Tortuga Tavern patron) intimidated others. **>71** Sign-up sheets for those wanting to sail on The Black Pearl or Blackbeard's Queen Anne's Revenge appear in books in a window display. On the Black Pearl sheet, a young Jack Sparrow has crossed out the name of its captain, Hector Barbossa, and replaced it with his own. **>72** Farther down that sheet, one of the Pearl's wanna-be crew members is "Jack (the monkey)," though Sparrow has also crossed that out. **>73** A small portrait of Arabella's mom sits on the mantel of a fireplace.

▶ Hidden Mickeys

>74 Mickey's three-circle silhouette appears as marks in a plaster wall in the Pirates of the Caribbean left queue, above and to the right of a fireplace mantel; **>75** as coins on a scale in the gift shop, just after you exit the ride on your right; **>76** as angled golden circles near the left shoulder of a woman's tunic, in a colorful painting in the far back corner of the shop; **>77** and as candles in a bowl in the Tortuga Tavern, in front of the sign-up sheets for the pirate ships.

76

Big Thunder Mountain Railroad

Now you blow things up.

RESEARCH BY **MICAELA NEAL**

Disney's highest-grossing film of the 1970s, "The Apple Dumpling Gang" was released in 1975.

BIG THUNDER MOUNTAIN RAILROAD is the rare roller coaster that tells a story, a tale of a frontier mining town whose relentless pursuit of riches upset the spirits of nature.

According to Disney lore, during the Gold Rush men from the Utah desert town of Tumbleweed were prospecting on a nearby mountain, a Native American burial ground. Though the ridge rumbled when mining took place— the Apache called the peak Big Thunder—the gold diggers were persistent. Adding insult to injury, they partied hard at night, drinking, playing poker and dancing with parlor girls.

Eventually the spirits had enough. Miners began to hear ghostly sounds, cave-ins became frequent and equipment mysteriously failed. One day a train suddenly spun out of control, and flew around the mountain like a bat out of hell. More desecration of the mountain led to a devastating flood—though some miners were too drunk to notice as they partied at the Gold Dust Saloon. Moments later an earthquake struck. Word of the mine's troubles eventually got out, and soon it, its trains and the little town of Tumbleweed were all abandoned.

Thirty years later, when eyewitness accounts of the incidents have faded into folklore, mining tycoon Barnabas T. Bullion has resurrected the company and is blasting into the mountain once again. Bullion comes from a wealthy and powerful East Coast family, and considers the gold in the mountain to be his very birthright by virtue of his oddly appropriate name.

Bullion has discovered new veins of gold and digs new shafts every day. He's also revamped the railroad and retooled some of its mine shafts to create a tourist attraction, giving sightseers a chance to tour his facility and ride the legendary trains. But as today's riders will soon learn, some legends are true. And if you don't learn from history you're bound to repeat it.

History

The roller coaster was originally planned to be part of a much larger expansion to Frontierland. "Thunder Mesa" would have also included an indoor Old West boat ride called the "Western River Expedition," a mule ride and hiking trails. Budget troubles eliminated everything but the coaster, though the boat ride idea lived on to become Pirates of the Caribbean.

Big Thunder Mountain Railroad opened in 1980. In 2013 it was spiffed up with an elaborate and interactive queue that's packed with hundreds of little things to look for, including many hidden references to Disney's 1975 live-action film about the Gold Rush, "The Apple Dumpling Gang."

Fun facts

A Big Thunder television series? It almost happened. Some trivia:

It was almost a TV show. In January 2013, a television pilot based on the ride—titled "Big Thunder Mountain"—was ordered by ABC. A "supernatural adventure drama," the "rock 'n' roll western" was to focus on a brilliant 19th-century New York doctor who relocates to a frontier mining town with his terminally ill son, whose health then begins to mysteriously improve. Casting was completed later that year—"Twilight" actor Alex Meraz was to play "a handsome Shoshone tribesman"—but the project was later scrapped.

It made the silver screen. The 1984 Steven Spielberg/George Lucas movie "Indiana Jones and the Temple of Doom" used the sounds of the Big Thunder trains in its mine cart sequence.

It holds one Disney 'first'. Big Thunder Mountain Railroad was the first Walt Disney World attraction designed with computers.

That's real gear. The old mining equipment that litters the premises was scoured from Old West ghost towns during the 1970s.

There's no mountain. Not even a hill. In reality, the "mountain" is a painted cement and wire-mesh skin over a concrete-and-steel frame. Inside are computers, electronics and water pumps. While passing through the flooded town of Tumbleweed, the track does several bunny hops, and the train seems to sway from side to side as if in water. The swaying is achieved by banking the track slightly.

Bossman Bullion is a fraud! The portrait of Big Thunder Mining Co. President Barnabas T. Bullion hanging in the queue actually portrays imagineer Tony Baxter, the chief designer of the attraction.

Today's Rain Forecast ▼ 40" ▼

40" (102cm)

36"

24"

3

Fun finds

Grounds: **>1** On the attraction's sign, broken wheel rims support hanging lanterns. **>2** Sticks of dynamite are strapped to the clock of the FastPass+ sign. A black fuse leads away from them. **>3** A height measurement bar reads "Today's rain forecast." It points to the ride's height minimum, 40 inches. **>4** Real century plants, agave and prickly pear cactus grow on the grounds. **>5** Authentic old ore carts scatter across the landscape; **>6** as do buckets, cogwheels and other pieces of mining equipment. **>7** A fine crusher sits to the right of the entranceway. It was made on March 10, 1885. **>8** Some equipment was manufactured by the Joshua Hendy Machine Works of San Francisco, a company that later became the leading supplier of engines for U.S. ships during World War II. **>9** Lanterns throughout the grounds continuously dim and flicker. **>10** Many signs read "Danger: Blasting Area." **>11** Crates and boxes of "Lytum & Hyde"-brand explosives are scattered around the entrance and within the queue. **>12** The Lytum & Hyde company is based in Sparks, Nevada. **>13** A crate of "Widowmaker"-brand explosives rests just off the walkway in front of the ride, between its entrance and exit. **>14** "O'verdigums Irish Blend" is the brand of whiskey in a crate nearby (as in the toast, "through the lips and over the gums, look out stomach here it comes!"). **>15** Reliance Hose Co.

Fire Chief Richard LePere Jr. is the intended recipient of a third crate, which sits next to a water fountain. In reality, LePere heads the fire department of the Reedy Creek Improvement District, the one at Walt Disney World. **>16** Potatoes are the third item on a "Clarksdale Dry Goods" wagon, which otherwise holds dynamite and a powder keg. **>17** Smoke rises from flues atop the corrugated tin roof of the mine office (it's actually steam). **>18** Barbed wire tops fences that surround the mountain. **Ambient music:** **>19** A song from the 1950s Disney television serial "Davy Crockett," "Old Betsy" (*"Bang goes ol' Betsy, my only gun is Betsy..."*) is one of the many instrumentals heard on the grounds. **>20** The 1844 tune "Buffalo Gals (Won't You Come Out Tonight?)" would usually have its title altered to reflect where it was being sung. So here it would be *"Tumbleweed Gals..."* **>21** It's a shame 1880's "Hand Me Down My Walking Cane (I'm Gonna Catch the Midnight Train)" appears here as an instrumental— the African-American work song has great lyrics (*"hand me down my bottle of corn, I'll get drunk as sure as you're born," "the beans are bad and the meat's all fat, oh my God I can't eat that!"*). The phrase "Hand me down my walking cane" has appeared in many lyrics since. It's the first line of the Spinners' 1976 hit, "The Rubberband Man." **Building entrance:** **>22** "No Drinking, Fighting or Whistling. No Kidding!" warns a sign in front of

Magic**Kingdom**

you. **>23** "Costas A. Lott" is the manager of the B.T. Bullion Company Store, where "all sales are mandatory" and "all sales are final," according to a sign on your left. **>24** "Meal provided daily, baths weekly" reads an adjacent sign for the Big Thunder Boarding House, where "all miners are required to bunk." **>25** Its proprietress is "Mrs. Liddy Stockley." That name is the first of many references in the queue to Disney's 1975 live-action comedy about the Gold Rush, "The Apple Dumpling Gang," the company's most successful movie of the 1970s. The character Liddy Stockley ran the boarding house in that film. **Office: >26** Once fully in the

building you come to the company's office, where the foreman has his desk and the business of the mine takes place. A list of pay rates on the wall reveals the foreman's name: G. Willikers. **>27** Willikers earns $10.84 per day ($250 a day in today's dollars), more than twice that of anyone else. **>28** Gold bars and ore fill an open safe. The mineral sparkles (and rumbles) whenever anyone nearby uses a Remote Distance Blasting Machine (see below). **>29** Bullion's land grant for the (supposed) 340 acres is posted near the safe. **>30** The land sits in the district of "the Western River Valley" and includes "Thunder Mesa"—references to the Thunder Mesa area of Magic

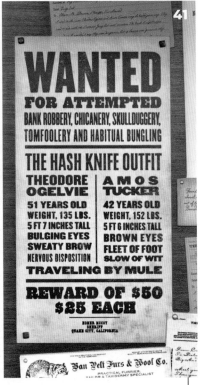

Kingdom that Big Thunder Mountain was once planned to be a part of, and the never-built Western River Expedition boat ride it was going to complement. **>31** A painting of the Big Thunder Mountain landscape appears in the rafters.

>32 A nearby notice from the T.W. Bullion Silver Mine warns of two rogue prospectors claiming to be metallurgists, who *"fouled up our whole operation and took off with ten pounds of lead. Complete incompetents."* An accompanying sketch of the thieves shows the faces of the two holdup men from "The Apple Dumpling Gang," Theodore Ogelvie (actor Don

Knotts, best known as deputy Barney Fife on the 1960s television series "The Andy Griffith Show") and Amos Tucker ("Carol Burnett Show" funny-man Tim Conway).

>33 Tommy knockers are in one of the Big Thunder mines, according to a large nearby Assay Report board. Commonly believed to be real by miners throughout the United States at the time, tommy knockers were mischievous leprechaun-like creatures who lived in mines. Often they would knock on the walls of their shafts, either to warn those above of an impending cave-in or to cause one. **Bulletin boards: >34** Several fun finds

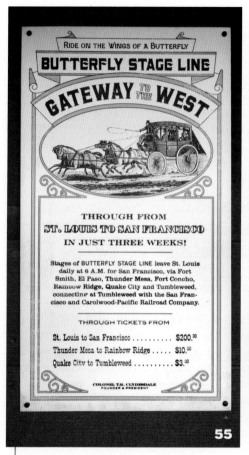

55

125

22

appear on two bulletin boards. A note from the Tumbleweed Mining Co. foreman G. Willikers warns that "All miners caught taking an early lunch will be put on the graveyard shift, permanently." **>35** "E.Z. Marks" has sent a letter to Professor Cumulus Isobar, the self-proclaimed "Rainmaker and Purveyor of Medicines and Elixirs" seen later on the ride. E.Z. asks for an alternative medicine for his bunions, explaining that the professor's last "cure" actually worsened his

health. **>36** Marks' address is 1313 Gullible Way. **>37** He mentions his children, Patsy and Rube. **>38** In a postscript, he adds that *"The entire Marks clan is planning a trip back east in order to see the bridge you so graciously sold me!"* **>39** A two-page patent for J. Olson's "Subterrascope" is in the middle of the bulletin board. Three of the devices appear later in the queue. **>40** T.W. Baxter is the inventor of the train's automatic brakes, according to a patent diagram.

MagicKingdom

Disney Imagineer Tony Wayne Baxter led the design and construction of the ride. **>41** On a second board, a telegram sent to the mining company from the sheriff of Tumbleweed reads *"A word to the wise. Theodore Ogelvie and Amos Tucker may be headed your way. They used to ride with the Stillwell*

'Cave-ins? Flash floods? Bad beans? Life of a miner is fraught with perils.'

gang but call themselves the Hash Knife Outfit. I wouldn't say they were dangerous, but if brains were dynamite…" Nearly all of that is a reference to "The Apple Dumpling Gang"—in that film Ogelvie and Tucker worked for evil Frank Stillwell (cowboy star Slim Pickens) before setting off on their own as the Hash Knife Outfit. (In real life, "the Hash Knife Outfit" was slang for Arizona's Aztec Land & Cattle Co. Its brand resembled a hash knife; its cowboys were known for their lawlessness. **>42** Chase M. Downs is the Tumbleweed sheriff. **>43** Just below that telegram, a wanted poster seeks the Hash Knife Outfit for its "attempted bank robbery, chicanery, skullduggery, tomfoolery and habitual bungling." The phrase "wanted for chicanery, skullduggery, tomfoolery and habitual bungling" was the tagline of "The Apple Dumpling Gang" on its promotional posters. **>44** The sign

says Ogelvie has "bulging eyes, sweaty brow, nervous disposition." **>45** Tucker is "fleet of foot, slow of wit." **>46** It was posted by Quake City Sheriff Homer McCoy—that's two more "Apple Dumpling Gang" shout-outs. Played by Harry Morgan (later Col. Sherman Potter on the 1970s sitcom "M*A*S*H") Homer McCoy was the sheriff of the town of Quake City. **>47** "Near the old mill" is where you'll find the Dan Pelt Furs & Wool Co., according to a small ad underneath the wanted poster. "The Old Mill" is a 1937 Disney Silly Symphonies cartoon. **>48** *"Dear Barney, I am indeed sorry to hear of the recent disturbances within Big Thunder Mountain, but I did warn you that you were prospecting at your peril when I sold you that drilling machine,"* writes Jason Chandler in a letter to Big Thunder Mining Co. President Barnabas T. Bullion posted at the top right of the board. *"I took the liberty of consulting with Madame Larhou at the Museum of the Weird, and it is her considered opinion that you should consider abandoning this entire operation at once… some forces simply are not to be trifled with."* Chandler, founder and president of The Society of Explorers and Adventurers, closes with *"I do hope to see you around the club a bit more often!"* During the 1960s, the Museum of the Weird was one of many Disney concepts for an attraction that became the Haunted Mansion. **>49** "Payments will not be made in advance no matter what trouble you are in with the law," warns the paymaster on a scrap of paper. **>50** *"Ready to head West, even if there are reports of Tommy-knockers and cave-ins in the mine,"* reads a yellowed telegram to Tumbleweed resident K. Derreis. In real life, Katy Harris is a Disney artistic director known for her willingness to travel. She's worked at theme parks around the world. **>51** *"I've got men here ready to go dig gold. Didn't tell them about the troubling problems you have,"* reads a telegram from "Ruthless Pete." That's a reference to the cartoon cat Pete, the shady long-time nemesis of Mickey Mouse and host of the Magic Kingdom attraction, "Pete's Silly Sideshow." **More signs and notices: >52** "Cave-ins? Flash floods? Bad beans? Life of a miner is fraught with perils," warns a sign promoting a "Boothill Layaway" service offered by the Tumbleweed Cabinet & Casket Co. "Boothill" meant graveyard in the Old West, where men were said to have died "with their boots on" if they did so in a gunfight or at work. **>53** "Speedy" funerals are $10, "proper" ones $30. Services that include a "plot with a view" are $42. **>54** "U.B. Underhill" is the owner of the company. **>55** A white sign advertises that the Butterfly Stage Line stops at Quake City, Thunder Mesa, Fort Concho and Rainbow Ridge. In "The Apple Dumpling Gang," bumbling thieves Ogelvie

and Tucker leave Quake City and enlist in the U.S. Cavalry at Fort Concho (a real fort in San Angelo, Texas). Thunder Mesa was, again, the large Fronterland expansion Disney planned but never built except for Big Thunder Mountain. Rainbow Ridge is a faux mining town at the Big Thunder Mountain ride at California's Disneyland. **>56** The Carolwood Pacific Railroad Co. connects to the stage line. Carolwood Pacific was the name Walt Disney gave a miniature railroad he built in his backyard. **>57** "Colonel T.R. Clydesdale" is the stage line's founder and president. That's the name of the stage-line owner (played by famed actor David Wayne) in "The Apple Dumpling Gang." **Fusing cage: >58** Names on a wooden door leading into this small room pay tribute to Disney imagineers who helped create the attraction. "Buckaroo Burke" is a shout-out to Pat Burke, a show-set designer. **>59** "Calamity Clem" refers to Clem Hall, a scenic designer and artist. **>60** "Little Big Gibson" denotes Blaine Gibson, who sculpted the ride's robotic figures. **>61** "Jolley the Kid" refers to art director Bob Jolley, ironically the "older brother" of the ride's imagineers. **>62** "Matchstick Marc" is Marc Davis, who designed the never-built Western River Expedition. **>63** "Skittish Skip" is rockwork expert Skip Lange, who designed the mountain's landscape. **>64** "Wild Wolf Joerger" refers to Fred Joerger, who created the

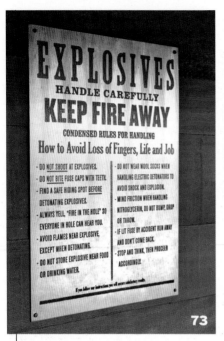

73

74

faux-rock work. **>65** In the cage, an ad for "Chandler's Magnificent Drilling Machine" refers to Jason Chandler, the writer of a letter to company president Bullion seen earlier in the queue and the device Chandler sold him. **>66** The piece itself appears in front of the ad. **>67** A bottle of sulphur sits on a table; nitroglycerin bottles rest on shelves. Sulphur and nitroglycerin are key ingredients of dynamite. **>68** "Western River Explosives: 40% Strength" reads a box on a nearby shelf. **Explosives magazine: >69** Boxes of Lytum & Hyde dynamite sticks are among the combustibles that pack this room. **>70** "Ol' Faithful"-brand blasting caps (labeled "Do Not Store With Any Explosives") are stored in the rafters, as is a bucket filled with dynamite sticks. **>71** Fire buckets are too. **>72** Powder kegs rest nearby. **>73** A sign lists ten "condensed rules for handling" explosives. **>74** "Remote Distance Blasting Machines" let you blast new mine shafts. You crank a contraption to prime it, then push a nearby plunger to trigger an explosion. The blasting machine shown in the photo above stands at the ride's entrance for disabled guests. **>75** A broken crank is in the rafters. **>76** Smoke billows into the air after each blast. **Foreman's post: >77** Steampunk-style "subterrascopes" let you look into shafts and spy on miners who aren't exactly working hard, using (supposedly) a complex series of

76

LYTUM & HYDE
EXPLOSIVES
High Explosives · Dangerous

69

72

MagicKingdom

lenses and mirrors. Patent notices state the devices were made in 1871—a reference to 1971, the year Magic Kingdom opened. **>78** Peer into Shaft 19 to see a miner knocking on the scope; **>79** one looking through papers who is handed a lit stick of dynamite; **>80** a man overloaded with papers; **>81** a man

Steampunk-style 'subterrascopes' let you look into shafts and spy on miners who aren't exactly working hard.

pulling a dynamite stick out of the air as in a magic trick; **>82** or a man taking a spoonful of medicine from a bottle and reacting to its odor. **>83** In Drift No. 30 a man and woman playfully whisper to each other, then she gasps and punches his arm; **>84** someone cleans the scope lens; **>85** a prospecting couple finds gold and the woman celebrates by kissing the man; **>86** a miner digs deeper into the mine; **>87** or a woman pulls hidden gold out of her hair and clothes, then places it in a bucket. **>88** The third subterrascope looks into Prospector's Pit. It reveals a man looking into the scope and cleaning it, only to smear a trail of grease on his forehead as he wipes his brow; **>89** a mine shaft ready for demolition, with dynamite sticking out of the walls; **>90** two

miners preparing to fight; **>91** or a man peeking out from behind some woodwork. **Foreman's log: >92** To the left of the subterrascopes, a log by foreman Willikers reveals that he's been spying on the miners for a week and a half. "Men working hard," he jots down on a Monday. **>93** Willikers records some men have "too many candles lit" on Tuesday, not long before an "unauthorized blast" destroys his lens. **>94** He notes "misuses of tools" on Wednesday. **>95** Thursday he records "mirror fogged up. Ratify immediately." **>96** On Friday Willikers observes some strange occurrences: "Shadow in shaft between shifts," "Ore cart tipped and spilled when no one near" and "Tommy knockers cleared out mine." **>97** Saturday he notes "some miners took an early lunch, again." Recording that they took their break at 11:56 a.m., he deems that "unacceptable." **>98** Sunday he notices "unsafe and careless dynamite use" and gives the miners an "impromptu safety lesson." **>99** "Donkey knocked over blasting powder. No one noticed," he notes that Monday, starting another week of spying. **>100** "Workers are acting unusual," he writes Tuesday, later adding "New vein of gold discovered by miners. And hid by miners." **>101** "Two miners stealing the same gold," he reports the next morning, adding "Bullet destroyed new lens." **>102** A detailed map of the mine's shafts and ventilation systems hangs on a wall farther down the queue. Locations include Behemoth Gorge, Coyote Gallery, Ganglion Gallery, Little Spark Shaft, Moon Ridge #2, Rabbit Foot Fissure, Rattler's Nest, Spur Shaft and Tumbleweed Tunnel. **>103** A tunnel on the left marked "Future Expansion" is headed straight for an underground lake. **>104** The map also names areas seen on the ride, including its Rainbow Caverns and bat cave. **More signs and notices: >105** Next to the map, sketches of a can-can girl lifting her leg and a buffalo at rest and at speed illustrate that "wounds, illnesses or missing limbs are not acceptable excuses to miss a work shift." **>106** "All friends, come celebrate my marriage to the prettiest lady in Tumbleweed, my wife Sue, at the Gold Dust Saloon. Drinks are on you!" invites a yellowed note from "Bill." That's legendary cowboy (and nearby fast-food proprietor) Pecos Bill, with news regarding his gal Slew Foot Sue. **>107** "Looking for a new roommate who doesn't snore or eat beans," solicits a second note. **>108** "Missing: One gold tooth and one non-gold tooth. Last seen in my mouth at the Gold Dust Saloon. Reward 5¢" offers a third note. **Ventilation room: >109** Equipment in this room supposedly ensures that the miners' air is safe. Crank some huge fans to

life and images on them animate like those of an old mutoscope. The animations include a dancing prospector who holds a pickaxe and a gold nugget, **>110** a bucking bronco, **>111** a stampeding buffalo, **>112** and a cowboy riding a horse. **>113** An old dirt-stained ad for the Big Thunder Mining Co. has been painted over on the wall to the right. **Autocanary Air Quality Analyzers: >114** You can check the air in eight mine shafts by turning cranks on these machines and seeing how canaries respond. **>115** Scents include sagebrush, smoke and leather. **>116** One Autocanary monitors the ride's train platform one floor below. **>117** "Formulated to keep your canary alert," sacks of "Cheep Cheep Cheep" Alarm Bird Seed are piled nearby. **>118** Hanging above the machines, empty bird cages belong to the feathered volunteers that are currently being used for testing—or have been and have met their fate. **>119** "Rosita" reads the nameplate on one cage. Its presence solves an age-old mystery among Disney fans—"Whatever happened to Rosita?" At Walt Disney's Enchanted Tiki Room, Mexican macaw José has been pondering that question since 1963, in a throwaway line he says just after that show's female cockatoos are introduced and she's not one of them. **>120** Another nameplate reads "X. Benedict." **>121** A "canary trolley" sits nearby, ready to shuttle new birds to their destinations. **More signs and notices: >122** "Prior to

Magic**Kingdom**

139

140

144

leaving the premises, all miners must empty boots, pockets and so forth," warns a sign. **>123** "Open day and night, rain 'ore' shine," teases a poster for Mother Lode's Gold Dust Saloon, the Tumbleweed bar later seen on the ride. **>124** "The biggest little boom town in the West!" it boasts of its town. **>125** More homage to "The Apple Dumpling Gang": "When in Quake City, shake things up at the Hard Times Cafe," another poster urges.

>126 The cafe's Specialty of the House is its apple-dumplings dessert—one more bow to "The Apple Dumpling Gang." **>127** "Belly up to the world famous 'mile long' bar!" promotes a poster for the Pecos Bill Tall Tale Inn and Cafe— an actual nearby fast-food spot that had a "Mile Long Bar" when it was first built. **>128** "Every order is a tall order!" at the Pecos Bill Cafe— an allusion to the folk-legend's habit of wildly exaggerating

DRY GOODS
D. HYDRATE & U. WITHER, PROPRIETORS

147

everything. **>129** Miner's Hall is the intended destination of a nearby crate of mining equipment. That's the building that houses the roller coaster's Gold Dust Saloon. **Boarding area: >130** Hung in the rafters, a portrait of mining company president Barnabas T. Bullion looks down at the boarding ramp. **>131** A crate full of whiskey and some used candlesticks are stored above the ramp. **>132** "You are using the best darn Black Powder made in these here United States" reads the writing on a barrel in the FastPass+ queue. It's on the right, just before the second touchpoint scanner. **>133** "Miners Only" and "Train Crew Only!" read doors restricted to cast-member use. **>134** "If you're wearin' hats or glasses, best remove 'em! 'Cause this here's the wildest ride in the wilderness!" the safety spiel warns. **On the ride: >135** As your train pulls out, sounds of working miners echo from behind a lantern on the right. **>136** In the bat cave, red eyes glare at you from crevices. **>137** Speakers hidden throughout the ride play the sound of trains with steam whistles, even though the ride's trains don't have them. **>138** Two opossums hang over your head as you enter the town of Tumbleweed, **>139** then donkeys bray to your left. **>140** A sign reports that the town's population has dropped from 2015 to "dried out." **>141** On your right, two javelinas have chased a bobcat up a saguaro. **>142** Wearing red long johns, prospector Cousin Elrod has washed into town in his bathtub. Hands behind his head, he leans back and enjoys the moment. **>143**

MagicKingdom

Chickens look down at him. **>144** On your left, rainmaker Professor Cumulus Isobar bails himself out of his flooded wagon. **>145** A twirling windmill, honking horns and whistling steam vents form a makeshift weather machine atop the wagon. Baby-boomer movie buffs may recognize it as similar to a machine in the 1964 Tony Randall comedy "The 7 Faces of Dr. Lao." (Okay, perhaps only totally insane baby-boomer movie buffs, such as the authors of this book.) **>146** "Dogs" is the amount of rain present at the time, according to a satellite-dish-like "Moisture Gauge" centered on the wagon. That's the gauge's highest reading, way beyond "drizzle" and "cats." **>147** D. Hydrate and U. Wither are the proprietors of the nearby Superior Mercantile Dry Goods store. **>148** An alcohol-fueled game of poker has been flooded out on the first floor of the adjacent Gold Dust Saloon. Its playing cards rest on a table behind the bar's open door. **>149** Carousing animated miners fire pistols in the air, toss laughing women off their feet and lift mugs of sudsy beer just above the saloon, in Miner's Hall. **>150** Five cents will buy you a hot bath with soap and a towel at the hall, according to a sign on its side. **>151** "Dave V. Jones Mine" is the name of the short tunnel you enter to exit Tumbleweed. According to legend Davy Jones is the devil of the seas, and being consigned to his locker meant drowning at sea. **>152** "Flooded Out" reads a "Flood-ometer" on your left as you round a bend, head into a shack and climb the coaster's second chain lift. **>153** Moving, rusty mechanics make a loud clanking sound. **>154** Barrels of railroad spikes and nails sit in the rafters. **>155** Also up there: a crate labeled "Burke Tools & Supply." The name refers to Disney imagineer Pat Burke. **>156** Mountain goats stand to your right at the peak of the lift hill. **>157** An iron stove, an old-fashioned oil can and a set of bellows are among the relics at the entrance to a mine, the third lift hill. **>158** The track in front of you appears to wind deep in the mountain thanks to the help of some forced perspective. **>159** A lantern on your left shakes as the mine begins to collapse around you. **>160** You hear rumbles and falling rocks. **>161** One in about every dozen Big Thunder Mountain Railroad trains passes right by the Liberty Square Riverboat as it steams down the Rivers of America. **>162** "Professor Fullery" (as in "tomfoolery") of the U.S. Geological Survey owns a crate that sits by the ride's T. Rex skeleton. **>163** Fossils of broken dinosaur eggs are scattered under the T. Rex and around the crate. **>164** "Furniture, Upholstery & Embalming" are offered by the Tumbleweed Cabinet & Casket Co., according to words painted on a gray wooden coffin. It rests atop a wooden storage shed on your right after you pass through the ride's hot springs. **>165** Lytum & Hyde dynamite is stacked in open boxes

149

in front of the shed, **>166** as are boxes of "Büme, Büme & Büme" dynamite ("BB&B," the "last word in dynamite"). **>167** Authentic antique blacksmithing equipment—including an anvil, a huge set of bellows and a hand pump—litters a small work area to your left. **>168** Tracks veering off the ride's rails lead to a smithing station. **>169** I.B. Hearty, I.M. Brave, I.M. Fearless, U.B. Bold, U.R. Courageous and U.R. Daring are the names of the ride's trains. Each appears on the side of its engine. **Exitway: >170** Back in the boarding area, Morris Code is the name of the mining company's telegraph

MagicKingdom

161

Micaela Neal

162

164

manager. His office is alongside the exit walkway of the left-side track. **>171** A canary's cage hangs above the exit for the right-side track. The bird inside isn't moving; sometimes he's not even there. **>172** As you leave the building you pass a plunger in the wall to your left, above a "Blasting in Progress" sign. It's pushed in. **>173** "Büme, Büme & Büme" dynamite crates are stacked outside the exit. **>174** A crate of "Stagecoach Fine Fruits" sits nearby. **>175** A single Remote Distance Blasting Machine is set up alongside the short outdoor handi-capped queue, which is next to the exit. It triggers an explosion close by, near a crate. **>176** A Nikon photo spot offers a nice overlook of the mountain, giving those who aren't riding the coaster a chance to snap a photo of friends or family members who are. It's also a sweet selfie spot. **>177** Just to its right is a small geyser that erupts every

180

176

169

few minutes. Stand too close and you'll get sprayed. **>178** Sacks of gold nuggets are strewn around the attraction's nearby smoking area, called Miner's Cove. **>179** Also there: a prospector's sifter and a small cannon. **>180** "Tumbleweed Boat Tour" reads the back of a small rowboat resting upside-down on the mountain's muddy river-bank. Tough to spot from the coaster's grounds, it's easy to see from the Liberty Square Riverboat.

Hidden Mickeys

>181 The three-circle shape appears on your right during the first chain lift, formed by stalagmites on the floor of the cave. **>182** The shape is easy to see toward the end of the ride, as it comes up when your train has slowed to a crawl. It's again on your right, as three rusty gears on the ground.

Also at Magic Kingdom

Main Street U.S.A.

Ambient music: **>1** Among the many period-correct instrumentals heard on the street: "Daisy Bell (Bicycle Built for Two)," an 1892 song that later gained fame in the iconic 1968 science-fiction movie "2001: A Space Odyssey" (in one of that film's key moments, the computer HAL 9000 sang the tune as it slowly deactivated itself); **>2** "The Entertainer," a 1902 piano rag which regained fame seven decades later as the theme to the 1973 movie "The Sting"; **>3** "Hello! Ma Baby," an 1899 Tin Pan Alley song later immortalized in the 1955 Warner Bros. cartoon "One Froggy Evening"; **>4** "It's a Long Way to Tipperary," a 1912 tune sung by British troops during World War I as well as by the cast of the 1970s television sitcom "Mary Tyler Moore" at the end of its final episode; **>5** "Meet Me in St. Louis," a 1904 song which commemorated that year's St. Louis World's Fair (…"we will dance the hoochie-koochie, I will be your tootsie-wootsie…"). **>6** Songs from Broadway musicals include "Surrey with the Fringe on Top" from 1943's blockbuster "Oklahoma" (also a 1955 movie); **>7** "Before the Parade Passes By," "Elegance" and "Put On Your Sunday Clothes" from 1964's "Hello Dolly" (a 1968 movie). "Put On Your Sunday Clothes" also played under the opening credits of the 2008 Disney/Pixar film

MagicKingdom

The Chapeau No.3 17

MAIN STREET
CHAMBER
OF
COMMERCE
· EST 1871 · 11

18

FLA 1915 D 0116 20

15

"Wall-E." >**8** Four Main Street U.S.A. tunes come directly from Disney movies: "Beautiful Beulah" "Flitterin'," and "Summer Magic" from Disney's 1963 film set in the Victorian Age, "Summer Magic"; and >**9** "Married Life," from the 2009 Disney-Pixar film "Up." **On Town Square: >10** Brass statues of Roy Disney and Minnie Mouse sit on a bench in the center of the square, though during peak periods Disney may move the bench over to City Hall or remove it altogether. >**11** The street's Chamber of Commerce was established in 1871, according to a sign above its door. That's a sly reference to 1971, the year Walt Disney World was established. >**12** Inside City Hall, a mural behind the guest counter depicts The Chicago World Exposition of 1893—a veiled homage to Walt Disney's father Elias, who worked at the Expo as a carpenter and inspired Walt with stories of it. >**13** The firehouse is "Engine Co. 71," another reference to 1971. >**14** Real 1920s barber chairs sit inside the Harmony Barber Shop, as does an 1870s shoe-shine chair. >**15** The canine stars of Disney's 1955 film "Lady and the Tramp" have pressed their paws in the pavement in front of Tony's Town Square Restaurant, just as they did in the movie. >**16** Inside Tony's, a window in the back right corner looks into the alley where the movie's iconic "spaghetti kiss" took place. >**17** The address of The Chapeau hat shop is No. 63—a reference to 1963, the year the movie "Summer Magic" was released. According to the store's little-known backstory, its proprietress

MagicKingdom

is Nancy Carey, the central character of that film played by teen star Hayley Mills. **>18** You can eavesdrop on an 1890s conversation between a mom and daughter by picking up the earpiece of an antique wall phone inside The Chapeau. The two complain about the price of hamburger (5 cents a pound) and discuss how to attract a man. Most phone calls were once just as public, as an entire neighborhood shared the same "party line." **>19** A checkerboard is set up on a table in front of the shop, ready for a game. **>20** "1915" reads the year of the license plates on the Main Street jitneys, firetruck and other vehicles, as that was the first year the state of Florida issued license plates. **Town Square Theater: >21** A perfect photo prop, a lifesize statue of Goofy sits on a bench in front of the theater, his hand tipping his tophat. "Well, howdy!" he sometimes chuckles when someone sits next to him. The bench is removed for space in peak periods. **>22** Tiles in its foyer reveal that the theater was established in 1901, the year Walt Disney was born. **>23** A poster for the upcoming act "Oswald the Disappearing Rabbit" hangs in the theater's waiting area to meet Mickey Mouse. Created a year before Mickey in 1927, Oswald was Walt Disney's first successful cartoon character. Disney lost the rights to him soon afterward, however, and didn't regain them until 2006. **>24** A poster for "Mickey the Magnificent" lists "Fred & Ward"

as its opening act. That's a reference to famed Disney animators Fred Moore and Ward Kimball, who appeared as themselves in a 1941 Disney short, "The Nifty Nineties." **>25** A poster for a "Special Halloween Spooktacular" promotes "Dippy Dawg as Ichabod Crane." Dippy Dawg was the original name of Goofy. **>26** A trunk in the queue labeled "Colonel Hathi's Trunk Co." refers to imperious Indian elephant Colonel Hathi, a character in Disney's 1967 movie "The Jungle Book." **>27** A letter from Angus MacBadger of J. Thaddeus Toad Motors Ltd. thanks "M. Mouse" for purchasing Toad's horseless carriage sits on a desk in the queue. That's a reference to a ride vehicle from the former Fantasyland attraction Mr. Toad's Wild Ride that was displayed in this building for years. **>28** A cubbyhole for "B. Justice" on the desk is a shout-out to animator Bill Justice, who created a giant mural of Disney characters that originally appeared in this area. A small rolled-up version of that appears in the cubbyhole. **>29** In Mickey's meet-and-greet area, look for Mary Poppin's parrot-head umbrella handle in a flipped-open trunk; **>30** the icons of the Disney World theme parks, depicted abstractly in a row on a shelf as a tree (Disney's Animal Kingdom), Mickey's sorcerer's hat (formerly at Disney's Hollywood Studios), a crystal ball (Epcot, though labeled "Leota crystals" a reference to the Haunted Mansion's Madame Leota) and a

line of uneven books that mimics spires of a castle (Magic Kingdom); and **>31** a sketch of Oswald the Lucky Rabbit standing next to Mickey, pinned to a nearby bulletin board. The drawing was made by Disney Imagineer Jason Grandt as a child. **>32** Unseen forest critters chitter throughout the waiting area to meet Tinker Bell. **>33** An upside-down oversized tea cup is labeled Honorable Barrie bone china, England, 1906, Kensington Gardens. The original "Peter Pan" book, which Tinker Bell's character originates from, was written in 1906 by J.M. Barrie while he lived beside London's Kensington Gardens. **>34** In Tinker Bell's meet-and-greet area, tiny white lights from indistinct fairies flicker in a hedge on the entrance wall. **>35** A birdhouse that sat for years in the garage of Mickey's Country House at Mickey's Toontown Fair (today's Storybook Circus area) appears high on a shelf in the Curtain Call Collectibles gift shop, which you exit into after meeting either Mickey Mouse or Tinker Bell.

MagicKingdom

Railroad station: >36 Framed photos showing the original industrial lives of the Magic Kingdom locomotives appear on the walls of the station's lower level. **>37** Walt Disney poses with his Carolwood Pacific Railroad—the miniature train and track he built in his California backyard—in nearby images. **>38** Collections of railroad trading cards hang nearby. Railroad cards were packaged with cigarettes during the early 20th century, much like baseball cards were with chewing gum. **>39** Tributes to old Disney live-action movies hide on a nearby Arrivals and Departures board. They include "Bullwhip" and "Griffin Gulch" (nods to 1967's "The Adventures of Bullwhip Griffin"); **>40** "Harrington" (the town of 1960's "Pollyanna"); **>41** "Hickory" (the town of the 1966 movie "Follow Me Boys") **>42** "Medfield" (as in Medfield College, the setting of 1961's "The Absent Minded Professor," 1963's "Son of Flubber" and 1969's "The Computer Wore Tennis Shoes"); **>43** "Pendergast Plains" (Mr. Pendergast, the villain of "Pollyanna"); **>44** "Rutledge" (Rutledge College, Medfield's rival); and **>45** "Siddons City" (Lemuel Siddons, the main character of "Follow Me Boys"). **>46** "Kimball Canyon" honors Disney animator and train enthusiast Ward Kimball; **>47** "Grizzly Bear Flats" is a reference to the Grizzly Flats Railroad, the model track and train Kimball built in his backyard. **>48** Inside the station's second-floor ticket booth, an early-1900s scissor phone

extends from a wall, its handset beneath it. **>49** Several copies of Harper's Weekly lay under the phone on a desk. They're dated 1862, the second year of the U.S. Civil War, a time when the magazine was the most-read publication in the country. **>50** Random paperwork from the Atlantic Coast Line Railroad Co. also rests on the desk. Included are fare schedules and luggage-like tags used to track repairs of radio equipment. For decades the train line provided the main way to travel between New York and Florida. **>51** The cypher DRR is stamped on a nearby brass cup, an old memento of the Disneyland Railroad in California. **>52** In the train station's waiting room, a 1927 nickelodeon sits against the front wall. Inside are castanets, a mandolin, a piano, a triangle and a xylophone. It's all brought to life by a turning paper roll, just like that of a player piano. **>53** Six mutoscopes line the walls of the room. Standing about 5 feet tall, these early "moving-picture machines" would, in exchange for coins, allow patrons to peer into them and crank through a series of photo cards, bringing to life comical (or often risqué) short scenes. Reels in the train station include "Oh! Teacher," "The Burlesque Bouncer" "Play Cowboy Rodeo Time" and "Old San Francisco," the latter starring Delores Costello, the grandmother of modern-day actress Drew Barrymore. **On Main Street: >54** Osh Popham is the proprietor of the Emporium gift

56

57

60

70

65

71

72

MagicKingdom

shop, according to a display window at its main entrance. As played by Burl Ives, Popham runs the general store in the 1963 Disney movie "Summer Magic." Ives, a popular actor and folk singer, was blacklisted during the 1950s by the House Committee on Un-American Activities and barred from employment during the 1950s for his Communist ties. He went on, however, to record the 1962 country pop hit "Little Bitty Tear," star in "Summer Magic," portray Sam the Snowman in the 1964 stop-motion animated television special "Rudolph the Red-Nosed Reindeer" and become a longtime spokesman for Luzianne iced tea. **>55** The window shows the Emporium was established in 1863, another reference to 1963, the year of "Summer Magic." **>56** A vintage U.S. mailbox hangs from a lamppost in front of the Emporium. It's fully functional; a U.S. postal worker collects mail from it six days a week. A second mailbox appears next to the News Stand gift shop outside the park entrance. **>57** Horse-hitching posts stand on both sides of Main Street, replicas of actual posts at a 19th-century New York mansion. **>58** Old-time photos of some of the Citizens of Main Street appear in the windows of Uptown Jewelers. Look for suffragette Hildegarde Olivia Harding, socialite Bea Starr and choir director Victoria Trumpetto. **>59** Sounds of a singer and dancer sometimes can be heard from two windows on West Center Street, a small court

halfway down Main Street. Lettering on them reads "Voice and Singing Private Lessons" and "Music and Dance Lessons, Ballet, Tap & Waltz." **>60** A cigar-store Indian stands in front of the Crystal Arts shop. It's there because a store in that spot sold cigars and other tobacco products during the 1980s and 1990s. Earlier the Indian stood across the street, in a front of a dedicated tobacco store. **>61** Two "peace medals" hang from the Indian's neck. Presented as tokens of goodwill, the medals were given to Native American leaders by the U.S. government throughout the 1700s and 1800s. **>62** Inside Crystal Arts, references to the 1893 Chicago World Exposition include framed photos of the event; **>63** a stereoscope showing it at night, on a high shelf; **>64** the number "1893" engraved on a red glass, on another high shelf. **>65** The brown Starbucks logo on the Main Street Bakery replicates the original 1971 Starbucks logo with two exceptions—its lower words read "Fresh Roasted Coffee" instead of "Coffee Tea Spices," and its mermaid's longer hair lays over her breasts. **>66** Bakery proprietors (and hinted Starbucks founders) Ishmael and Clara Pike pose in portraits just inside the shop's entrance. Their surname refers to Seattle's Pike Place Market, the spot where the real first Starbucks opened in 1971. Ishmael was name of the narrator of "Moby-Dick," the classic 1851 Herman Melville whaling novel in which a first mate is

named Starbuck. **>67** Photographs and collected coffee gear reveal how the Pikes traveled the world in the late 1800s and learned about coffee. **>68** A "vintage" photo of the supposed opening of the bakery hangs between the Pikes' portraits. **>69** Mermaid-themed plates and dishes hint at the couple's interest in that sea creature. **>70** A statue of famed baseball player Casey stands outside the Casey's Corner fast-food spot. In the poem "Casey at the Bat," the confident player comes to the plate in the bottom of the ninth with two outs, with runners on second and third and his Mudville team behind by two runs.

He refuses to swing at the first two pitches, then swats triumphantly on the third... and misses. *"Oh, somewhere in this favored land the sun is shining bright. The band is playing somewhere, and somewhere hearts are light. And somewhere men are laughing, and somewhere children shout. But there is no joy in Mudville—mighty Casey has struck out."* **>71** Casey's Corner was established in 1888, the year the poem was written. **>72** Vintage posters, pennants and other baseball paraphernalia line the walls of Casey's indoor eating area. **Hub garden: >73** Nine Disney characters stand as small brass statues in the plaza at the end of Main Street: the two chipmunks Chip 'n Dale; **>74** Donald Duck; **>75** Dumbo; **>76** Goofy; **>77** Minnie Mouse; **>78** Pinocchio; **>79** Pluto; and **>80** Brer Rabbit. **>81** A topiary of a dragon swims in the grass at the far left of the plaza, just before the bridge to Tomorrowland. Disney fans will recognize it as Elliot, the star of the 1977 movie "Pete's Dragon." **>82** The logo of a Palm Springs guest ranch adorns Walt Disney's tie tack on a statue of him with Mickey Mouse ("Partners") in the center of the plaza, in front of Cinderella Castle. The logo is that of the Smoke Tree Ranch, a rustic retreat where Disney had a cottage. **Halloween decor: >83** The Mayor of Main Street is among the jack o'lantern-faced scarecrows in the center of Town Square. **>84** Others include the drum major of the Main Street Philharmonic marching band; **>85** the band's bass drum player; **>86** a chef and a baker from the Main Street Confectionery; **>87** a tiny-waisted townswoman; **>88** a Casey's Corner baseball player, who holds a baseball in his mouth; and **>89** a shopper who holds a bag from the Emporium. **>90** Many unusual jack o'lanterns sit on the ledges, balconies and railings of the Main Street U.S.A. buildings. In Town Square, these include a dalmatian (complete with a collar with a bone tag) on the fire station; **>91** a fire-hydrant one nearby; **>92** a rest-room jack o'lantern, complete with the universal male and female rest-room symbols and an arrow pointing to actual facilities to its right; **>93** Dapper Dans jack o'lanterns atop the Harmony Barber Shop (where the group sometimes sings), two of which have old-fashioned curly mustaches. **>94** On Main Street itself, look for a snowman formed by three stacked white pumpkins (complete with carved candy-corn buttons) above the Main Street Confectionery; as well as jack o'lanterns that resemble **>95** lollipops and candy-canes in windows above the confectionery; **>96** a diamond-ring on a third-floor railing above Uptown Jewelers; **>97** a musical-note in the window of a dance instructor on Center Street; **>98** a paint-brush and drawing pencil in front of the nearby Art Festival; **>99** a basketball, football and soccer ball above the Hall of Champions facade of the Emporium; **>100** a baseball,

baseball bat, hot-dog, french fry, peanut and soft drink along the top of the Casey's Corner hot dog spot; **>101** an ice-cream-cone, sundae and waffle cone above the Plaza Ice Cream Parlor; and **>102** the Dapper Dans above the Plaza Restaurant, where the group also occasionally performs. **>103** Some jack o'lanterns are matched to the office windows in which they sit. On the right side of Main Street, two sailing-themed ones sit in the sailing-office windows of Roy E. Disney; **>104** a film-projector jack o'lantern (an abstract 3-D projector turned on its side so it faces down) sits in front of Iwerks and Iwerks Stereoscopic Cameras. **>105** An elephant's face is created by two side-by-side jack o'lanterns above the window for Sully's Safaris Guide Service, a nod to Disney exec Bill

Sullivan, who got his start at Disney at the Jungle Cruise. **>106** On the left side of Main Street, a stack of pale pumpkins forms a clown in front of the windows for Ridgway Public Relations, a tribute to mischievous Disney media man Charles Ridgway. **>107** In the hub's garden plaza are four small pedestal statues of costumed Disney characters, each of which has their own jack o'lantern. Dressed as a princess, Minnie Mouse has carved hearts into her pumpkin; **>108** Musketeer Donald Duck has carved his to look like Daisy Duck; **>109** Musketeer Pluto has made his look like a bone; while **>110** Jester Goofy is balancing atop his, squashing it.

Christmas decor: >111 Life-size toy soldiers from the 1961 Disney film "Babes in Toyland" stand alert in Town Square.

MagicKingdom

State Archives of Florida, Florida Memory

Walt Disney, Florida Gov. Haydon Burns and Roy O. Disney announce their "Florida Project" in Orlando, Nov. 15, 1966. Walt Disney died 30 days later.

Window tributes

On almost every building on Main Street U.S.A., second- and third-story windows front various businesses that supposedly operate there. In reality, though, these windows serve as Walt Disney World's credits—an acknowledgment of the real people who created or inspired the resort that "scrolls" past you as you walk by. Each is affixed with the names of one or more Disney alumni or family members.

The inscriptions are often witty but always cryptic. Many use puns; some refer to an honoree's personality or hobbies. Walt Disney's name shows up three times. Taken as a group the windows offer a unique glimpse at Disney history.

The idea of honoring people with

windows came from Walt Disney himself. On the opening day of California's Disneyland in 1955, he had arranged for some of its Main Street windows to salute his main artists, costumers and construction chiefs. Today to get his or her name on one, a cast member must attain "the highest level of service, respect or achievement" according to current park executives and imagineers; and be retired.

Some windows hint at things they probably weren't meant to, as each is a product of its time. Though the Disney company is based in California and is the largest employer in Florida, the windows have only one Hispanic name; nearly all are Anglo-Saxon. And they're very male. Of their 186

Roy O. Disney surveys the land with Joe Potter and Card Walker in 1967; Dick Nunis (left) and Bob Matheison (right) meet with a Florida tourism exec in 1968.

names only 14 are female, and of those 10 are spouses and daughters. The window for Walt's nephew Roy E. Disney is the only one to mention manners, referring to his sailing hobby as "gentlemanly" though during the 1980s and 2000s he used hardball "Save Disney," efforts that were largely successful.

Here's a rundown of every window, who it honors and where you can find it, listed in alphabetical order by faux-business name. Unless indicated, each is on its building's second floor: **>112** *The Back Lot. Props & Scenic Backdrops. Frank Millington, Chuck Fowler, Hank Dains, Marshall Smelser.* Honors the original Disney World decorating team. West Center Street (a brick court about halfway down Main Street, on the right), above Crystal Arts. **>113** *Big Top Theatrical Productions. "Famous Since '55." Shows for World's Fairs and International Expositions. Claude Coats, Marc Davis, John de Cuir, Bill Justice.* Key attraction developers at

Disneyland (which opened in 1955) and the 1964 New York World's Fair. Above Hall of Champions. **>114** *The Big Wheel Co. "One-of-A-Kind." Unicycles, Horseless Carriages. Dave Gengenbach, Bob Gurr, George McGinnis, Bill Watkins.* Designers of Disney World ride systems and vehicles. Above Main Street Fashion Apparel. **>115** *B. Laval & Associates. Partners in Planning. "What We Build Together Can Last Forever."* Bruce Laval helped create Disney's Fastpass system. Above the watch shop. **>116** *Broggie's Buggies. Hand Made Wagons, Surreys, Sleighs. Roger Broggie, Wheelwright.* Walt Disney's first imagineer, Broggie sparked Walt's interest in railroads, designed park vehicles. Ground floor, Town Square Car Barn. **>117** *Buena Vista Construction Company. State Bonded Licensed. Schedules Changed While-You-Wait. General Contractor. Bill Irwin, Field Calculations. Larry Reiser, Synchronizer. Pete Markham, Engineer. Francis Stanek,*

BUENA VISTA
MAGIC LANTERN
SLIDES

Treat Your Friends
to Our Special
Tricks

YALE GRACEY
BUD MARTIN
KEN O'BRIEN
WATHEL
ROGERS

MAIN ST. CONFECTIONERY

118

Prognostications. Dan Dingman, Reckoning. Executives of Buena Vista Construction Co., still today the general contractor for Disney World construction. Above the Main Street Confectionery, facing Town Square. **>118** *Buena Vista Magic Lantern Slides. Treat Your Friends To Our Special Tricks. Yale Gracey, Bud Martin, Ken O'Brien, Wathel Rogers.* Four special effects men. Gracey designed the effects for the Haunted Mansion and Pirates of the Caribbean. Martin headed Disney's special effects department. O'Brien focused on facial and mouth movements of robotic figures, notably in the Hall of Presidents. Among other projects, Rogers created the animals in the Jungle Cruise. Above the Main Street Confectionery's left-most door, near the Main Street Cinema. **>119** *Graphics Complete. Catalogue of Brochures for Every Occasion. Layouts on Request. Burbank. C. Robert Moore, Norm Noceti.* Moore designed the Walt Disney postage stamp. Noceti was a graphic designer who worked with Moore. Above the Main Street Confectionery, facing the Emporium. **>120** *The Camelot Corp. Road Show Installations. Tony Baxter, Dave Burkhart, Ed Johnson, Gary Younger.* These men supervised attraction installations. Baxter went on to become executive VP of design for the Disney parks. Burkhart was a VP of show quality assurance at Walt Disney Imagineering. Johnson was a project show designer, and worked in the model shop. Younger was a production director and system developer. Above Casey's Corner, near the First Aid station. **>121** *Center Street Academy of Fine Art Painting & Sculpture. Collin Campbell, Blaine Gibson, Herbert Ryman, Mary Blair, Dorothea Redmond.* Some of Disney's finest artists. Concept artist Campbell worked on the Haunted Mansion and Pirates of the Caribbean. Gibson was Disney's premiere sculptor; his creations include the "Partners" statue of Walt Disney and Mickey Mouse in front of Cinderella Castle and the Cinderella fountain in Fantasyland. Concept artist Ryman was the chief designer of the castle. Blair designed the scenes and dolls of It's a Small World. Redmond created the murals for the mosaics inside Cinderella Castle. East Center Street. **>122** *Central Casting. "No Shoes Too Large to Fill." James Passilla, Director. Tom Eastman, Pat Vaughn.* Developed Disney World's casting and training program. Above Main Street Cinema. **>123** *Chinese Restaurant. Fine Food, Imported Tea. Jim Armstrong, Vegetable Buyer.* Did the first Epcot menus. Above Casey's Corner, facing the Plaza Ice Cream Parlor. **>124** *Community Service Recruitment Center. Bob Matheison. Quality, Integrity & Dedication.* Created Disney World's executive training program. Above the Plaza Ice Cream Parlor's right-most door. **>125** *General Contractor Bud Dare. We "Dare"*

MagicKingdom

You to Find a Better Deal. *Reedy Creek, Bay Lake, Lake Buena Vista.* Disney World's senior VP for operations development. East Center Street. **>126** *Daughterland Modeling Agency. Instruction in the Arts & Crafts. "What Every Young Girl Should Know!" Bob Sewell, Counselor. Malcomb Cobb, Jack Fergus, Fred Joerger, Mitz Natsume.* The Imagineering model shop. Above the Crystal Arts shop, facing Center Street. **>127** *Elias Disney. Contractor. Est. 1895.* Walt's father, Elias Disney formed his own business in 1895, a contracting company that built houses. East Center Street, above a sign reading "China." **>128** *Roy E. Disney. Sailmaker—Sailing Lessons. Specializing in the Gentlemanly Sport of Racing at Sea Aboard the Ketch Peregrina. Patty Disney,* First Mate and Gourmet Cook. *Roy Patrick, Abigail, Susan, Timothy.* Walt Disney's nephew, Roy E. Disney was the son of Roy O. Disney and an avid sailor. His often harsh "Save Disney" campaigns organized the ouster of two CEOs: Ron Miller in 1984 and Michael Eisner. In 2005 he also sued the company. Listed with his wife Patty (who was known for her home cooking) and their children. Above the Main Street Bakery's rightmost entrance. **>129** *Dolls by Miss Joyce. Dollmaker for the World. Shops in New York, California, Florida, Japan & Paris. Owner and Founder Joyce Carlson.* Created the dolls of It's a Small World, which has been installed in New York (the 1964 World's Fair), California (Disneyland), Florida (Walt Disney World), Japan (Tokyo Disneyland)

and Paris (Disneyland Paris). Above the Emporium, facing the watch shop. **>130** *The Double Check Co. "A Penny Saved is a Penny Earned," B. Franklin. Auditors and Bookkeepers. Larry Tryon, Mike Bagnall, Carl Bongirno, Jim McManus, Warren Robertson.* Men responsible for Disney World's early financial health. Tryon was treasurer of the Disney company; Bagnall CFO; Bongirno the president of Disney Imagineering. West Center Street, above Crystal Arts. **>131** *Draughting Corporation. Doug Cayne, Delineator. "A Straight Line is the First Rule." Associates Ron Bowman, Glenn Durflinger, Don Holmquist, Dick Kline, George Nelson.* Designers who produced sets of working drawings for attractions and other projects. Above the Main Street Confectionery, facing Town Square. **>132** *Dreamers & Doers Development Co. "If We Can Dream It We Can Do It!" Roy O. Disney, Chairman.* Roy O. Disney single-handedly ensured Disney World would be built after his brother Walt died by foregoing his retirement and seeing the project through. Above the Main Street Confectionery, facing Town Square. Third floor. **>133** *Dyer Predictions & Prestidigitation. "A Florida Institution Since '67." Bonar Dyer, President.* Handled Disney World industrial and union relations when it set up its first office in 1967. West Center Street, above Crystal Arts. **>134** *Evans & Assoc. Tree Surgeons. "We Grow 'Em, You Show*

'Em." Morgan Evans, D.T.S. Tony Virginia, A.T.S. Evans designed the landscaping for Walt Disney's home; later became director of landscape design for all Disney parks. Topiary was a passion. Virginia was head of Disney World landscaping. Above Crystal Arts, facing Main Street Fashion Apparel. **>135** *Family Mortgage Trust. Municipal Stocks and Bonds. Loans and Debentures. Interest Low; Terms Favorable; No Dodges. Nolan Browning, Counselor.* Financial consultant Browning introduced Roy O. Disney to the concept of debentures—bonds which can be converted into stock. Using debentures allowed Disney to raise the cash to build Disney World without having to merge with another company—in other words, to keep it in the family. East Center Street, above Uptown Jewelers. **>136** *Fashions by John. Dressmaking, Hemstitching & Picoting. Tom Peirce, Orpha Harryman, Ken Creekmore, Alyja Paskevicius and John Keehne.* Leaders of Disney World's first costume department. Above the Chapeau Hat Shoppe, near the Confectionery. **>137** *Fense Bros., Attorneys at Law. D. Fense O. Fense, Partners. Legal Associates: Neal McClure, Dick Morrow, Spence Olin, Jim Ross, Phil Smith.* Walt Disney Co. attorneys. West Center Street, above Crystal Arts. **>138** *FPC Academy. Featuring the Culinary Arts. Specializing in the 86 Steps to Gastronomical Expertise. Larry*

MagicKingdom

149

Magic Kingdom
CASTING
AGENCY

"It takes People
to Make the Dream
a Reality"

WALTER ELIAS DISNEY
Founder & Director Emeritus

161

OWEN
POPE

Harness Maker

FEED &
GRAIN · SUPPLIES

LEATHER GOODS

SADDLES A SPECIALTY

116

BROGGIES
BUGGIES

Hand Made

WAGONS · SURREYS

ROGER
BROGGIE · SLEIGHS

Wheelwright

129

Dolls BY
Miss Joyce
Dollmaker for the World
Shops in

New York, California,
Florida, Japan & Paris

OWNER & FOUNDER JOYCE CARLSON

171

SULLY'S SAFARIS
&
GUIDE SERVICE
Chief
Guide

Bill Sullivan

124

COMMUNITY SERVICE

Bob
Matheison

Quality Integrity
& Dedication

RECRUITMENT CENTER

136

FASHIONS
BY
JOHN

DRESSMAKING

HEMSTITCHING
& PICOTING

TOMPIERCE   KEN CREEKMORE
OPHA HARRYMAN   ALTA PASKEVICIUS
                 JOHN KEEHNE

145

IWERKS-IWERKS
STEREOSCOPIC
CAMERAS

UB IWERKS
DON IWERKS

REPAIRS

MODIFICATIONS

178

WASHO
&
SON

STONEMASON

BUD WASHO

DICK WASHO

Slocum, Headmaster. Slocum headed Disney World food services. Above the Plaza Restaurant, facing Cinderella Castle. **>139** *General Joe's Building Permits. Licensed in Florida. Gen. Joe Potter, Raconteur.* The first employee hired by Walt Disney in Florida, Potter oversaw the massive Disney World construction project. Above the Main Street Confectionery, directly above the "Y" in "Confectionery," facing Town Square. **>140** *Golden State Graphic Arts Studio. Latest Artistic Principles Employed. Ken Chapman, Paul Hartley, Sam McKim, Elmer Plummer, Ernie Prinzhorn.* Graphic designers at the Imagineering home office in California (the "Golden State"). East Center Street, above a sign reading "China." **>141** *Hollywood Publishing Co. Manuscripts and Melodramas. F.X. Atencio, Al Bertino, Marty Sklar.* Show writers and designers. Xavier ("X") Atencio was a key developer of the Haunted Mansion, Pirates of the Caribbean and Space Mountain. Bertino was a show writer for the Country Bear Jamboree and (since closed) Mr. Toad's Wild Ride. Sklar wrote dialogue for many attractions, and became the head of Walt Disney Imagineering. Above the Main Street Confectionery, facing the Emporium. **>142** *Home Sweet Home Interior Decorators. Emile Kuri, Proprietor.* Disney World's chief interior and exterior decorator. Above the Emporium, left of the "Toys" sign. **>143** *The Human Dynamo Calculating Machine Co.*

Michael Bagnall, Office Mgr. David Snyder, Program Supervisor. Bagnall was chief financial officer for the Disney company. Snyder, a manager of scientific systems for Disney Imagineering, developed DACS (the Digital Animation Control System), an underground computer system that controls rides, shows, parades, lighting and more. Above the Emporium, directly above the "Collectibles" sign. **>144** *Hyperion Film & Camera Exchange. World's Largest Film Library. Screenings Daily at 4 p.m. Dick Pfahler, Bob Gibeaut, Bill Bosche, Jack Boyd, McLaren Stewart.* Men in charge of the film elements at Walt Disney World attractions. In Los Angeles, Walt Disney's first studio was on Hyperion Ave. Above the Main Street Confectionery, facing the Emporium. **>145** *Iwerks-Iwerks Stereoscopic Cameras. Repairs, Modifications. "No Two Exactly Alike." Ub Iwerks, Don Iwerks.* Ub Iwerks was Walt Disney's original partner and animator; he drew Mickey Mouse. He created the first Mickey cartoon, 1928's "Plane Crazy," by drawing 600-700 drawings an evening—after he finished his regular day shift drawing Oswald the Lucky Rabbit—and animated most early Disney cartoons entirely by himself. Using car parts and scrap metal, he created the first multi-plane camera, a device that added depth to animated films by moving layers of art past a lens at various distances and speeds, and was the first to realistically

153

synchronize live action with animation. Later he developed illusions for the Haunted Mansion and Pirates of the Caribbean, and the Hall of Presidents' widescreen projection system. Son Don created CircleVision 360 film recording and projection systems, the original Star Tours projection system and the huge rear-projection system employed at the Epcot attraction "The American Adventure." Above the Main Street Bakery main entrance. **>146** *Jefferds' Mail Order Service. We Sell-Trade Anything Under the Sun.* In 1973, Vince Jefferds repackaged Disney's animation cels so they could be sold to the public at art galleries, college bookstores and via mail order at up to $75 each. Previously the cels were sold only at Disney theme parks for $3 each. Above

Uptown Jewelers, facing Center Street. **>147** *Lazy M Cattle Company of Wyoming. Ron & Diane Miller & Partners Christopher, Joanna, Tamara, Jennifer, Walter, Ronald Jr., Patrick.* Diane Disney Miller was Walt Disney's eldest daughter. Husband Ron was president of Disney during the 1980s; the "partners" are their children. The Lazy M is the couple's Wyoming ranch. Above the Main Street Bakery's left-most window. **>148** *Little Gremlins Mechanical Toys. Toy Makers & Associates. "We Build 'Em, You Run 'Em." Bob Booth, Roger Broggie Jr., John Franke, Neil Gallagher, John Gladish, Rudy Peña, Dave Schweninger, Dick Van Every, Jim Verity.* Men who headed the Imagineering manufacturing arm. Above the Emporium, facing

the watch shop. **>149** *Magic Kingdom Casting Agency. "It takes People to Make the Dream a Reality." Open Since '71. Walter Elias Disney, Founder & Director Emeritus.* Disney is often quoted, "You can design and create, and build the most wonderful place in the world. But it takes people to make the dream a reality." Meant to honor all Disney World cast members. Ground floor door between Main Street Fashion Apparel and Disney Clothiers. **>150** *The Main Street Diary— "True Tales of Inspiration." Lee A. Cockerell, Editor-in-Chief.* Disney's longtime senior operations exec published the Main Street Diary, a weekly cast-member newsletter that highlighted stories of those who went the extra mile for guests. He later wrote the books "Creating

Magic," "Time Management Magic" and "The Customer Rules." Above the watches shop. **>151** *Main Street Music Co. Ron Logan, Conductor. "Leading the Band into a New Century."* The first Disney World music director, later VP of entertainment. Above the Emporium, directly above the "Books" sign facing Town Square. **>152** *Main Str. Water Works. "Let Us Solve Your Plumbing Problems." Control Systems, Maintenance. Ted Crowell, Chief Engineer. Arnold Lindberg, Foreign Rep.* Crowell came up with the concepts of compact "Q" lines that snaked guests into attractions and ticket books that divided rides into "A," "B," "C," "D" and "E" designations. He helped develop Disney World's highway system by sitting in his car on the then-new Interstate 4 and counting cars in both directions. Lindberg was the first Disney World shop manager. Between Main Street Fashion Apparel and Hall of Champions. **>153** *Main Street Youth Athletic League. "Preparing Youngsters for the Game of Life." Al Weiss, Head Coach.* President of Disney World from 1994 to 2005, Weiss spent his entire professional life with the Disney company, starting as an hourly Walt Disney World cast member when he was 18 years old. Above the Hall of Champions. **>154** *Merchants Hotel. First Class Particulars. Steam Heat Throughout. Howard Roland, Furnishings. John Curry, Owner Representative. Stan Garnes, Engineering.* Led the team that built Disney World's first resort hotels, the Contemporary and Polynesian Village. Above Casey's Corner, facing Cinderella Castle. **>155** *M.T. Lott Co. Real Estate Investments. "A Friend in Deeds is a Friend Indeed." Donn Tatum, President. Subsidiaries: Tomahawk Properties, Latin American Development, Ayefour Corporation, Bay Lake Properties, Reedy Creek Ranch Lands, Compass East Corporation.* This window pays tribute to the devious way the Disney company acquired the land for Walt Disney World, by pretending to be various small fictional firms—the "subsidiaries" listed on the window are the names of these dummy corporations. Disney paid an average of $180 dollars an acre for the land. Soon after Disney

World was announced, a nearby acre sold for $300,000. "Ayefour" is a reference to Interstate 4, which was then under construction. Donn Tatum was president of Disney during Disney World's construction. Above Crystal Arts main entrance. **>156** *New Era Band & Choir Studio. If It's New, It's the Latest. Instruction, Talent Agents. Robert Jani, Bandmaster. Charles Corson, Casting Director.* Jani was the director of entertainment at both Disneyland and Disney World; he produced the Main Street Electrical Parade among many other projects. Corson was a Disney World entertainment executive. Above the Emporium's left-most door, facing Town Square. **>157** *Olsen's Imported Novelties & Souvenirs. "World's Largest Collection of Keychains." Jack Olsen, "The Merchant Prince."* Olsen ran the Disneyland and Walt Disney World merchandise operations. West Center Street, above Crystal Arts. **>158** *The Original Dick Nunis Gym. Turkish Baths, Massage Parlor. 24-Hour Service. Supervisor Dick Nunis. Night Manager Ron Miller. Masseur O. Ferrante.* Three Disney execs known for their athletic prowess. In charge of Disney World's outdoor recreation programs, Nunis was an Academic All-American football player at the University of Southern California (USC). President of the Disney company in the 1980s, Miller played for USC and the Los Angeles Rams. Ferrante played at USC, for the Rams and the San Diego Chargers

166

before creating PICO, the Project Installation Coordinating Office at Imagineering. Above the Main Street Bakery, facing Main Street Fashion Apparel. **>159** *Peterson Travel Agency. Reservations by Cable Anywhere in the World. Passages Boarded by Sea & Rail. "Exclusive Representatives for the*

Titanic." Jack Lindquist, Purser. The first advertising manager of Disneyland, Lindquist eventually handled the marketing of Disney parks worldwide. Above Disney Clothiers. **>160** *Plaza School of Music. Sheet Music B. Baker. Band Uniforms B. Jackman. Music Rolls G. Bruns.* Buddy Baker composed

SEVEN SUMMITS
Expedition

Frank G. Wells
President

"For those who
want to do it all"

170

the Haunted Mansion's "Grin Grinning Ghosts," the song "If You Had Wings" from that 1970s attraction and arranged a medley of classical music that accompanies the Epcot film "Impressions de France." Bob Jackman managed Disney's music department, and co-wrote "Swisskapolka," the tune played by the organ in the Swiss Family Treehouse. George Bruns composed the music for many Disney songs, among them "Yo Ho (A Pirate's Life For Me)" for Pirates of the Caribbean. Above the Emporium, near the Harmony Barber Shop. **>161** *Owen Pope, Harness Maker. "Saddles A Specialty." Leather Goods. Feed & Grain Supplies.* Pope established and ran the horse operations at Disney World, including the Tri Circle D Ranch at Fort Wilderness. On the left side of the Car Barn. Ground floor. **>162** *Project Detective Agency, Private Investigations. We Never Sleep. Ed Bullard, Investigator.* The first head of Disney World Security. Above the Emporium, directly above the "Toys" sign, facing Town Square. **>163** *Pseudonym Real Estate Development Company. Roy Davis, President. Bob Price, Vice-President. Bob Foster, Traveling Representative. Offices in: City of Lake Buena Vista, City of Bay Lake, Kansas City.* A second reference to the ways Disney acquired the land for Disney World (see M.T. Lott Co., above), in this case to how its executives used aliases in their negotiations with Florida land

owners. Walt Disney's brother Roy O. Disney called himself "Roy Davis." Disney attorney Robert Price Foster went by "Bob Price." Foster would stop in Kansas City—the supposed home base of one land purchaser—to visit his mother on the way back to California. Created purely for business and tax reasons, Lake Buena Vista and Bay Lake are legal Florida towns on Disney property that have no true residents. Price named Lake Buena Vista. East Center Street, above Uptown Jewelers. **>164** *Rainbow Paint Co. Polychromatists. Lonnie R. Lindley. World's Largest Collection of Color Samples.* Known for his keen eye for color, Lindley headed the Disney World paint shop. Above the Emporium, directly above the "Records" sign, facing Town Square. **>165** *Ralph Kent Collection: Fine Art and Collectibles. Anaheim, Lake Buena Vista, Tokyo.* Initially a designer of marketing materials at California's Disneyland, Kent became known as "the Keeper of the Mouse" after creating the first adult Mickey Mouse watch. In Florida he designed theme-park souvenirs and later became the head of Walt Disney Imagineering East, where he oversaw staff at Disney World and Tokyo Disneyland. Above Casey's Corner, facing Cinderella Castle. **>166** *Ridgway and Company, Public Relations. Charles Ridgway, Press Agent. "No Event Too Small."* The first director of press and publicity for Disney World, Ridgway helped launch the resort in 1971 and hosted thousands of reporters at some of the smallest (and largest) media events ever staged. Above the Arcade. He later wrote the book "Spinning Disney's World." **>167** *Robinson's Repairs. "No Job Too Large or Too Small." Restorations and Renovations.*

Instead of arrows and an olive branch, Phelp's eagle clutches a spool of thread and a pair of scissors.

Cecil Robinson, Proprietor. A Disney engineer who helped lead the creation of Epcot. Above Disney Clothiers. **>168** *Safe & Sound Amplification Co. Gordon Williams, Ed Chisholm.* Williams was an audio designer and Audio-Animatronics expert. Chisholm worked for Imagineering as a mechanical engineer. Above the Main Street Confectionery, facing the Emporium. **>169** *Sayers & Company. College of Business. Satisfied Graduates from Coast to Coast. References on Request. Jack Sayers, National Rep. Pete Clark Western Mgr. Norm Fagrell, Eastern Mgr.* Sayers was VP of lessee relations for Disneyland and Disney World, Clark the director of lessee relations for Disneyland, Fagrell that position at Disney World. West Center Street, above the Arts Festival. **>170** *Seven Summits Expeditions. Frank G. Wells, President. "For Those Who Want To Do It All."* Wells ran the Disney company before his death in a 1994 helicopter accident. Known for his sense of adventure, his goal was to climb the seven tallest summits in the world. He conquered all but Mt. Everest. His Main Street window is the highest one of all. Above the Crystal Arts store. Third floor. **>171** *Sully's Safaris & Guide Service. Bill Sullivan, Chief Guide.* Bill "Sully" Sullivan started at Disney as a ticket taker and ride operator on the Jungle Cruise. He became the head of Magic Kingdom. Above the Plaza Ice Cream Parlor's right-most door. **>172** *Super Structures Inc. Engineers and Associates. Don Edgren, John Wise, Partners. Associates: Morrie Houser, Lou Jennings, John Joyce, Ken Klug, Stan Masiak, John Zovich.* Key Imagineering engineers who helped open Disney World. Above the Emporium, directly above the "Teddy Bears" sign. **>173** *Town Square Tailors. Tailors to the Presidents. Bob Phelps, Prop.* Designed costumes for many attractions, most notably the Hall of Presidents. His window art includes an American bald eagle similar to one seen on the Great Seal of the United States, but instead of arrows or an olive branch, Phelp's eagle clutches a spool of thread and a pair of scissors. Above the Main Street

TOWN
SQUARE
TAILORS

TAILORS
TO THE
PRESIDENTS
★ ★ ★
BOB PHELPS
PROP.

173

RAILROAD OFFICE

Keeping Dreams on Track

WALTER E. DISNEY

CHIEF ENGINEER

POPULATION 600,000,000 THE MAGIC KING

DISNEY WORLD

176

Confectionery, facing Town Square. **>174** *Dr. Card Walker. Licensed Practitioner of Psychiatry and Justice of the Peace. "We Never Close Except for Golf."* President of the Disney company in the 1970s, Walker was known for his skills as a mediator and his love of golf. Between Main Street Fashion Apparel and Hall of Champions. **>175** *Walsh's Chimney Sweep & Pest Control Co. Burbank, Calif. Cincinnati, Ohio. Professor Bill Walsh. The Bug Lover.* The producer and writer of many Disney productions, including 1964's "Mary Poppins" with its chimney sweeps and 1968's "The Love Bug." Above the Emporium, directly above the "Soft Toys" sign. **>176** *Walt Disney World Railroad Office. Keeping Dreams on Track. Walter E. Disney, Chief Engineer.* Honors Walt Disney's passion for trains, which included building a 1/8th-scale working model railroad in his backyard in California, which he ran as "chief engineer." On the clock tower of the train station as you view it from outside the park. **>177** *Walter E. Disney Graduate School of Design & Master Planning. "We Specialize in Imagineering." Headmaster, Richard Irvine. Dean of Design, John Hench. Instructors: Edward Brummitt, Marvin Davis, Fred Hope, Vic Greene, Bill Martin, Chuck Myall.* Honors Walt Disney and the key imagineers who created the Disney World master plan. Above the Plaza Restaurant, facing Cinderella Castle. **>178** *Washo &*

Son. Stone Mason. Our Motto: "No Stone Unturned." Bud Washo, Bill Washo. Bud served in the plaster shops at Fox, Columbia, Universal and Paramount Studios before becoming foreman of the Disneyland plaster shop when that California park broke ground. He and his son later moved to Florida to manage the Disney World Architectural Ornamentation department. They focused on artificial stone facades. Above the Main Street Bakery's main entrance. **>179** *William and Sharon Lund Gallery. Exhibiting Only Authentic Works of Art. Genuine Antiques. Selected by Victoria, Bradford & Michelle.* Honors Walt Disney's younger daughter Sharon (a trustee of the California Institute of the Arts), her husband William and their three children. Above the watch shop. **>180** *Windermere Fraternal Hall. "Lodge Meetings Every Friday." Charter Members Bob Allen, Pete Crimmings, Dick Evans, Bill Hoelscher, Bob Matheison, Bill Sullivan.* The operating committee that opened Disney World. Windermere is a wealthy suburb north of Disney World. West Center Street, above Crystal Arts. **>181** *Yucatan Engine Works. "Highest Grade Steam Power." Boiler & Engine Specialists. Earl Vilmer, Consultant.* Vilmer oversaw the overhaul of the four steam locomotives in the Mexican state of Yucatan that became the engines of the Walt Disney World Railroad. All are still in use today. Above Main Street Fashion Apparel.

Magic**Kingdom**

185

205

225

182

210

183

209

Adventureland

Grounds: **>182** Banana palms border the entranceway bridge as well a small plaza just before it on the right. **>183** Just inside the Adventureland entrance, gift stand Bwana Bob's honors Bob Hope. The star of the 1963 movie "Call Me Bwana," the comedian had a long associated with the Disney company. In 1971 he dedicated the Contemporary Resort. **>184** Skeins of yarn festoon a cupola on a roof to the right of the Agrabah Bazaar. Rugs hang off the roof, apparently made from the yarn.

Swiss Family Treehouse: >185 Prehistoric-style drawings of people, animals and a sailboat decorate volcanic rocks near the entrance. **>186** Cannons sit at the ready at the entrance and throughout the treehouse. In the 1960 Disney movie "Swiss Family Robinson," the family used them to fight off pirates. **>187** Lush flowers attract wild hummingbirds and butterflies around the base of the tree. **>188** Huge bullfrogs often live under its suspension bridges. **>189** The shipwrecked boat's oars and sails cover the entranceway. **>190** Its ropes hold the treehouse together. **>191** Bamboo buckets carry water to the top of the home as part of an ingenious plumbing system. **>192** The ship's bell hangs beneath you to your right as you climb the first staircase. **>193** Other remnants of the boat include its lantern, **>194** log book **>195** and captain's wheel. **>196** A Bible lays on a table in the tree's living room. **>197** A cask of rum sits in the rafters above it. **>198** The room's pull-stop organ is a true antique. **>199** The song it plays is "Swisskapolka," a lively tune heard in the movie as family members race each other riding wild animals, including ostriches. **>200** During November and December the organ plays "O Christmas Tree" and "Deck the Halls." **>201** Giant clam shells serve as sinks in the living room and kitchen. **>202** Smaller ones hold soap. **>203** The ship's sails provide cover for the library and kitchen. **>204** A barrel of water cools the kitchen's refrigerator.

Magic Carpets of Aladdin: >205 A golden statue of a camel spits at passersby from behind the ride's sign, mimicing real life camels that, when irritated, also spit at people. **>206** In the boarding area, an elaborate red medallion lies embedded in the concrete near the No. 5 carpet. **>207** Aladdin and Jasmine stroll into the boarding area, chose a guest family and ride with it around 9:30 a.m. most mornings. **>208** As you fly, a pool of water underneath your carpet reflects your image, just like those of Aladdin and princess Jasmine reflect in the movie. **>209** Camel heads drool water into the pool. **>210** Aladdin's pet monkey Abu cartwheels around the ride's genie-bottle hub in a sequence of images which recall early zoetrope animation. **>211** A second camel statue spits water at you as you fly. **The Enchanted Tiki Room: >212**

Magic**Kingdom**

Preshow host toucan Claude invites you to enjoy a "Tropical Serenade," the original name of the attraction, as he and his counterpart Clyde perform the original preshow. **>213** Baby boomers will recognize Claude's voice as that of Sebastian Cabot, butler French on the 1960s television series "Family Affair." **>214** "Lurk! Lurk!" calls Clyde, claiming to imitate a lurking crocodile. **>215** In the main show co-host José, a Mexican macaw, asks "I wonder what happened to Rosita?" as female cockatoos begin to sing, though a bird with that name has never been in the show. **>216** During "Let's All Sing Like the Birdies Sing," José and the show's three other host macaws parrot vintage crooners. José mimics Bing Crosby; **>217** Irish Michael channels Jimmy Durante; **>218** German Fritz scats like Louis Armstrong; **>219** and French Pierre becomes—but of course!— Maurice Chevalier. **>220** When the flowers croon, their petals form lips and their stamens form tongues. **>221** Some orchids have baby singing with them. **>222** Wall tikis move their eyes and mouths as they chant. **>223** Upside-down masks on the walls depict Negendei, the Earth Balancer, who is always portrayed standing on his head. **>224** The *"phew! phew!"* sounds of the pressurized air that animates the birds and flowers are easy to hear. Though modern Audio-Animatronics figures use hydraulic oil-filled valves, those in the Tiki Room still use air valves—to ensure they don't leak on their audience. **>225** The Orange Bird appears in the sign of the Sunshine Tree Terrace, a snack stand near Tiki Room. He was created by Disney in 1970 for the Florida Citrus Commission, in return for a ten-year sponsorship of the attraction.

Liberty Square

Grounds: >226 The rousing theme song to the BBC television show "Monty Python's Flying Circus" plays as part of the Liberty Square ambient music. That's because it's actually a vintage John Philip Sousa tune, "The Liberty Bell." **>227** Snaking down the center of the main walkway, a curved squiggle of brown pavement symbolizes the sewage that flowed on 18th-century streets. **>228** It leads to restrooms. **>229** Cast in 1987 from the same mold as the original, a replica of The Liberty Bell hangs in a small plaza in front of the Hall of Presidents. **>230** A version of Boston's historic Liberty

Tree elm looms nearby. Disney's tree is a 160-year-old Southern live oak, transplanted in 1971 from its original location 8 miles away.

>231 Thirteen lanterns hang from the tree's branches, representing the 13 British colonies that formed the United States. **>232** Their flags circle the Liberty Bell, each with a plate showing the date its state ratified the Constitution. **>233** Perfect for photos, stocks for adults and children stand in front of the riverboat dock. Throughout history, criminals have been put in stocks to publicly humilate them.

The Hall of Presidents: >234 Along the left side of the hall, a rag doll in a window re-creates a Colonial-era signal to firefighters that the room belongs to a child. **>235** A rifle in a second-story window sends a message that the owner is home and ready to fight. **>236** Nearby, two lanterns in a window recall the "two if by land, one if by sea" phrase from the 1860 Longfellow poem "Paul Revere's Ride." **>237** Beyond the building, a plaque of interlocked hands tells arriving firefighters that the building's firemans-fund fee has been paid. **>238** In the lobby, displays showcase authenticpresidential memorabilia. **>239** In the show, the robotic President Warren G. Harding nervously bounces his foot. **>240** Before reciting the Oath of Office, President Obama glances at his notes. **Liberty Square Riverboat: >241** Visible on the boat's lower deck, a diesel boiler turns river water into steam.

MagicKingdom

229

234

242

237

246

248

Howling Dog Bend

>242 Driven by the steam, a large paddle-wheel makes the boat move. You can watch it up-close from the exit. **>243** An steam whistle toots from atop the riverboat. **>244** Old maps, etchings, photos, antique playing cards and poker chips are displayed in a small second-floor lounge. **>245** The dock of the long-closed attraction Mike Fink Keel Boats still sits on the left, just before Big Thunder Mountain. **>246** Real great blue herons often scour the river for fish.

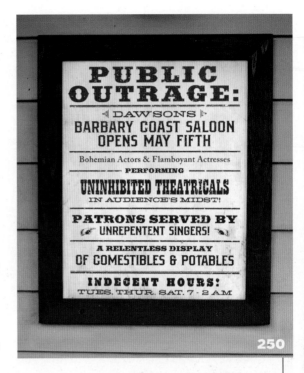

PUBLIC OUTRAGE:
◄ DAWSONS ►
BARBARY COAST SALOON OPENS MAY FIFTH
Bohemian Actors & Flamboyant Actresses
— PERFORMING —
UNINHIBITED THEATRICALS
IN AUDIENCE'S MIDST!
PATRONS SERVED BY
☞ UNREPENTENT SINGERS! ☜
A RELENTLESS DISPLAY
OF COMESTIBLES & POTABLES
INDECENT HOURS!
TUES. THUR. SAT. 7 - 2 AM

250

>247 "Beacon Joe" rests on a dock in Alligator Swamp, a gator hide tacked to his shack. **>248** "Howling Dog Bend" reads a river marker floating in front of The Haunted Mansion, from which wafts the sounds of a howling wolf.

Frontierland

Grounds: >249 Texas John Slaughter's Academy of Etiquette "will make 'em do what they oughta," vowss a poster to the left of the Frontierland Shootin' Arcade. That's a shout-out to the theme song of the 1950s television serial "Texas John Slaughter"— *"Texas John Slaughter made 'em do what they oughta, and if they didn't, they died."* The western ran as part of "The Wonderful World of Disney," a long-running anthology. **>250** Another sign feigns Public Outrage over the opening of a saloon, between the Frontier Trading Post and Frontier Mercantile. **>251** A second cigar store Indian stands in front of the Trading Post. **Frontierland Shootin' Arcade: >252** "A. Carpenter. Trapped when in his coffin he napped," reads a gravestone. Other epitaphs: **>253** "Rest in peace Henry Baker. He has gone to meet his maker"; **>254** "One last drink was his demand. Died a-reaching, Red-Eye Dan"; and **>255** "He loved to dance, he drank his fill. He lives no more; he dances still." **>256** Most targets animate

ONE LAST DRINK
WAS HIS DEMAND
DIED A REACHING
RED EYE DAN
DEC 21

AN ARROW SHOT
STRAIGHT

rest in Peace
Henry Baker

he has gone
to Meet his Maker

A. CARPENTER

TRAPPED
WHEN IN HIS COFFIN
HE NAPPED.

252

when hit. Among them: a prisoner escapes a jail; **>257** an ore car rolls out of its mine; **>258** a skeletal grave-digger pops out of his hole; **>259** skeletal hand in a glowing coffin tries to reach a bottle of whiskey; **>260** a hotel lights up to reveal dancers inside; **>261** a bank lights up to expose a robbery; **>262** prairie dogs pop out of burrows and chitter; **>263** baby birds rise out of a nest; and **>264** a skeletal ghost cowboy flies across the sky. **>265** Each electronic gun is loaded with a secret free round to start the day.

Country Bear Jamboree: >266 Outside the theater, two bear rugs hang on the wall of a second-floor balcony. **>267** To the right of the entrance, the swinging pendulum on a clock is engraved with the letters CBJ—Country Bear Jamboree.

>268 A fur coat sale from Scalp Bros. Furriers is advertised on the show's curtain. Other ads promote **>269** corsets that "cinch like a bear-hug"; **>270** a cure for "paw rot" that's "good for bear or man"; and **>271** dentures with a "built-in grizzly grip" from Dr. Winch, the "painless dentist." **>272** "Ya'll come up and see me sometime!" flirts temptress Teddi Barra as she swings in a chair above the audience to channel actress Mae West. "As soon as I can find a ladder!" replies the emcee. **Pecos Bill Tall Tale Inn and Cafe: >273** "Diarrhoea or worms" are solved by Herrick's vegetable pills, according to a poster outside the cafe, to the right of its main entrance. **>274** The legend of Pecos Bill— the toughest cowboy who ever lived, and featured in the Disney

1948 movie "Melody Time"—hangs inside the main entrance on the right. **>275** Display cases hold artifacts of Bill's famous friends, who have left them behind for him to remember them by. Among them, Johnny Appleseed left the pot he used for a hat; **>276** folk hero Davy Crockett left his powder horn and satchel; **>277** lumberjack Paul Bunyan left his axe; **>278** scout and showman Buffalo Bill left his boots; and **>279** the Lone Ranger left his mask and a silver bullet (and, of course, didn't identify himself). **>280** A cast member bangs a triangle to welcome diners each day when the restaurant opens (typically 10:30 a.m.), just outside the main entrance. **>281** "Respect the land, defend the defenseless... and don't ever spit in front of women and children."

That's Bill's Code of the West, which hangs on a wall just inside the restaurant's middle entrance. **>282** His coat and hat hang nearby. **>283** A drawing of Peco Bill jumping the rope of his lasso while on his horse Widowmaker hangs above several coils of rope. **>284** "Defender of the Defenseless" is Bill's occupation, says a "warrant of authenticity" from the state of Texas on a wall to the far left of the condiment bar. **>285** The warrant was signed by Texas Gov. Sam Houston in 1894—a tricky thing, since Houston died in 1863. **Splash Mountain: >286** Birdhouses and other tiny critter homes hang in trees along the ride's winding outdoor queue. **>287** Nineteenth-century ambient music includes "Polly Wolly Doodle" (*"Oh, I went down South*

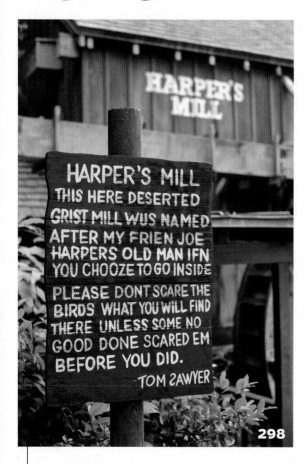

298

the ceiling as you enter the flooded Laughing Place. That's a literal shout-out to Florida State University, the alma mater of one of the ride's imagineers. **>293** "If you've finally found your laughing place, how come you're not laughing?" vultures above you ask as the big drop approaches. **Tom Sawyer Island: >294** Old tin signs decorate dock areas. **>295** A crate addressed to "S.L. Clemens, 208 Hill St., Hannibal Missouri" sits on a dock. Using the pen name Mark Twain, Hannibal native Samuel Langhorne Clemens wrote "Tom Sawyer" in 1876. **>296** Made in part from spools, cloth and rope, an antique toy boat tucks into the rafters of a dock. **>297** Often set up and ready to play, checkerboards sit on tables near the island docks and at Fort Langhorn. **>298** Not much of a speller, Tom Sawyer himself painted the island's signs. **>299** Inside Harper's Mill, creaks and groans very slowly croak out the tune "Down By The Old Mill Stream." **>300** A bird nesting in its cogs of recalls the 1937 Disney short "The Old Mill." **>301** A hooting owl in

for to see my Sal, singin' Polly wolly doodle all the day…") and **>288** "Froggy Went A' Courtin'" *("Froggy went a-courtin' and he did ride, uh-huh…").* **>289** "You can't run away from trouble… ain't no place that far," reads a sampler on a queue wall. **>290** On the ride, "Fleas, flat feet and furballs" are all cured by a Critter Elixir heralded on a wagon past the second lift hill. **>291** The snores of an unseen Brer Bear come from a house around a corner. **>292** "F… S… U!" cheer two gophers who pop down from

297

294

308

the rafters resembles one in that cartoon. **>302** In the mine, water appears to run uphill. **>303** A scary face hides in Injun Joe's Cave, made of indentations in a wall that fill with glowing light. **>304** Eerie wailing winds echo through the cave. **>305** Undiscovered by most visitors, a small playground hides on top of the cave's hill, up a short path. Most young children love it. **>306** At Fort Langhorn, the women's restroom is labeled "Powder Room." **>307** Kids shoot electronic rifles free of charge in the fort's watchtowers. Targets include Big Thunder Mountain Railroad trains and the Liberty Square Riverboat. **>308** An escape tunnel hides at the back of the fort.

309

Fantasyland

Cinderella Castle: >309 A mosaic mural tells Cinderella's story in a series of panels alongside the castle's open hallway. **>310** As Cinderella tries on the glass slipper, stepsister Drusilla's face is green with envy, while Anastasia's is red with anger. **>311** Faces of two Disney imagineers hide in that scene. The page holding the slipper has the profile of castle designer Herb Ryman. **>312** His assistant is Walt Disney World master planner John Hench. **>313** Molded sculptures of Cinderella's animal friends decorate columns alongside the art. **>314** Cinderella's wishing well sits to the right of the castle, along a stone-walled walkway that connects to Tomorrowland. **>315** A statue of her stands in a small fountain behind the castle to the left.

Thanks to a sketch of a crown on the wall behind it, toddlers who stand in front of the fountain see the princess wearing her crown. **Prince Charming Regal Carrousel: >316** Cinderella's personal horse prances in the second row, a golden ribbon on its tail. **>317** Medieval weapons carried by the horses include a flail with a spiked steel ball, a lance and a war hammer. **>318** Eighteen hand-painted illustrations recount Cinderella's story on the Carrousel's inner rounding board. **>319** The namesake of the ride when it was built a hundred years ago, dignified blonde Miss Liberty adorns the side of its lone chariot. Now vivid pink, her duds were originally red, white and blue. **>320** She also appears in the top rounding boards. **>321** Cinderella's bumbling stepsisters

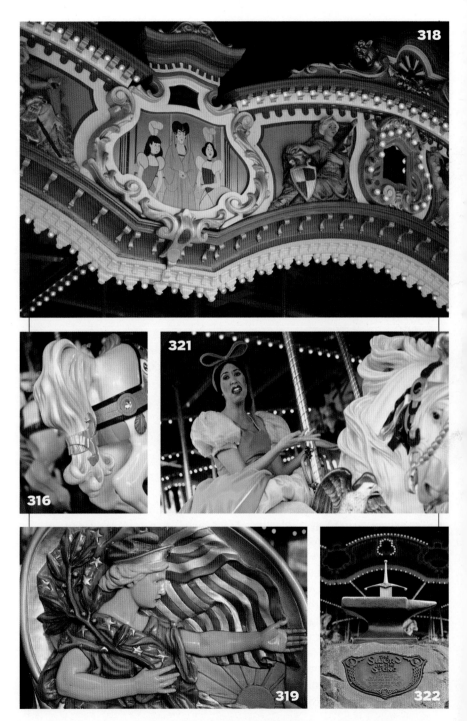

323

324

327

328

331

and haughty stepmother Lady Tremaine ride the Carrousel with guests nearly every morning, just after the park opens. **>322** A large stone with a sword stuck in it sits beside the Carrousel. As in the 1963 movie "The Sword in the Stone," the sword doesn't budge for anyone—or rather *almost* anyone.

Princess Fairytale Hall: >323 A huge golden tiara is formed by the attraction's sign, attesting to the royalty within. **>324** Shields on the building display symbols, one for each Disney princess. There's a seashell (for Ariel), **>325** a spinning wheel (Aurora), **>326** an open book (Belle), **>327** a slipper (Cinderella), **>328** a bow and arrow (Merida), **>329** a dragon (Mulan), **>330** blowing leaves (Pocohontas), **>331** the sun (Rapunzel), **>332** an apple (Snow White) **>333** and a lily pad (Tiana). **>334** For some reason, Jasmine's symbol (Aladdin's lamp)

represents her guy, not her. **>335** At the end of the main hallway, Cinderella's glass slipper sits in a spotlighted case. Nearby, tiny slippers adorn wallpaper and windows. **>336** Queen Elsa often says "Freeze!" as she poses for a photo, instead of "cheese."
>337 A Snow White storybook in each greeting room is a nod to the former attraction in this spot, Snow White's Scary Adventures. **It's a Small World: >338** In the boarding area, a giant clock comes to life every 15 minutes. **>339** On the ride, in the European room a pink poodle ogles French can-can girls;

338

>340 a bespectacled doll under the Eiffel Tower represents the ride's artist, Mary Blair; **>341** a Bobby guards the Tower of London with a cork gun; **>342** a crazy-eyed Don Quixote tilts at a windmill as Sancho Panza looks on in dismay; and **>343** a Swiss yodeler wields an ax. **>344** In Asia, one flying carpet has a steering wheel. **>345** In Africa, a reclining Cleopatra winks at you; and **>346** the eyes of three tongue-wagging frogs spring from their sockets. **>347** In Latin America, three basket people sing near a

saguaro cactus that's playing a guitar. **Mickey's PhilharMagic: >348** Willie the Whale performs "I Pagliacci" on a poster in the lobby of a previous show in the theater—a reference to the "Whale Who Wanted to Sing at the Met" segment of Disney's 1946 movie "Make Mine Music." **>349** Inside the theater a crowd murmurs even when there's no one there, as faint audience noise plays from hidden speakers. **>350** Unseen stage manager Goofy hums "The Mickey Mouse March" as he works backstage.

379

380

>**351** "Sorry little feller!" he says sheepishly after stepping on a cat. >**352** When Donald Duck grabs an unruly flute from the orchestra, its other instruments collectively gasp, watch as he tosses it into the audience, and laugh when it circles back to the stage and whops the duck on the head. >**353** At the finale of the "Be Our Guest" number, Lumiere jumps down to the table and rolls forward on a tomato that wasn't there a moment earlier. >**354** When Donald kisses an electric eel during "Part of Your World," strobes in the ceiling flash. >**355** After a crocodile sends Donald flying, you hear the duck circle behind you before he returns to the stage. >**356** Jasmine waves to someone in the audience as she starts to sing "A Whole New World." >**357** Toward the end of the movie, Donald is tripped into a tuba by the flute he abused at the beginning of the show. >**358** As you exit, Goofy says goodbye to you in five languages, a nod to the last scene in the nearby attraction It's a Small World. **Peter Pan's Flight:** >**359** In the queue, a bedside calendar from December 1904 has the 27th circled—the date of the first stage performance of J.M. Barrie's novel "Peter Pan." >**360** Nearby, your shadow can ring the shadow of a bell; >**361** have the shadow of a butterfly land on it; >**362** tap the shadow of Tinker Bell, which will cause her to take flight; >**363** be topped by the shadow of a top hat >**364** or Capt. Hook's feathered

hat—and if that happens the shadow of your hand will become a hook. **>365** Tinker Bell appears as a sparkle of light and the tinkle of a bell and moves around the nursery. Among her exploits, she enters a toy sailboat and almost knocks it off a bookshelf; **>366** splashes into a pitcher of water; **>367** slips inside the keyhole of a trunk and a dresser and bumps around; **>368** primps on top of Wendy's hand-held mirror; and **>369** straightens a painting she earlier caused to hang crooked. **>370** Tink's spark turns into a heart in front of Peter Pan's silhouette. **>371** Pixie dust sprinkles on you as you leave the nursery; more will fall if you clap your hands. **>372** On the ride, the Indians' shadows are painted onto their teepees. **The Many Adventures of Winnie the Pooh: >373** In the boarding area, a mirror creates the illusion that riders travel into a storybook and disappear. **>374** Mr. Toad hands Owl the deed to the space in a framed photo on the left wall of Owl's house, a reference to the building's previous attraction, Mr. Toad's Wild Ride. **>375** Toad's

413

friend Mole bows to Pooh in a photo on the right floor. **>376** A checked heffalump morphs out of a checked wall during Pooh's Nightmare. **>377** The air chills as you enter the Floody Place. **>378** Shelves appear to drip honey on the floor of the gift shop at the ride's exit. **Mad Tea Party: >379** A soused mouse pops out of a central teapot, just like he does in the 1951 movie "Alice in Wonderland." **>380** The film's Japanese tea lanterns hang overhead. **Enchanted Tales with Belle: >381** Oswald the Lucky Rabbit hides in the walkway across from the entrance, as three embedded pebbles. **>382** A tiny windmill drives the arms of Lumiere on the entrance sign. **>383** Belle's dad Maurice built a fence in her yard using whatever was handy, including broken wagon wheels. **>384** Birds whistle and chitter in the yard, courtesy of unobtrusive speakers. **>385** Inside her cottage, wall markings in French display Belle's height as she grew up; **>386** a teapot and teacups sit on a shelf, a nod to Mrs. Potts and Chip; and **>387** a painting shows Belle as a young girl posing with her mom and a book telling Sleeping Beauty's story, "La Belle au Bois Dormant." **>388** Also in French, a book recounting the Cinderella tale lies open on a table. **>389** Inside Maurice's workshop, Belle's father has created light fixtures from buckets, **>390** gears and **>391** a failed flying contraption. **>392** His blueprints for the wood-chopping machine seen in the 1991 film

"Beauty and the Beast" hang on the back wall. **>393** In the library, images of roses project onto the carpet. **Seven Dwarfs Mine Train: >394** In the queue's gem-sorting trough, an errant bar of soap shoots off the screen when you touch it—a reference to the segment in the 1939 film "Snow White and the Seven Dwarfs" when Grumpy displays his aversion to soap. **>395** Just past it, interactive water nozzles play music when you place your hands under them. **>396** Nearby, when you spin one of seven gem-filled barrels one of the seven dwarfs appears above it on the mine's ceiling. **>397** When all seven dwarfs appear at the same time, Snow White does so too, in the center of the ceiling. **>398** As your coaster leaves the mine, the shadows of the dwarfs leaving it with you appear on your left. **>399** A full-figure Oswald the Lucky Rabbit hides on a log to your left past the crest of the second lift hill, right after you pass Doc. **>400** Two vultures stare down at you as you climb a lift hill; they're the same ones who stared down at riders in the attraction Snow White's Scary Adventures. **Under the Sea: >401** On the building, huge octopus tentacles appear to hold up tower balconies on Prince Eric's castle. **>402** In the queue, Prince Eric's boat sits on the beach on your right; his footprints lead away from it. **>403** An impression of Jules Verne's Nautilus submarine—from his 1870 novel "Twenty Thousand Leagues Under the Sea"

418

419

416

Julie Neal

424

421

and the 1954 Disney movie—hides in the rocks along the far side of the pool. It's a sly reference to the ride that used to be on this spot—20,000 Leagues Under the Sea: Submarine Voyage. **>404** A cartoon crab urges you to help him sort Ariel's collection of gadgets and gizmos on a series of video screens in the indoor queue. **Ariel's Grotto: >405** In the queue, seashells are embedded in the floor; **>406** light fixtures resemble underwater lily pads **>407** and, as you approach Ariel, sea cucumbers. **Be Our Guest: >408** All sporting horns, six medievel stone figures line the outdoor entranceway. **>409** In the ballroom, snow falls

outside the tall arched windows. **>410** The enchanted rose slowly drops its petals inside a glass bell jar in the dim West Wing, just as it does in the 1991 film "Beauty and the Beast." **>411** In a portrait over the fireplace, the Prince transforms into the Beast when lightning flashes. **Gaston's Tavern: >412** Gaston uses antlers in all of his decorating, just like he boasts that he does in his song. **Tangled restroom area: >413** Rapunzel's fanciful tower rises over the area. **>414** Posters promote a concert by Hook Hand and **>415** an exhibit of Vladamir's ceramic unicorns. **>416** Rapunzel's long golden hair wraps around the sign for the

BACK BY POPULAR DEMAND!
(BECAUSE HE INSISTED)
HOOKHAND
At the Piano

Tearing Up the Keyboard Nightly

414

423

422

ladies' room, which is topped by her comb. >417 Rapunzel has painted the ladies' room interior; her paints and brushes sit on a shelf. >418 Flynn Rider's satchel hangs outside the men's room, on the building's second floor. >419 Inside the men's room, his wanted poster acknowledges that he has been pardoned. >420 Frying pans hang throughout the area. >421 A stern portrait of the horse Maximus guards a door reading "Kingdom Staff Only." >422 He's pulled an apple out of a nearby bag and taken a bite out of it. >423 His hoof prints appear in the concrete walkway. >424 Chameleon figures blend into the landscape, especially around the stream.

MagicKingdom

425

427

429

Storybook Circus

Grounds: >425 Portable signs, banners and tents support the circus, which has been set up in a park in a small 1940s American town. **>426** Posters identify the spot as "Carolwood Park," a nod to the "Carolwood Pacific" model railroad Walt Disney built in the backyard of his California home, which was on Carolwood Drive. **>427** Wooden ticket booths front most attractions and the Big Top Souvenirs tent. **>428** An important date in Disney history is subtly honored by the number on each circus wagon snack stand. For example, the hot dog stand's number 55 is a reference to 1955, the year Disney's first theme park (California's

436

442

440

Disneyland) opened to the public. **>429** On the side of the yellow pretzel cart, the number 34 refers to 1934, the debut year of Donald Duck. **>430** Walkways that look like muddy paths are embedded with the hoof and paw prints of circus animals, including camels, monkeys, ostriches and tigers. **>431** Elephant tracks, including those of a baby pachyderm, lead to Dumbo the Flying Elephant. **>432** Impressions of banana peels appear in the walkways too; **>433** as do peanut shells, especially near Dumbo. **>434** Bear tracks lead into Big Top Souvenirs. **>435** Horseshoe marks and wagon-wheel tracks also wind through the concrete. **>436** Many vintage Disney animal stars

MagicKingdom

450

456

455

perform in the Big Top Souvenirs tent, according to posters in the park. They include 1950s cartoon star Humphrey the Bear as a juggling unicyclist (apparently the source of those bear tracks); **>437** 1930s cartoon star Salty the Seal horn-honking a "Symphony of the Seas"; **>438** "Ballerina of the Big Top" Hyacinth Hippo (star of the "Dance of the Hours" ballet in the 1940 film "Fantasia"); **>439** Lambert "The Man Eater" Lion (star of the 1952 short "Lambert, the Sheepish Lion"); **>440** and "Lifter of All Things Heavy" Pete (the nemesis of Mickey Mouse, host of nearby Pete's Silly Sideshow, and as his circus poster reveals, a cheat at lifting). **>441** Other posters

promote Clara Cluck and Horace Horsecollar (1930s cartoon stars who have regained fame in the Disney Junior television series "Mickey Mouse Clubhouse") and Pluto. **>442** Water pails for some of the circus stars appear overturned as seats in the open circus tent next to Pete's, including those for Feifer, Fiddler and Practical Pig (from the 1933 cartoon "The Three Little Pigs"); **>443** Ali Gator (from 1940's "Fantasia"); **>444** Timothy Mouse (from 1941's "Dumbo"); and **>445** Pete's Silly Sideshow stars the Amazing Donaldo, **>446** Great Goofini, **>447** Madame Daisy Fortuna, **>448** Minnie Magnifique as well as **>449** Pete himself.

Dumbo the Flying Elephant: **>450** From the back, the attraction's ornate, gilded sign (Dumbo is clearly the star of this circus) reads "Believe & Soar"—a phrase that appeared on the longtime Dumbo ride behind Cinderella Castle. Timothy Q. Mouse spins above the sign, holding Dumbo's "magic feather." **>451** The feather also serves as the hour hand of the ride's Fastpass+ clock. **>452** Up high on the two ride's hubs, flying storks

463

hold blanket-wrapped baby Dumbos in their beaks. **>453** Her golden face beaming down on her flying son, Mrs. Jumbo adorns the center of the hubs, **>454** as do stylized elephant trunks, feathers and many peanuts. **>455** Down low on the hubs, eight murals tell Dumbo's story. **>456** Circling the hubs, the firehoses of the clowns from Dumbo's original circus act spray water into pools (in the movie, he's initially in a skit with clown firemen who force him to jump off a building). **>457** Multicolored lights illuminate the pools at night. **>458** "Sorry, Flying Solo!" reads a banner that's draped on a Dumbo ride vehicle when it's out of commission. **>459** Between the two hubs, a climb-in ride vehicle makes a perfect photo prop. **>460** In the circus-like indoor playground, a little

fire trunk in the center ring has a honkable horn and tap-touch lights. **>461** Nearby animal prints make noises when stepped on. **>462** To the left of the playground, fireworks in a bin shoot off when children pull a cord. Firebursts then appear above the bin, on a ceiling so low only kids can see them. **The Barnstormer Starring the Great Goofini: >463** Definitely *not* the star of the circus, Goofy has put together his daredevil-pilot act on the cheap. His entrance is a hodgepodge of Dumbo leftovers, rusting metal and scrap wood. **>464** His ticket booth is closed because he's "out flying!" **>465** The back of his entrance sign reveals that it's made from the sign of the previous crop-duster-themed version of the ride, The Barnstormer at Goofy's Wiseacre Farm. **>466** Other

464

465

466

467

low-budget indicators include a rusting Fastpass+ display and **>467** tarnished Fastpass touch-points. **>468** Goofy's long johns and socks hang out to dry above the entrance, just as they did over the old ride's entrance. **>469** "An Acrobatic Skyleidoscope" proclaims a small slogan on a billboard for the ride which Goofy's plane crashes through. Unnoticed by most pass-ersby and apparently most longtime Disney executives, the slogan is a rare case of unintended Disney dark humor—"Skyleidoscope" was a 1980s aerial show at Epcot featuring ultralight aircraft, at which in 1987 an actual stunt pilot crashed and

died. **>470** Goofy juggles tigers on a poster in front of the ride. It alludes to the 1945 cartoon "Tiger Trouble," in which he and Delores the Elephant hunt for the large cats. Goofy gave a bath to Delores when she was a circus elephant in the 1948 cartoon "The Big Wash." **>471** Goofy's face is smothered by an octopus on another poster, which promotes his "Aquamaniac" water-skiing routine. That's an allusion to a 1961 Goofy cartoon about water-skiing, "Aquamania," in which the same octopus did just that. **>472** A terrified chicken hangs on to Goofy's stunt plane on another poster out front, this one for the

Barnstormer ride itself. The fear-filled fowl is a reference to a moment in the earlier Barnstormer ride, when Goofy's plane crashed through a barn and startled a group of chickens. **>473** Coco the monkey, Goofy's "coconutty" companion on Disney Junior's "Mickey Mouse Clubhouse," appears on several posters as Goofy's assistant. **>474** The smoking remains of a rocket Goofy saddled and straddled in a "Fearless Rocketeer" attempt at stardom sits along the standby entrance. **>475** Its name is Delores. **>476** It's followed by Goofy's Wheel of Peril, a wooden target he once strapped himself onto so others could toss knives at him. **>477** The cannon from a previous "Canine Cannonball" act sits

alongside the Fastpass+ entrance. **>478** Its "Launch-O-Matic" lever is set past "High" to a makeshift setting, "To The Moon." **>479** One of its cannonballs is Goofy's bowling ball. **>480** Giant wooden matches lay in a container behind the cannon. **>481** Its fuse occasionally lights and fizzles. **>482** A round target torn apart by Goofy's silhouette appears directly in front of the cannon, near the train station. **>483** Similar targets provide shade for the last part of the queue. **>484** As your plane takes off you relive Goofy's most recent flight, first heading straight for a red-and-white racing pylon, then crashing through it and losing control. **>485** As you step out of your plane, Goofy's "Aquamania"/Aquamaniac

472

470

483

MAN... OR MAN'S BEST FRIEND?

It's a question that baffles Disney enthusiasts, or at least those who love Goofy, a character who has the body of a human but the nose, snout and long ears of a dog. Disney has never actually said, though most fans agree Goofy is human, as the company's signature cartoon dog is obviously Pluto. And besides, Goofy is so much a MAN—a clumsy, gullible good-hearted simpleton who has a hard time concentrating and—despite his bad posture and ill-fitting clothes—loves to mug for a camera. During the 1930s and 1940s Goofy starred in many of Disney's best theatrical shorts. Then in the 1950s, in one of Disney's more bizarre moves, it finished up Goofy's theatrical cartoon career by transforming him into George Geef, a suburban everyman with none of the physical traits of a dog and, at times, no ears at all. Good ol' dogman Goofy returned in 1965, in the educational film "Goofy's Freeway Troubles."

477

479

481

water skis stand in a barrel on the left. **>486** A Yah-Hah-Buoy-brand life preserver is a nod to Goofy's signature yell, "yah-hah-hooey!" **>487** Its small print indicates it was made by Geef Industries. That's a reference to George Geef, Goofy's odd alter ego who starred in "Aquamania" (see the sidebar "Man... or Man's Best Friend?").

>488 Props on the right side allude to Goofy's failure as a stunt pilot. Among them are a small First Aid crate on top of a large Second Aid crate, a bottle of High Flyer Altitude Discomfort Remedy (it "Gets Your Head Out of the Clouds"), a green glass bottle of How to Fly-brand air sickness pills with only a few pills left in it (a reference to the many

484

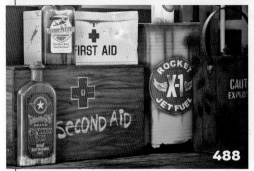
488

490

Goofy "How To" instructional cartoons) and a barrel of X-1 rocket fuel for Delores. **>489** An image of Pedro, a Chilean mail plane in the 1942 Disney film "Saludos Amigos," decorates a can of fuel from the Pedro Empresa Gasolinera (Pedro Gasoline Company). **>490** Goofy's crash helmets hang outside the boarding area. They've definitely crashed and burned. **>491** When seen together, the numbers on the tails of the coaster's airplanes—5, **>492** 19 and **>493** 32—form the date of Goofy's first cartoon appearance: May 1932 (in "Mickey's Revue"). However the planes are never seen together, as only two are on the track at once. **>494** With its uncowled radial engine and open cockpits, the Barnstormer airplane looks like a 1940s Stearman/Boeing Model 75, a World War II trainer. After the war,

MagicKingdom

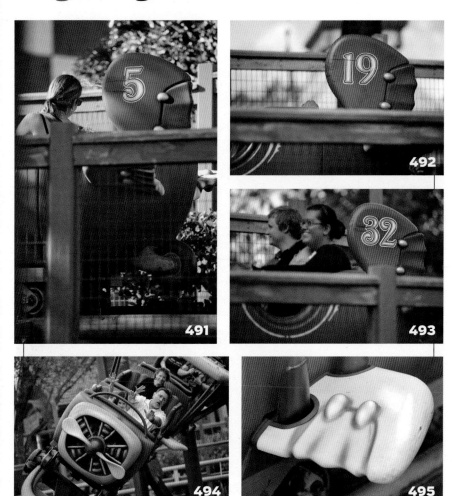

surplus versions of it became popular as crop dusters and stunt planes. **>495** Not-quite-so-based in reality, the wings have raised ridges like those of a bird. **Pete's Silly Sideshow: >496** In front of the tent, round tabletops are painted to look like the iconic Pixar ball—yellow with a fat red star. **>497** Numbers on the wait-time signs are appropriately weathered, even though they're projected from behind. **>498** The sideshow is "Nearly World Famous," according to another sign on the tent. **>499** A "Toot, Whistle, Plunk and Boom" calliope at the tent entrance refers to a (great!) 1953 Disney short by that name. **>500** The device features the "Melody Time Brass Horn Band," a nod to a 1948 Disney film, "Melody Time." **>501** The calliope

496

497

498

499

503

505

507

504

508

was manufactured by the "Melody Time Brass Horns Co." according to words on its side. **>502** "Tell the mouse, ducks and that silly-looking dog to be ready ready ready… on account-a it's show time! Hmm? Whaddya mean the mic's on?" Pete barks out of a loudspeaker above the calliope. **>503** "No Re-entry Unless You Buy Another Ticket"

warns the back of the tent's entrance partition. **>504** A magic act performed by Mickey Mouse at the Town Square Theater—a dove in a cage that vanishes into thin air—appears on nearby fortune-telling cards used by Daisy Fortuna. **>505** You walk through the mouth of Pete to enter the tent's meet-and-greet area. **>506** Its inside walls

Magic**Kingdom**

509

510

512

are stamped with instructions on how to assemble them. **>507** Exhaust fumes spew from the motorcycle of the Great Goofini, which he has crashed into a globe of death behind his meeting spot. **>508** If you ask, the Amazing Donaldo will "charm" you just as he does his snakes. **Casey Jr. Splash 'n' Soak Station: >509** Numbers on the train cars and clown wagon refer to the opening years of the four Walt Disney World theme parks. A "71" on the elephant car refers to 1971, the year Magic Kingdom debuted. **>510** An "82" on the clown wagon refers to 1982, the year Disney added Epcot. **>511** On the giraffe car, "89" refers to the 1989 debut of Disney's Hollywood Studios, then known as Disney-MGM Studios. **>512** On the camel car, "98" refers to 1998, the opening year of Disney's Animal Kingdom.

511

515

513

514

>**513** Numbers on the merchandise cart ("7") and >**514** locomotive ("9") are those of the engines of the Casey Jr. Circus Train ride at California's Disneyland. >**515** Mrs. Jumbo (Dumbo's mom) peeks out of the elephant car. >**516** Most of the animal-car murals also appear behind the check-out counters of the Big Top Souvenirs gift shop. >**517** The song "Casey Jr." (*"Casey Junior's coming down the track..."*) is performed each morning during the Magic Kingdom's opening ceremony. >**518** The locomotive alludes to the song by puffing steam from

FANTASYLAND STATION

CAROLWOOD PARK   ELEVATION 102 FT.

520

THE BIG BAD WOLF
BALLOONOLOGIST EXTRAORDINAIRE

"He'll Huff & He'll Puff...
& Create the Animal of Your Choice!"

524

its smokestack *("...with a smoky stack...")* **>519** and tooting steam from its whistle *("Every time his funny little whistle sounds...")*

Fantasyland railroad station:
>520 A sign above the entrance locates the station in Carolwood Park (see No. 426). **>521** A clock on the roof indicates it's in a "Fair Weather Place"—a nod to Walt's slogan for his backyard train, the "Fair Weather Route." **>522** A silhouette of Casey Jr. tops the station's weather vane. **>523** Spur tracks connect its roundhouse (its restroom) with the Walt Disney World Railroad. **>524** Carts on the left side of the station hold the luggage of Disney characters, most of whom have arrived to be in the circus. A trunk for the Big Bad Wolf—the villain of 1933's Silly

Symphonies cartoon "The Three Little Pigs"—reads "Balloonologist Extraordinaire. He'll Huff & He'll Puff... & Create the Animal of Your Choice!" **>525** A red trunk is stamped with the logo for Red's Amazing Juggling Unicycles—a reference to the unicycle-riding juggler in Pixar's 1987 short "Red's Dream." **>526** The birdcage from the disappearing dove act of Mickey Mouse at the Town Square Theater sits on the trunks (see Main Street U.S.A.). **>527** One holds "Melody Time Brand Brass Horns" (which are "Always in Toon")—the horns in the Pete's Silly Sideshow calliope (see No. 500). **>528** Leather hat boxes are from the company Ten Schillings and Sixpence—the price of the Mad Hatter's hat in the 1951 film "Alice in Wonderland." A tiny

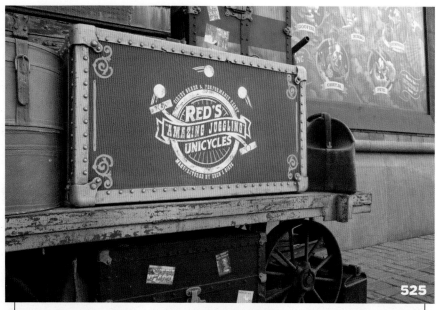

525

526

527

528

529

slogan reads "Hats for all occasions… birthdays, unbirthdays and all days between." **>529** "Property of Hyacinth Hippo, the Most Exquisite Aerial Sensation of the Big Top" reads another trunk. **Big Top Souvenirs: >530** Overhead trapeze ropes; hanging ladders; a stretched high wire with a stool,

towel and rosin containers; and a laced-mat and grass floor indicate that a circus act does indeed take place here. **>531** Overturned water pails for Hyacinth Hippo, Salty the Seal and other Disney animal characters form the bottoms of the store's portable merchandise towers. **>532** Wall displays and checkout areas recall circus wagons. **>533** The penguin wagon is a cooler for soft drinks. **>534** A Big

Top cast member often holds what looks like a full tray of a popcorn vendor. It's really a selection of pins to trade with guests. **>535** The Firehouse 5 Fire Department supplies the fire extinguishers in Big Top Souvenirs (and, for that matter, all of Storybook Circus). The name is a shout-out to the Firehouse 5 Plus Two, a longtime band at California's Disneyland that was comprised of Disney animators.

MagicKingdom

548

543

536

539

537

Tomorrowland

Grounds: >536 "Extry! Extry! Read all about it!" calls a New Yawk newsboy of the future near the PeopleMover ride. If you listen closely, you can hear him talk to you. "Your face looks familiar, let me check my scanner," he may say. "That's it! I've seen youse in the funny papers!" **>537** Alien Coca-Cola logos mark crates in front of a drink stand. **Carousel of Progress: >538** In the 1920s scene, Cousin Orville has the same voice as Bugs Bunny—famed voice talent Mel Blanc. **Monsters Inc. Laugh Floor: >539** Just inside the second queue room on the left, a vending machine offers treats such as Sugar Salt & Fat, Same Old Raccoon Bar and a Polyvinyl Chloride candy bar, which small print on its wrapper notes is artificially flavored. **Buzz Lightyear's Space Ranger Spin: >540** A backpack of batteries gives your space cruiser its power. **>541** As you enter Zurg's Planet Z, the bendy snake from the "Toy Story" movies appears in front of you, then **>542** man-eating plant Audrey 2 from the 1986 movie "Little House of Horrors" circles to your right. **>543** "Guards! Seize them! And their little green friends, too," orders Zurg, channeling the Wicked Witch of the West (from 1939's "The Wizard of Oz") as you cruise through his spaceship. **>544** Stitch's spaceship flies on the first mural on your right as you exit the ride. It's tiny. **Astro Orbiter: >545** The ride's orange steel-mesh elevator resembles the rocket gantries used at launchpads in early manned space missions at nearby Cape Canaveral, Fla. **Space Mountain: >546** Just inside the building, destinations on a departure board include Star Sirius, Real Sirius, World Ceres and Beta Beleevit. **>547** "Star Port Seven-Five" reads panels inside the mountain, a nod to the attraction's opening year, 1975. **>548** The hallway's angled plastic clapboard walls duplicate those of the Discover One spaceship in the 1968 film "2001: A Space Odyssey." **>549** A video game in the queue lets you blast asteroids to clear runways for your flight. **>550** In the boarding area, "Check Invisible Oxygen Dome" is among the pre-flight instructions flashed on a backlit sign next to your open-air vehicle. **>551** On the ride, next to the chain lift a large docked spaceship is named MK-1, a nod to the fact that this Magic Kingdom ride was Disney's first Space Mountain attraction. Similar versions have since been built at Disney theme parks in California, China, France and Japan. **>552** That ship's registration number is H-NCH 1975, a reference to the ride's designer, imagineer John Hench, as well as the year the ride opened. **>553** After you exit the ride, former Magic Kingdom attractions are alluded to on a console to your left, at the beginning of a moving walkway. These "closed sectors" of the universe include FL-28K (Fantasyland's 20,000 Leagues Under the Sea), FL-MMR (the Mickey

MagicKingdom

Mouse Revue), FL-MTWR (Mr. Toad's Wild Ride), MSU-UB (Main Street U.S.A.'s Swan Boats), TL-M2M (Tomorrowland's Mission to Mars) and TL-SK2FL (the Skyway to Fantasyland). **>554** "Open sectors" refer to attractions added to the park: AL-AFC (Adventureland's Aladdin's Flying Carpets), FL-MAWP (Fantasyland's Many Adventures of Winnie the Pooh), FL-MPM (Mickey's PhilharMagic), FRL-SM (Frontierland's Splash Mountain) and TL-BLSRS (Tomorrowland's Buzz Lightyear's Space Ranger Spin). **>555** A skinless robotic dog along the moving walkway was originally the RCA dog Nipper, listening to a record player with his head cocked. A real dog, the fox terrier was the RCA Victor mascot for more than 100 years. RCA sponsored the ride for its first 20 years.

Parades and fireworks

Disney's Festival of Fantasy Parade: >556 The dancing couples at the beginning of the procession mimic swans—the women's hair and dresses are draped in white feathers; the men have swan appliques on their chests. **>557** Cinderella's bird and mouse friends help stitch her giant-pink-dress backdrop into shape. **>558** Firefly Ray hides in Tiana's flower backdrop. **>559** Rapunzel's scaly friend Pascal rides just above a "Snuggly Duckling" sign at the front of her float; **>560** a skeleton in a casket brings up that float's rear. **>561** Following the Peter Pan float, Tick-Tock the Crocodile

makes a faint "tick-tock" sound. **>562** The "Brave" float is a huge bagpipe. **>563** Three arrows stick out of the center of a target seen on the right side of the float. **Main Street Electrical Parade: >564** A caterpillar smokes a hookah on the Alice in Wonderland float, just as he does in the film. **>565** Cinderella's stepsisters awkwardly hold their legs high in front of Prince Charming as they beg to try on his glass slipper. **>566** Huge cigar store Indians line the back of Pinocchio's float. **>567** Red-white-and-blue chorus girls salute parade watchers as they high-step alongside the final Electrical Parade float, a patriotic flag so brightly lit it seems straight out of Vegas.

Wishes: >568 Blue fireworks form stars in the sky during the song "When You Wish Upon a Star." **>569** As each Disney character reveals his or her wish, the fireworks are the color of his or her signature wardrobe. Cinderella's are blue; **>570** Ariel's are green. **>571** Red fireworks form hearts at the end of a melody from "Beauty and the Beast." **>572** During the show's "Sorcerer's Apprentice" sequence, lights transform Cinderella Castle into Mickey's magical hat from Disney's 1940 movie "Fantasia." **>573** Images of the Evil Queen's mirror appear on the castle as she commands "Slaves in the magic mirror, come from the farthest space..."; **>574** then fireworks form a frowning face and the mirrors become faces, when the Queen commands "Let me see thy face!"

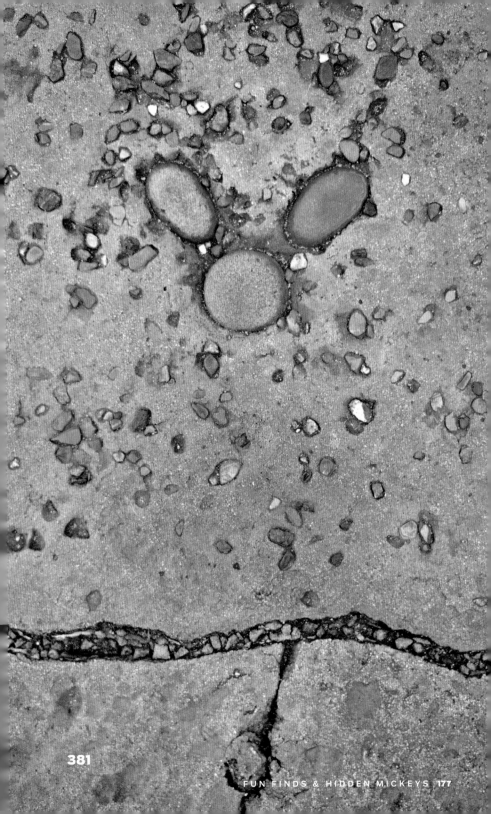

MagicKingdom

Park entrance: ➤1 Under the train station, each of the large metal gates that close off the two entrance tunnels are topped with an obvious row of the three-circle silhouettes. As the gates themselves are hidden whenever the park is open—they fold up accordion-style behind each tunnel's wide central pillar—some Disney fans consider these clear references to Mickey Mouse to be Hidden Mickeys.

Main Street U.S.A

Walt Disney World Railroad: ➤2 Once inside the park, turn around and look up to find some Mickeys that are much more hidden. The shape is formed abstractly, in a repeating pattern of metal scroll-work that lines the train station's second-floor roof. **➤3** Inside the second-floor ticket window of the station, a mischievous Disney cast member has inked two small circles above a large printed "O" on an actual piece of old paperwork—a baggage-tag-like ticket used by the Atlantic Coast Line Railroad Co. **Main Street Vehicles: ➤4** Small brass three-circle shapes adorn the harness and leather straps of the horses that pull the Main Street Trolleys. **Town Square Theater: ➤5** In the greeting room for Mickey Mouse, look for the shape in an open chest of props and magic tricks, as large metal rings in an upper-right compartment. **➤6** In the greeting room for Tinker Bell, the shape hides in the texture of some huge picked raspberries that rest on a tree trunk; **➤7** it's also formed by three embossed roses on a giant spoon. **Tony's Town Square Restaurant: ➤8** Outside the restaurant, the shape hides in plain sight on a wooden access panel on the back of its hanging sign, the center of a filigreed Victorian design. It's tiny, but obvious once you spot it. **➤9** Inside the restaurant, bread loaves in a basket form the shape on a server; **➤10** as does a minuscule indentation on the floor, in a black floor tile in front of the cappuccino machine. **Left side of Main Street: ➤11** A round pinkish flower pattern forms Mickey's head; plain panels his ears in each of the stained-glass windows in the cupola above the Emporium's "Gallery," its "new" Center Street expansion. **➤12** A "Steinmouse & Sons" piano hides Mickey's shape above its keys, in a logo shaped like a sheet music stand. The piano appears in a window to the left of the main entrance to the Emporium Gallery, just below a sign that reads "Collectibles" **➤13** Some Hidden Mickey hunters claim that the obvious three-circle shape that trims out the artwork for the Magic Kingdom Casting Agency door counts as a Hidden Mickey (or actually two, since it's at the top and the bottom of the design), though nothing about it is hidden or incongruent. It's small though, too small to notice with just a casual glance.

MagicKingdom

The white door appears past the tiny East Center Street space, to the left of the Emporium's "Hall of Champions" facade. **Right side of Main Street:** >**14** Outside the Confectionery three lollipops on a poster form the shape when viewed upside down. The poster is in a ground-floor window facing Main Street; it's also in the shop on a wall that fronts Town Square. >**15** In front of the Crystal Arts shop, the shape appears as a tiny impression in a gray flagstone. About the size of a quarter, it's right in front of the shop's main door, between the sidewalk and the bricks of the Center Street courtyard. **Holiday decor:** >**16** Mickey hides throughout the Main Street Halloween decor, in spots that are easy to find as well as difficult. In yet another not-so-hidden "Hidden Mickey," he's a three-circle jack o'lantern that tops many of the area's streetlights—a lit carving that flashes in rhythm to the park's ambient music during its Mickey's Not-So-Scary Halloween Party. >**17** In terms of *hidden* Hidden Mickeys, there's one in the center of Town Square—a scarecrow doll wearing Mickey ears that's being held by a scarecrow dressed as a shopper. >**18** Mickey appears in three Main Street U.S.A. jack o'lanterns, first atop the Main Street Cinema marquee as frames of a film strip; >**19** then as a Mickey Mouse watch, in a window above the "Watches" sign of Uptown Jewelers; >**20** and finally in the plaza hub in front of Cinderella Castle, as part of a small statue of Minnie Mouse. >**21**

The shape also hides in plain sight as you leave the park, in the first and last of two lines of jack o'lanterns that spell out "See Ya Real Soon!" above the archways that lead under the train station to the park exit. >**22** Mickey's silhouette shows up repeatedly along Main Street U.S.A. in its Christmas decor, most obviously as three-circle wreaths mounted on street lamps; >**23** and then, tougher to see, as solid white circles in the framework of metal arches that hold traditional wreaths in front of the buildings.

Adventureland

Grounds: >**24** A smiling Mickey face graces a Tiki in front of the Adventureland entrance, in some tropical landscaping in a small plaza on the right (lately a designated smoking section). >**25** The three-circle shape appears on the top portion of two shields on the entrance bridge—the first shield on the right and >**26** the second shield on the left. **Magic Carpets of Aladdin:** >**27** Mickey appears as three tiny yellow dots on a small, faded four-piece bracelet, which is embedded in a walkway behind the camel statue that faces the ride; >**28** nearby as three circles on a small teardrop-shaped silver charm in the walkway, between the ride exit and a pole outside the Agrabah Bazaar open-air shop; and >**29** as three tiny round concave ceramic tiles embedded in the floor of the shop, in front of a door that reads "Elephant Tales" (the store's former name). **Swiss Family Treehouse:** >**30** Mickey

appears as a spiral and two small holes in the lava rock to the left of the attraction, facing the Adventureland entrance. **>31** On the tree, a right-facing profile of him is formed within a patch of green moss on the trunk. Tough to see on a sunny day, it's on your right just after you leave the tree's second room and go down some stairs. **The Enchanted Tiki Room: >32** On the entrance doors, the shape is formed by berries on a stem underneath a bird's tail, about 4 feet off the ground; and **>33** on the side of the attraction facing the Magic Carpets of Aladdin, as the center of an elaborate stone pillar.

Liberty Square

The Hall of Presidents: >34 In the lobby, the three-circle shape hides in a painting on the wall to the right of the theater entrance, in the tip of George Washington's sword. **Columbia Harbour House: >35** It appears as painted grapes atop a spice rack in the lobby, to the right of a fireplace; and **>36** as circular wall maps on a wall in a room across from the order counter.

Frontierland

Splash Mountain: >37 The shape appears as stacked barrels along the right side of the second lift hill; **>38** inside the mountain, just past Brer Frog toe-fishing on top of Brer Gator, as a bobber to the left of a picnic basket; and **>39** as a hanging rope in the flooded cavern, just past a turtle. **>40** In the riverboat

31

scene, a full-figure reclining Mickey hides in a cloud to the right of the boat. **Walt Disney World Railroad:** **>41** Coming into Frontierland from Main Street U.S.A., three wheels on the ground form the three-circle shape, on the train's left just past the first road crossing. **Frontier Trading Post: >42** Loops of rope form the shape above a cash register, to the left and above a sign that explains "How to Pin Trade."

Fantasyland

Fairytale Garden: >43 The three-circle shape hides in etchings in the base of axe blades scattered throughout the Meet Merida area. **It's a Small World: >44** Purple flower petals form Mickey's shape in Africa, along a vine between the giraffes on your left. **Mickey's PhilharMagic: >45** The three circles hide multiple times as paint splotches in the lobby mural across from the main entrance. From the right, the circles appear between the third and fourth bass violins, **>46** between the second and third clarinets, **>47** above the second trumpet, **>48** below the second trumpet, **>49** to the left of the fourth trumpet, **>50** and twice to the left of the sixth clarinet. **>51** In the theater, it's in the French horn tubing in the right stage column. **>52** In the film's "Be Our Guest" segment, Lumiere's hands cast a shadow shaped like Mickey's ears and his base forms Mickey's face. It's visible for just a moment, as Lumiere sings the word "it's" in "Try the gray stuff, it's delicious!"

>53 The shape appears as a hole in a cloud created by Aladdin's carpet as he and Jasmine fly through it; **>54** as three golden domes atop a tower when the magic carpets dive toward Agrabah; and **>55** as music stands along the top of the walls of the Fantasy Faire gift shop at the exit to the attraction. **Peter Pan's Flight: >56** Three chocolate-chip cookies arranged on a plate in the nursery at the beginning of the ride form Mickey's shape. **The Many Adventures of Winnie the Pooh: >57** Mickey's three circles are formed by watermelon drums in the queue; **>58** as a radish marker in Rabbit's garden; and **>59** etched into the brown wood of Mr. Sanders' tree outside the attraction. It's behind a fence on the far side of the tree, to the left of a window. **Enchanted Tales with Belle: >60** Three yellow roses at the neckline of Belle's gown form Mickey's shape. **>61** A book in the library sports a gold Mickey shape on top of its spine. It can be found in the right rear corner of the room, the fifth book from the right above a blue-and-gold border. **Seven Dwarfs Mine Train: >62** Mickey appears inside the mine on Dopey's left, level with his head, as markings on a support beam; **>63** as three jewels slightly to the right of Grumpy; **>64** and as a full-bodied figure holding a pickaxe atop the second lift hill down low on your right, across from a hidden image of Oswald. **Under the Sea: >65** Three circular indentations in the rock form Mickey's shape in the

60

upper right of the attraction's sign at the Standby entrance. **>66** Also as indentations, Mickey hides in the top right side of a rock in the middle of a small pool, directly in front of a waterfall. It's on the right side of the queue. **>67** Sunlight projects the three-circle shape on a wall from holes in a rock above it. It is just past a carved figure from a ship's figurehead in the Standby queue. But the shape only appears once a year—at noon on Nov. 18, Mickey Mouse's birthday. **>68** The three-circle shape appears as holes in the rock above some bottles on a table, on the left side of the Standby queue. The image is tilted to the left. **>69** Oval purple corals attached to a rock hide Mickey's shape in the "Under the Sea" room. It's on your right, just to the left of a chorus line of upright fish. **>70**

Along the outdoor exitway, a large, abstract, three-dimensional Mickey as Steamboat Willie is formed by a series of rocks on your right that border a small pool of water. Mickey's left leg and shoe are closest to you; his right leg and shoe are on the rock behind that one; his pale face, pointing left, is on a farther rock (Mickey's hands grip a ship's wheel left of his face); his hat is on a rock even farther away. Buttons on his shorts are formed by indentations in the rocks. The whole image is flattened, as if it was meant to be seen from overhead. **Ariel's Grotto: >71** Sculpted in relief, a side profile of Mickey's face looking to the left appears in the queue just after you take the last right turn before entering Ariel's chamber. It's on the lower part of the left rear wall near the floor. **Be Our Guest: >72** The three-circle shape appears as a tattered hole in the fabric hanging from the ceiling in the West Wing dining room. You'll spot it if you stand directly in front of the rose at the rear of the room, then turn around and look up to your right. **>73** The shape also shows up as textured swirls in a rock on top of a low wall to the left of the check-in area outside. **Gaston's Tavern: >74** On Gaston's statue in front of his tavern, the three-circle shape is formed by dark impressions in the rock below Gaston's left leg, near the water line.

Storybook Circus

Grounds: >75 Tiny adults and children hold Mickey Mouse balloons in a Storybook Circus mural on the side of the train station and in the open tent next to Pete's Silly Sideshow. **Dumbo the Flying Elephant: >76** Elephant tracks form the three-circle shape in the walkway just in front and to the left of the Fastpass+ entrance. **The Barnstormer: >77** The shape appears as the center of a whirling airplane propeller on the far right of the billboard Goofy's airplane crashes through, just above the phrase "A Staggering Series of Stupendous Stunts"; and **>78** in the scrollwork above the corners of the Barnstormer ticket booth. **Casey Jr. Splash 'n' Soak Station: >79** It appears as three tilted puffy white clouds behind a giraffe, in a mural on the side of the giraffe train car that faces the train

station; and **>80** as overlapping elephant footprints several times near the Casey Jr. gift cart. **Pete's Silly Sideshow: >81** The three circles hide in Daisy Duck's blouse, in a pattern just beneath her face, on a Daisy Fortuna poster on the outside of the tent.

Tomorrowland

Buzz Lightyear's Space Ranger Spin: >82 A Mickey Mouse profile appears on a poster in the queue room as a green land mass on the planet Pollost Prime. The planet and its mass also appear three more times: **>83** to the left of the Viewmaster in the queue, **>84** on the right as you battle the video Zurg **>85** and in the final battle scene (room 5) on the left. **>86** Another Mickey profile appears on your left as you enter Zurg's spaceship, behind the battery-delivering robot and under the words "Initiate Battery Unload." **>87** The three-circle shape appears as a star cluster on a painted video monitor on a mural across from the souvenir-photo viewing area; **>88** also in that room, on a painted window to the left of the full-size pink character Booster, as a cluster of three stars at the top center of a star field; and **>89** as a second star cluster at the bottom right of that field. **Carousel of Progress: >90** A cloth decoration forms Mickey's shape above a mirror in daughter Patricia's bedroom in the first scene. **>91** The sorcerer's hat from 1940's "Fantasia" sits near an exercise machine in the 1940s segment.

MagicKingdom

>**92** Mickey-shaped items in the finale include a nutcracker on the mantel, >**93** a plush under the Christmas tree, >**94** a salt shaker on the bar, >**95** an abstract painting on the wall, >**96** a hand-drawn shape on a pink note tacked to a bulletin board on the far right wall, >**97** and at the start of a video game the son and grandma play, as engines of a spaceship.

PeopleMover: >**98** A belt buckle in a beauty salon forms Mickey's shape, on your right just after you enter the building that holds Buzz Lightyear's Space Ranger Spin.

Parade

Disney's Festival of Fantasy Parade: >**99** The shape appears as balloons in the upper left corner of the parade banner; >**100** a blue jewel and two smaller white jewels in the center of a large snowflake above "Frozen's" Elsa; >**101** barnacles underneath the saluting fish on Ariel's float; >**102** purple jewels in the bottom purple band on the right side; >**103** blue jewels in the light-blue band on the left side; >**104** bolts on the elbow of the left fore-leg of the dragon Maleficent; and >**105** indentations on a gear on its belly.

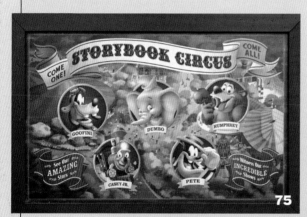

GIRAFFES

79

Epcot

Epcot

50

BASED AS IT IS on science and world culture, much of Epcot lacks a sense of humor and so has fewer fun things to find. It does have some, however. Here are about 50:

Future World

Grounds: >1 Mimicking the left-right division of the human brain, Future World splits its grounds into two distinct themes. The left side has analytical pavilions and straight, linear walkways; the right has more imaginative, naturalistic pavilions and curved walkways. **>2** The Innoventions fountain dances to music in a five-minute show every 30 minutes. **>3** Quench your thirst at one of three Future World drinking fountains and you'll hear wisecracks such as "Hey, save some for the fish!" or perhaps submarine sounds or an opera singer. One sits in front of the MouseGear gift shop; **>4** a second is close to the restrooms behind Innoventions West; **>5** the third is near a kids' water-play area between Future World and World Showcase. **>6** Fiber-optic lights shimmer and flicker in the sidewalks in front of the Innoventions buildings. The lights are always on, but aren't that noticeable until after dark. Large changing patterns appear in front of Innoventions West. **>7** Epcot's Inventor's Circle honors 38 discoveries and inventions. The five concentric circles are embedded into the walkway that leads from Innoventions Plaza to The Land pavilion. Inner-ring inventions lead to outer-ring advancements—the inner Alphabet leads to the outer World Wide Web. **Electric Umbrella: >8** Voices talk to you from a trash can inside the fast-food restaurant. Push open the lid of the only receptacle marked "Waste Please" and you may hear a surfer dude complain "Like, your trash just knocked off my shades!" or a Frenchman exclaim "Zis ees my lucky day! French fries!" The trash can usually sits next to a topping bar to the left of the order counter.

Spaceship Earth: >9 The radio station's call letters are WDI—as in Walt Disney Imagineering. **>10** In the computer mainframe scene, a placard on the right wall reads "Think," the one-word motto created by IBM founder Thomas J. Watson in 1911, after he met with some sales managers who lacked ideas. By the 1950s THINK signs cluttered the desks and walls of countless IBM offices. In the 1990s the slogan inspired an Apple Computer catchphrase, "Think Different." **>11** Nearby is a manual for IBM's System 360 Job Control Language used on 1960s mainframes and **>12** a 1960s Selectric typewriter. **>13** Items in the garage where a shaggy-haired young man invents the personal computer include a photo similar to a classic Microsoft shot of Bill Gates and Paul Allen; **>14** a Fleetwood Mac poster; **>15** Popular Mechanics magazines; and **>16** many empty pizza boxes.

The Seas with Nemo & Friends: >17 "Mine! Mine! Mine!" squawk seagulls in front of the pavilion, just like they do in the 2003 Disney-Pixar movie "Finding Nemo." As it is in the film, the voice is that of "Nemo" director Andrew Stanton. **>18** Just inside the building a sign along the queue reads "Please do not feed the seagulls." **>19** "To air is human!" claims a sign for the "Tanks A Lot" dive shop. **>20** Appearing above you in the dark queue, a floating boat, **>21** darting fish and **>22** swimming sea turtles give you the sense of being underwater. **>23** Cinderella Castle—complete with bursting fireworks behind it—is one of many recognizable images formed by a video school of fish on a wall just before the boarding area for the ride into the aquarium. **>24** "Hey wait! Take me with you!" sea star Peach begs as you pass her, clinging to the aquarium glass as the fish around her continue to sing the song "Big Blue World." "It's a nice song," she explains, "but they just never stop! Never, never, ever, ever, ever!" **>25** As you exit the ride, a swimming ray's silhouette appears on the moving walkway instead of safety footprints. **>26** "Oooooo! That's good!" moans shark Bruce when you rub his sandpapery skin in Bruce's Sub House. **Living with the Land: >27** Bananas, Brussels sprouts, coffee and jackfruit are among the plants growing in the greenhouses. **Soarin': >28** Your silhouette turns into a glowing outline when you play the interactive video games in the queue. **>29** Waving your arms causes animals to appear; **>30** plants to grow; and **>31** beach balls to bounce. **>32** A flying bird is guided through mountains by the mass of people in line if they lean in unison from side to side. **>33** In the theater, lights blink

Epcot

in the floor, making it resemble a runway. **>34** Your flight is "Number 5-5-0-5," a reference to the ride's opening date of May 5, 2005.
Journey Into Imagination with Figment: >35 Lining the entrance hall are the office doors of Professor Wayne Szalinski, the subject of a former nearby 3-D movie, "Honey, I Shrunk the Audience"; **>36** inventor Dr. Phillip Brainard from Disney's 1997 theatrical movie "Flubber"; and **>37** Dean Higgins, the principal in the 1969 film "The Computer Wore Tennis Shoes." **>38** "Your monkey is on the loose!" warns a page in the waiting line. It's for Merlin Jones, a teacher of chimps in Disney's 1965 movie "The Monkey's Uncle." **>39** On the ride, red tennis shoes outside a computer room refer to "The Computer Wore Tennis Shoes." **Ellen's Energy Adventure: >40** Ellen's lips don't move when she yells "Freeze!" just after Alex Trebek says to her, "Your first correct response!" **>41** Bill Nye's lips stay shut when, in front of a solar mirror, he says "all right." **>42** Michael Richards—Kramer on "Seinfeld"—makes a cameo as a caveman who discovers fire.
Mission Space: >43 A 35-foot-tall Gravity Wheel slowly rotates on its side in the queue. It's a prop from Disney's 2000 film "Mission to Mars." **>44** The logo for Horizons—the previous attraction on this site—dots the wheel's hub.

World Showcase

Canada pavilion: >45 Split in two with a hole for you to stick your face through, a carved head of a bird makes a fun photo spot. It sits in front of the pavilion, alongside the World Showcase promenade.
United Kingdom pavilion: >46 Three red British phone booths dot the pavilion grounds. Two stand near the restrooms; one is near the Rose & Crown restaurant. The booths are not, alas, operational.
Morocco pavilion: >47 A mistake in the tiling of each room is intentional. Moroccan artists made deliberate flaws in their work to reflect the Muslim belief that only Allah creates perfection. **>48** The Twilight Zone Tower of Terror at Disney's Hollywood Studios looks like another Moroccan building when seen from across the lagoon, near the Mexico pavilion. The tall, reddish building lines up with the Morocco buildings; they share a Spanish influence. **American Adventure pavilion: >49** The pavilion tricks the eye into appearing smaller than it is through reversed forced perspective. Unless you're up close to the building it looks like it's only three stories tall, though it actually rises more than 70 feet. **Germany pavilion: >50** Four working trains roam the rivers and woods of a miniature outdoor village to the right of the pavilion. A walkway leads over track tunnels and alongside the little town, which has its own live landscape. **China pavilion: >51** Giant bullfrogs often hide under the lily pads in the pond.
Norway pavilion: >52 Scattered with blooming flowers, sod forms the roof of the outdoor eating area.

49

53

THE BALL OF PRESIDENTS

>**53** Many of the Audio-Animatronic figures in Spaceship Earth are duplicates of those who portray U.S. Commanders in Chief at Magic Kingdom's Hall of Presidents. Look closely (and often, beyond the scruffy beard) to notice that the ride's Greek actor is actually William Henry Harrison, the Roman soldier really Zachary Taylor, the Roman senator Theodore Roosevelt. Study two seated Islamic scholars to find Franklin Pierce and John Tyler; look at their leader and you'll see William Taft. Later, a monk writing on parchment is John Adams; Alexander Gutenberg is James Buchanan. As you enter the Renaissance check out the lute player on your right—why it's Dwight D. Eisenhower—and the sculptor on your left—Ulysses S. Grant! Three figures on the ride are duplicates of historic characters seen in Epcot's American Adventure show—the prehistoric shaman (Native American Chief Joseph) Gutenberg's pressman (Andrew Carnegie) and the telegraph operator (Matthew Brady).

Epcot

Hidden Mickeys

Spaceship Earth: >**54** The three-circle shape appears as the ends of stacked scrolls in the room with Islamic and Jewish scholars, at the far right of some bookshelves on the second shelf from the bottom; >**55** as parchment blots made by a sleeping monk; and >**56** as bottle rings on the table of the first Renaissance painter. >**57** Across from the radio booth, a Mickey Mouse comic is mentioned in a newspaper being read by a movie-theater ticket seller. >**58** A chalk-board marquee promotes the 1935 Mickey Mouse short "The Band Concert." It's on your right. >**59** In Project Tomorrow (the ride's post-show), the three circles appear as bubbles on overhead screens.

Innoventions: >**60** The shape shows up in the final room of the Vision House, as dark foliage in a green hedge wall. **The Seas with Nemo & Friends:** >**61** Tiny water bubbles form the circles on a poster on the lower level of the manatee viewing area, near the warning "Manatee Zone... Slow Speed"; and >**62** by pearls in an oyster on the bottom right of two posters in Bruce's Sub House. One is titled "Did You Know?" >**63** the other "Bruce's Scrapbook." **Living with the Land:** >**64** A Mickey Mouse profile hides in a queue mural, as bubbles under the word "nature." >**65** The three circles appear as green and blue orbs in the mural behind the loading area. They're near the right wall, close to the

floor. **Soarin':** >**66** There's a blue Mickey Mouse balloon in the Palm Springs scene, behind a golf cart in the far lower left; >**67** and there's a Mickey silhouette on that errant golf ball. >**68** The shape appears in the fireworks over Disneyland, in the second burst. **Mission Space:** >**69** The three circles show up as overlapping craters on the moon sphere in the courtyard, above and to the left of the Luna 8 impact site; and >**70** as tiny round tiles in the courtyard patio, 40 feet from the Fastpass+ entrance (the ears blue; the head black). >**71** In the queue, "Mickey and Goofy are scheduled to launch at exactly 3 p.m." reads a notepad on a desk. >**72** The shape appears as craters on Mars on the far left and right monitors above the desks; and >**73** after the ride as part of the grid on a circuit board, to the upper left and right of the joystick consoles for the post-show game Expedition Mars. **Test Track:** >**74** In the Standby queue, the three-circle shape of Mickey Mouse appears on two photo collages on the right side of the walk-way—in one of designers, to the left of the drawing hand of a man wearing glasses and writing with a marker; and >**75** in one of concept artists, above a vertical white dashed line. **Journey Into Imagination ... with Figment:** >**76** The three circles are head-phones in the Sight Lab, atop the left wheeled table; and >**77** two circular carpets and a flowered

84

toilet seat in Figment's bathroom. **Canada pavilion: >78** The shape appears twice on the left entrance-way totem, underneath its top set of hands; and **>79** as wine-rack bottles behind the check-in counter of the Le Cellier restaurant. **United Kingdom pavilion: >80** A soccer ball, football and racket form the three circles on a sign above the promenade entrance to the Sportsman's Shoppe. **France pavilion: >81** The circles appear in the courtyard's metal tree grates; **>82** as a bush in the fleur-de-lis hedge garden; and **>83** in the movie, in a second-floor window of a house in the background of a wedding reception. **Morocco pavilion: >84** The shape is formed by brass plates on the left door of the Souk-Al-Magreb shop on the promenade; and **>85** as a marking in a window in the dome of a mina-ret on the backdrop in Aladdin and Jasmine's indoor meet-and-greet area. It's in the upper right-hand segment, next to a small ladder. **Japan pavilion: >86** The circles appear in the courtyard's metal tree grates; and **>87** as holes in the center of a koi-pond drain cover, near a bamboo fence. **American Adventure pavilion: >88** Three rocks form the shape at the beginning of the first film in the show, behind and to the right of a kneeling Pilgrim woman. **Germany pavilion: >89** The circles are formed by jewels in the center of the crown of the left-most Hapsburg emperor statue, on the second story of the Das Kaufhaus shop. **>90** A little figurine of Mickey often hides in the train village, usually in a window of a hilltop castle.

MAX. CLEARANCE

TO UPPER LEVELS
HEAD IN
ONLY!

Disney's Hollywood Studios

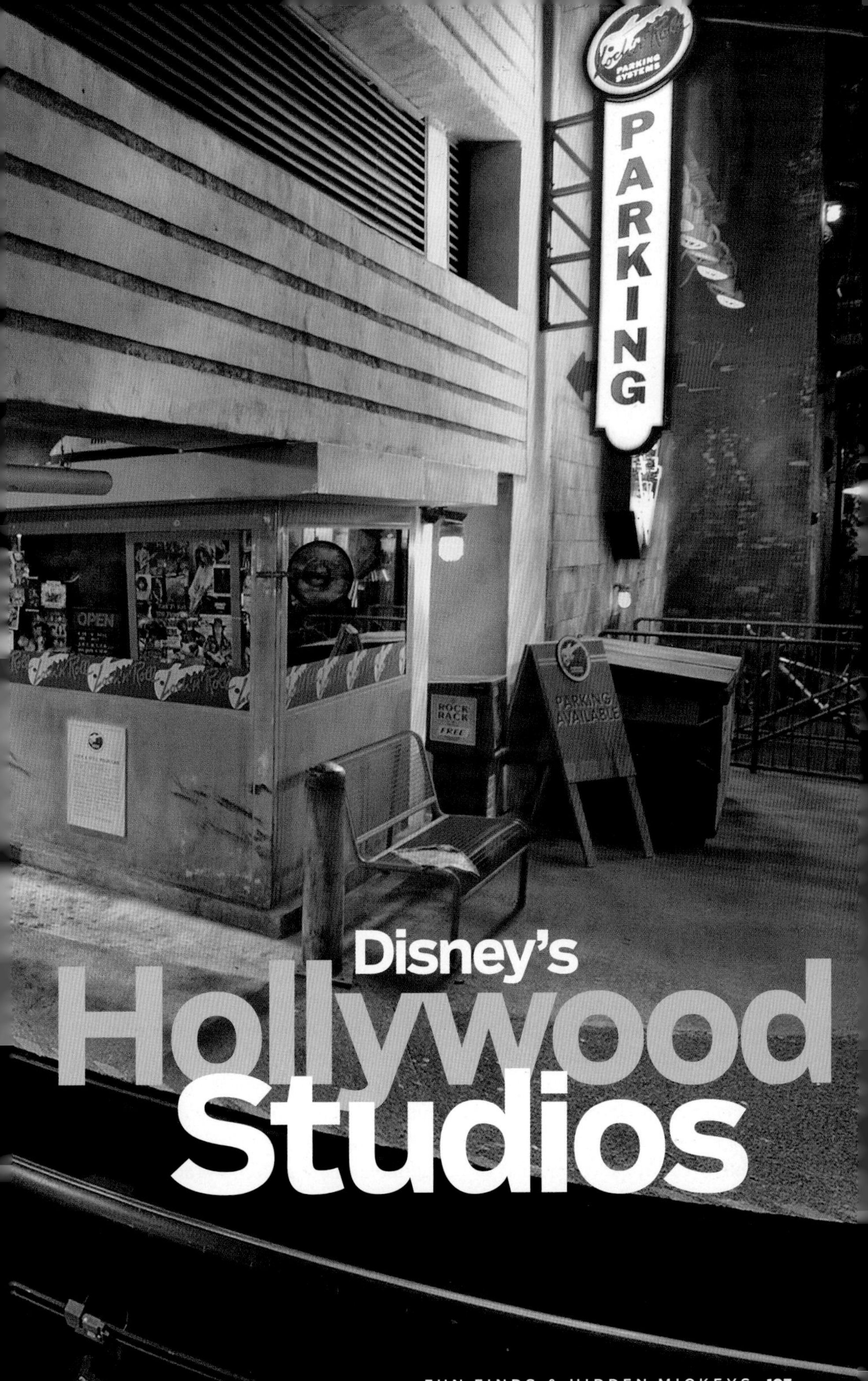
PARKING SYSTEMS
PARKING
OPEN
ROCK RACK
FREE
PARKING AVAILABLE

Star Tours

By Micaela Neal

TAKING OFF ON A TOURIST TRIP where everything goes wrong, you'll be immersed in the "Star Wars" universe by this 3-D motion simulator, which Disney and George Lucas redid a few years ago with lots of love, care and technical expertise.

Its scenes and destinations change with each flight. You might head to Tatooine, Coruscant, Naboo or even a Death Star, you may be stopped by Darth Vader, you may receive a hologrammed message from Princess Leia. In the Star Wars storyline, your adventure takes place between the events of "Episode III: Revenge of the Sith" and "Episode IV: A New Hope."

Entering the building and in the queue, you're a space tourist walking through a bustling spaceport terminal. As you learn in a video shown in the terminal, you're scheduled to travel aboard a Starspeeder 1000, piloted by one of the latest AC-series Tour Droids, AC-38, better known as Ace.

As a video in the boarding room reveals, however, Ace gets called away from your ship at the last minute, leaving only C-3PO in the cockpit, and he has absolutely no flight experience. Even worse, your takeoff is interrupted when members of the Galactic Empire discover that there is a Rebel spy aboard your Starspeeder, and stop your flight in the hangar. You escape, but instead of heading off on a vacation, you're off to deliver the spy to the safety of the Rebel Alliance, with Darth Vader and the Galactic Empire hot on your tail.

Some classic Star Wars vehicles and weapons play key roles in your flight. Rebel forces fly the X-Wing starfighter, which has double-layered wings that separate to form an "X" during combat. The bad guys use the TIE starfighter, named for its twin ion engines. These barebolts machines lack hyperdrives and deflector shields. The Empire's most horrific weapons are its Death Stars. Powered by a fusion reactor in its center, each of these moon-sized space stations is staffed with over a million troops. Its main weapon is a superlaser housed in a crater-like cannon well.

Characters

An assortment of Star Wars characters appear in the attraction, among them:

Admiral Ackbar. A veteran of the Clone Wars, Admiral Ackbar is the commander of the Rebel Alliance Fleet. A member of the Mon Calamari species, Ackbar and his people manned the distinctive warships supplied to the Rebellion by that aquatic culture. Beyond the qualifications of his great skills and sterling character, Ackbar is a symbol to the rest of the galaxy: a symbol that the Alliance is fighting for everyone, no matter what their background or origin. The Empire, in contrast, has made discrimination against non-humans a long-standing policy.

Ali San San. The spokesdroid for Star Tours, Ali ensures it remains the premiere intergalactic tour service. Friendly and enthusiastic, she hosts its promotional videos as well as its safety and boarding announcements.

Boba Fett. A mysterious, notorious bounty hunter who's well paid and highly sought after, this infamous mercenary scours the galaxy for profit and personal reward. He's frequently employed by crime lord Jabba the Hutt.

C-3PO. Fluent in over six million forms of communication, the golden protocol droid is rarely seen without his squat counterpart R2-D2, and together the two make a remarkably capable team. Because of R2's limited communication abilities, C-3PO must often interpret his companion's electronic sounds for his human masters. Though preferring to remain far from any potential threat, the anxious droid frequently finds himself in the midst of the action. C-3PO had been the personal attendant to Senator Padmé Amidala of Naboo, who died of a broken heart after her husband, Jedi Knight Anakin Skywalker, turned to the Dark Side and became Darth Vader.

Chewbacca. Chewbacca is first mate and co-pilot of the Millennium Falcon, the ship of rogue pilot Han Solo. A natural mechanic, "Chewie" is essential for the often-temperamental Falcon and its constant need for repairs and upgrades. Over 200 years old, he communicates in a series of growls, grunts, and fierce roars; Solo is one of few humans who understands the Wookiee's native language.

Darth Vader. A Dark Lord of the Sith responsible for wiping out the Jedi and executing the Emperor's evil bidding, feared by Rebels and Imperials alike, Darth Vader is a terrifying union of man and machine hidden beneath black robes and forbidding armor. Determined to hunt down and extinguish the Rebel Alliance, he commands the massive Imperial fleet and rules his forces through unquestionable terror. Once, this ominous figure was a young Jedi apprentice named Anakin Skywalker who trained under Obi-Wan Kenobi to become a Jedi. Too impatient with his Jedi Master and consumed with anger and aggression, Anakin chose a path that could only lead to the Dark Side.

Princess Leia. The beautiful Leia Organa is a symbol of diplomacy, strength and hope within the Rebel Alliance. The youngest member of the Imperial Senate, she secretly helps lead the struggling Rebellion in their mission to overthrow the Galactic Empire.

R2-D2. A feisty astromech droid of surprising determination and resourcefulness who nevertheless can communicate only in beeps and whistles, R2 has a cylindrical body that's equipped with multiple instruments and sensors. He earlier served Anakin Skywalker.

Stormtroopers. The highly trained soldiers of the Galactic Empire, these elite shock troops are deployed in overwhelming numbers to carry out the Emperor's will and maintain oppressive order throughout the galaxy. Armed with standard Imperial blasters, they wear anonymous white armor over black body gloves.

Yoda. In the days of the Old Republic, he was the most wise and powerful of all Jedi. Diminutive and unassuming, Master Yoda had no equals in his insight into the Force, or in his skill with a lightsaber. For over 800 years he instructed young Jedi and instilled in them a profound sense of discipline, strength and unity. Once the Dark Side re-emerged he moved to Dagobah, a mysterious swamp planet.

Inspirations

A space fantasy that takes place "a long time ago, far, far away," the Star Wars films tell a timeless story of good versus evil. Combining a space-opera plot like those of the Buck Rogers serials of the 1930s and '40s with the use of special effects and modeling similar to the 1968 film "2001—A Space Odyssey," the films created a mix of wit, mythology and simulated reality that has entranced audiences worldwide for decades. A key element is the Force, an omnipresent, controllable energy field that, as described in the first film, "binds the galaxy together." Mythical planets include the desert-landscaped Tatooine, home of Anakin and Luke Skywalker, and the metropolitan Coruscant, the capital of both the old and new republics.

Fun finds

Grounds: >**1** A climb-on Speeder bike, the woods-weaving vehicle in 1983's "Episode VI: Return of the Jedi," sits across from the Star Tours entrance. It's perfect for photos. >**2** Ewoks chatter in their village above the queue at night. They play music, too. >**3** Aurebesh, a Star Wars alphabet, appears throughout the attraction. It translates directly to English. >**4** A blooper! Red blasts fire from TIE fighters on the building's poster. As fans of the Force know, true TIE blasts are green. **Inside the building:** >**5** The cipher JK0966 appears on a circular plate on the wall on your right, just before you reach the arrivals and departures screen. It's a nod to "Star Trek" character James Kirk and the month and year that television series debuted, September 1966. >**6** Just below that mark in gray above a second plate, N1C7C01 is a mixed-up version of the registration number of the Enterprise, NCC-1701. >**7** IG0088 on that plate is a cryptic call-out to bounty hunter IG88 from 1980's "Episode V: The Empire Strikes Back." **Terminal screen:** >**8** Departure information is displayed in English and Aurebesh. >**9** "See Agent" is the status of flights to Alderaan, a planet that, in the Star Wars storyline, is about to be destroyed in "Episode IV: A New Hope." >**10** Alderaan was "recently voted Safest Planet in the Galaxy by 'Hyperspace Traveler,'" claims a later commercial. >**11** Flights to Endor— the destination of the original version of the ride, which took place after Episode VI—are "delayed." >**12** News regarding "Flight 1138 to Chandrila" pops up on the bottom left of the screen. That's a reference to the first film directed by George Lucas, 1971's "THX1138." >**13** The host of a Starspeeder promotional video looks like the Dex's Diner waitress in "Episode II: Attack of the Clones," but has red markings. Her name is Ali San San, a nod to her voice actor Alison Janney. >**14** She interviews "Ace," the scheduled pilot for your flight, droid AC-38. >**15** She also introduces the IC-360, the ship's 360-degree camera droid. **Starspeeder area:** >**16** Below and to the left of the screen, "TWB-3000" honors Tony Wayne Baxter, the imagineer who championed the Star Tours ride and its first ride simulator, the Starspeeder 3000. >**17** A nearby 21B3ABY is a barely disguised enthusiastic shout-out to the 213 area code of Los Angeles, which includes the headquarters and studios of the Walt Disney Co. >**18** Near the bottom of the Starspeeder, some white Aurebesh type on a registry plate translates to "WDI" and "WED"—WDI for Walt Disney Imagineering, WED for its original name WED Enterprises, which was founded by Walter Elias Disney. >**19** Aurebesh type under R2-D2's Starspeeder port reads "Astromech Droid Socket." **Dialogue between C-3PO and R2-D2:** As they perform some last-minute maintenance on your Starspeeder, the

20

© Disney

© Disney

STAR TOURS

4

FROM THE CREATIVE FORCES OF DISNEY AND GEORGE LUCAS

8

ARRIVALS				
ARRIVING FROM	FLIGHT	TIME	STATUS	GATE
BESPIN	727	0835	ON TIME	1A
BESPIN	119	1120	DELAYED	1G
BESPIN	922	1350	ON TIME	2D
BIMMISAARI	1203	1305	CANCELED	2B
CAROSI XII	104	0720	LANDED	2A
CAROSI XII	519	1050	ON TIME	1A
CAROSI XII	801	1650	ON TIME	1B
CATO NEIMOIDIA	1007	0650	LANDED	1K
CATO NEIMOIDIA	320	1415	ON TIME	2M
CHANDRILA	1138	0815	ON TIME	2B

iconic Star Wars droids have a running conversation. Highlights include: **>20** C-3PO, after a promotional video for Coruscant: "Now that sounds like a fascinating tour… On second thought, I just remembered how much I hate space travel"—an allusion to his comment in Episode IV as he rode in Han Solo's Millennium Falcon: "Oh my, I'd forgotten how much I hate space travel." **>21** C-3PO, after a promotional video for Naboo: "Ah, Naboo… a most beautiful planet. But frankly R2, I find the Gungans to be rather annoying." R2-D2 chirps. C-3PO: "No, not just Jar Jar. All of them." **>22** The number of your flight— "1401"—is another selfie shout-out to Walt Disney Imagineering, which is headquartered at 1401 Flower St. in Glendale, Calif. **Pages and announcements: >23** "Will the owner of a red and black landspeeder, vehicle ID THX1138, please return to your craft?" is another nod to the first George Lucas movie. **>24** "Departing Tatooine passenger Sacul, Mr. Egroeg Sacul, please see a Star Tours agent at gate 2D." Egroeg Sacul is "George Lucas" backward. **>25** "Paging Star Tours passenger Mot Worrom, please pick up the nearest flight courtesy comlink" refers to Tom Morrow, a pun of a name with a long Disney history. Initially, Tom was the Audio-Animatronic "operations director" of Mission Control in the 1970s Tomorrowland attraction Flight to the Moon (today's Stitch's Great Escape). In the 2000s, a tiny transparent Tom Morrow 2.0

hosted the Innoventions area of Epcot as well as a series of "Imagineer That!" shorts on the Disney Channel television network. Today, Mr. Morrow is paged both at Star Tours and on the PeopleMover, a ride in Magic Kingdom's Tomorrowland. In the Star Wars realm, human T. Morrow appeared in the Star Wars Galaxies online role-playing game (2003–2011), as a general in the Rebel Alliance during the Galactic Civil War. **Droid Customs: >26** As you enter a second queue room, Rex, the pilot of the Starspeeder in the original Star Tours ride, sits to your left in an open crate. **>27** "Defective— Return to Factory" reads a sticker on him, revealing that his later problems got their start very early. **>28** Every now and then a power surge causes him to burst out a line of his old dialogue: "Welcome-welcome-welcome-Welcome aboard!" **>29** He sometimes sparks. **>30** "Reubens Robotics" is the name of the factory Rex is being returned to—a nod to his voice talent Paul Reubens (best known as 1980s childlike comedian Pee-wee Herman). **>31** The Aurebesh at the top of his shipping label translates to "Boyd's Be There In A Minute Delivery Service." **>32** Type behind the defective droid reads TK-421731-81." That's a reference to TK-421, the Stormtrooper in Episode IV who wasn't at his post because he was actually Luke Skywalker in disguise. **>33** To the left of Rex, the type swD77808399020508 breaks

Hollywood**Studios**

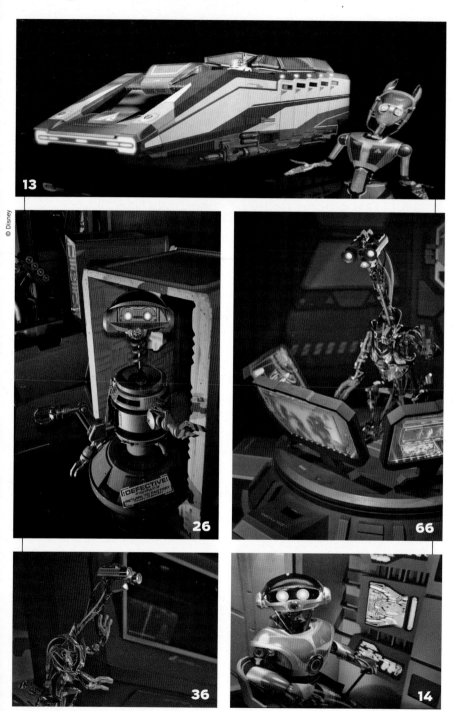

13

26

66

36

14

down as "Star Wars dates" and the year each of the first six Star Wars movies debuted (i.e., the first one came out in 1977). The "08" refers to the television series "Star Wars: The Clone Wars." **>34** Just past Rex, some bird-like robots sit in cages. In the earlier attraction they sat above the entrance to the boarding area, squawking at guests beneath them. **Baggage scanner: >35** The scanning station's ID is ST109-87, a reference to the opening date of the original Star Tours at California's Disneyland, Jan. 9, 1987. **>36** "This job is a lot better than, say, fixing broken droids all day" chatty droid G2-9T may proclaim— an inside joke, as his job in the original Star Tours queue was exactly that. G2-9T is voiced by Tom Fitzgerald, the attraction's lead imagineer. Among his other comments: **>37** "Anyone heading to Kashyyyk for the big Holochess tournament? Well, a little bit of advice: let the Wookiee win"—a strategy C-3PO came to embrace in Episode IV. **>38** "Everything's perfectly alright now. We're fine. We're all fine here now, thank you. How are you?" reassuring a Star Tours supervisor on an intercom who calls him after alarms go off. In Episode IV, Han Solo said the same thing to a Death Star supervisor on an intercom, maintaining cover after decimating some guards. **>39** "Boring conversation anyway," hanging up on his supervisor with the phrase Solo muttered after blasting his intercom. **>40** Occasionally he breaks out

into song. "Star Tours! Nothing but Star Tours!" he sometimes sings to the instrumental Star Wars theme, parroting the performance of cheesy lounge singer Nick Winters (comedian Bill Murray) in a 1978 skit on the television show "Saturday Night Live." **>41** When he sings "I've been looking at the same bags, all my livelong day…" he's hinting at his first job at Disney, as a goose in a musical attraction at California's Disneyland, America Sings, who warbled "I've Been Working on the Railroad." Other hints he was once a goose: his yellow beak, webbed feet and wagging tail. Upcoming passenger-scanning droid G2-4T has the same history. **>42** Among the items his scanner finds in the luggage for your flight (and reveals on a screen behind him) are the white gloves of Mickey Mouse; **>43** the Christmas lights, toaster with cassette tape, and plant in a boot from the 2008 Disney/Pixar movie "WALL-E"; **>44** WALL-E himself; **>45** the helmet of Zurg, Buzz Lightyear's nemesis in the "Toy Story" films; **>46** the original logo of The Living Seas pavilion at Epcot (today The Seas with Nemo & Friends) on a decal on a football helmet; **>47** Madame Leota's crystal ball from Magic Kingdom's Haunted Mansion; **>48** Figment, the dragon from Epcot's "Journey Into Imagination with Figment"; **>49** Major Domo, the robotic security officer in the 1986 Michael Jackson spectacle "Captain EO," an Epcot 4-D movie produced by

© Disney

86

George Lucas; **>50** a superhero suit from the 2004 Disney/Pixar movie "The Incredibles"; **>51** the whip and fedora of Indiana Jones; **>52** Wally B (the insect star of the groundbreaking 1984 cartoon "The Adventures of André and Wally B" created by the Graphics Group, a division of Lucasfilm that was later re-named Pixar), as well as André's red hat. **Silhouette window: >53** Figures passing behind a window include Watto, the junk dealer from Episodes I and II; **>54** a cloaked Jedi who performs a Jedi mind trick on a Stormtrooper; **>55** two floating camera droids that crash into each other; and **>56** Jar Jar Binks, encased in carbonite. **Passenger scanner: >57** Voiced by deadpan actor Patrick Warburton—David Puddy on the 1990s sitcom "Seinfeld" and Kronk in the year-2000 Disney movie "The Emperor's New Groove—droid G2-4T's comments to passersby include "Keep it moving, humans! Those of you traveling with

domesticated creatures, this is not your line. I'm talking to you, miss… Oh, is that your boyfriend? I'm terribly sorry." **>58** "Hold it right there, do you know who I am? Seriously, I just accidentally wiped my memory, I could use a little help here. I'm kidding! Or am I?" **>59** "My name is G2-4T. That's short for G2-4TT45579982DWP-403ST. That's just my first name. I'd tell you my last name, but I don't wanna hold up the line." **>60** "I can't think of anything more fun than scanning you people. Wait, I just thought of something." **>61** "I've got my eyes on you. Not just these two, I've got others." **>62** "To those of you traveling with small children—good luck with that." **>63** "You would not believe what some humans try to get away with. The other day a woman tried to waltz right by me with two cinnamon buns in her hair! Everyone knows there's no food allowed past this point." **>64** "Move along… move along. Nicely done. You've done this before, haven't

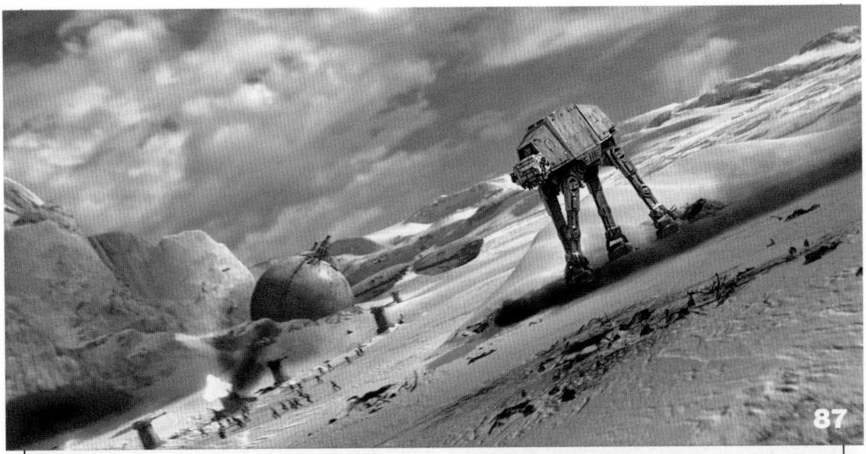

87

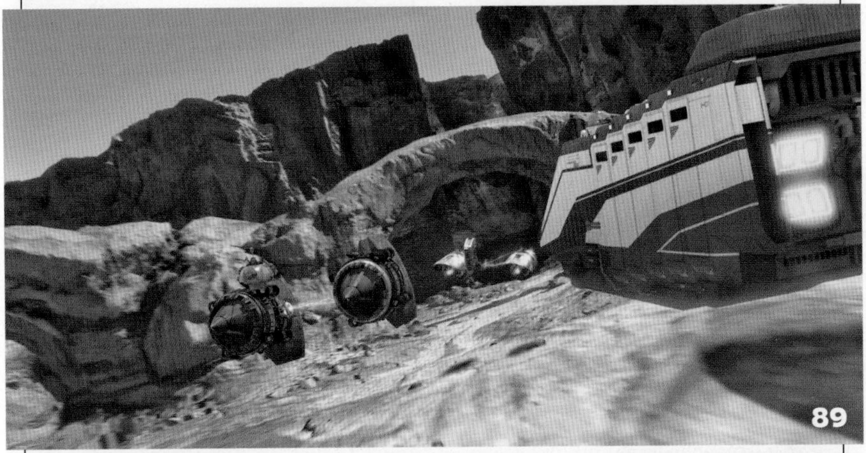

89

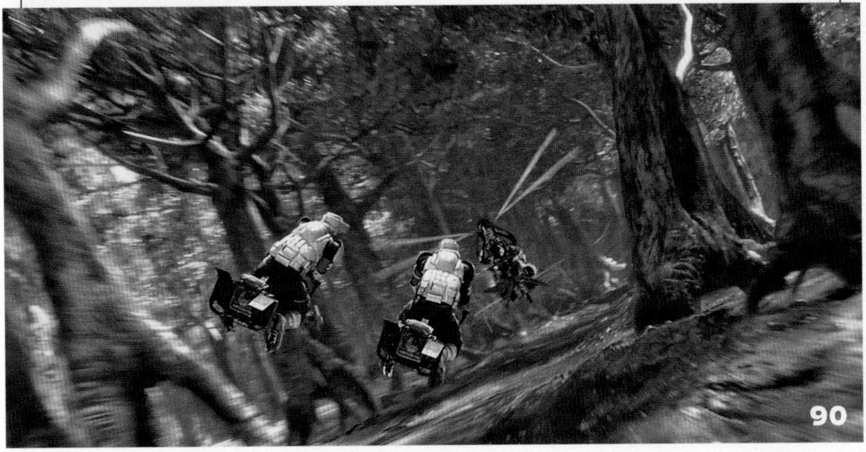

90

Hollywood**Studios**

you? You people seem to know what you're doing! Almost like you've been doing it all day long. I'm impressed. Move along…" **>65** "Nice work, pal"—the same praise Warburton gives a boy as the host of the pre-flight video of the Soarin' ride at Epcot. **>66** G2-4T's thermal scanners may determine that your past includes "excessive use of a blaster in an Ewok sanctuary"; **>67** that you're "considered armed but not dangerous, aim is poor"; **>68** or that you're wanted for "questioning on Mos Eisley," **>69** "parking too close to a black hole" **>70** or "housing a bantha in a residential neighborhood." **>71** A stylized "71" on G2-4T's pedestal refers to the 1971 opening of Walt Disney World. **Boarding area: >72** Baggage workers toss your flight's luggage around like basketballs, as shown on a security-cam monitor above the doors to your flight's loading bay. **>73** As the workers pull away, some remaining cargo falls off their moving carts. **>74** Using a bucket and a squeegee, inept pit droids continually attempt to clean the ship's windshield, their final effort a slapstick disaster. Eventually, a human shows them how it cleans itself at the touch of a remote. **>75** A camera inside your Starspeeder shows pilot droid AC-38 leaving his cockpit to let C-3PO repair a binary motivator, and then getting called away from the area. **>76** In the ride's safety video, the flight attendant's coy tone of voice and wagging finger match those of the host of a Delta Airlines safety video that

went viral in 2008. **>77** After the video, the monitors show your ship rising into its loading bay. **In the Starspeeder: >78** Fixtures in the ceiling recall the reading lights and tiny fans in the passenger cabins of commercial aircraft. Also similar are illuminated icons that convey "no smoking," "buckle up" and "stow carry-ons under seat." **>79** Sounds of your Starspeeder preparing for flight can be heard as you take your seat. **>80** C3PO frets to himself in the cockpit before you see him. **Stormtrooper encounter: >81** On the left side of the hangar, guards carelessly knock luggage off a cart. **>82** On the right, Han Solo stands in front of the Millennium Falcon, which sits ready for takeoff but is detained by guards. **>83** A spotlight shines on the Rebel spy in your cabin as Stormtroopers show his or her mugshot. **>84** Aurebesh on the mugshot reads "Wanted: Rebel Spy." **>85** As the mugshot appears, Han Solo shoots at the guards delaying him, boards his ship and flies off. Your Starspeeder follows him briefly before he goes into hyperspace. **Darth Vader encounter: >86** A Mon Calamari waves at you from a control window to your left. **Hoth: >87** Just after you enter the atmosphere beneath you run a herd of tauntaun—the creature ridden by Luke Skywalker in Episode V. **>88** An AT-AT Walker tumbles when a Rebel fighter pilot tangles its legs, a trick Luke Skywalker used in Episode V. **Tatooine: >89** "I've always wanted to do this!" C-3PO exclaims about

93

98

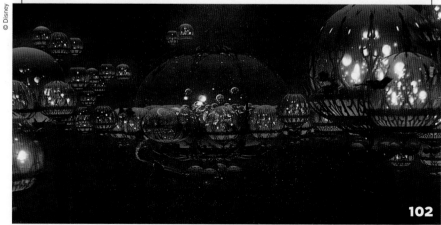

102

Hollywood**Studios**

being in a podrace, the same thing earlier Star Tours pilot Rex said about heading into the surface of a Death Star. **Kashyyyk: >90** C-3PO hits the brakes to catch a trooper behind him, just like Luke Skywalker did in Episode VI. **>91** Crashing into a tree, a clone trooper does the Wilhelm scream, a yelp from 1951 that's actually the voice of character actor Sheb Wooley. Heard in more than 150 movies, including every Star Wars and Indiana Jones film, the scream was named for Private Wilhem, a cowboy who "yelled" it as he got shot with an arrow in 1953's "The Charge at Feather River." Wooley later found fame as the singer of a 1958 novelty tune, "The Purple People Eater." **>92** A Wookiee shakes his fist at you as you leave the planet. **Above**

Geonosis: >93 Bounty hunter Boba Fett chases you through an asteroid belt much like Jango Fett chased Obi-Wan Kenobi in Episode II. **>94** "I have a bad feeling about this," C-3PO says as you approach the Death Star, repeating a line uttered in every Star Wars movie. **>95** You fly through the Death Star just like the Rebels did in Episode VI. **>96** Darth Vader's parked shuttle appears on your right, just before you exit the Death Star. **>97** You drop off your spy on Home One— Admiral Ackbar's ship from the Battle of Endor in Episode VI. **Coruscant: >98** The first half of this segment mimics the opening to Episode III. Your ship is attacked by buzz droids, just like Obi-Wan Kenobi's ship was in that film. Again, R2-D2 shoots one in its center eye. **>99** The second half recalls a chase sequence of Episode II, and includes the tunnel flown through by bounty hunter Zam Wessel. **>100** "Tomorrowland" reads an Aurebesh billboard on your left. **>101** You nearly collide with a yellow fuel truck as you land on the planet, just as passengers in the first Star Tours did at the end of their trip. **Naboo: >102** Just after you plunge underwater Jar Jar Binks waves at you, then ducks to avoid your ship. "We nearly hit that poor Gungan!" C-3PO exclaims. **>103** Episode I's opee sea killer, sando aqua monster and cobo claw-fish also appear. **>104** The sea killer snags your bongo-submarine escort with its tongue, just as it did in Episode I. **Hologram messages: >105** "Help me, Star Tours. You're my only hope" Leia says, recalling her plea in Episode IV, "Help me, Obi-Wan Kenobi. You're my only hope." **>106** All the holograms use the correct pronoun for the Rebel spy—"him," "her" or "them." **Exitway: >107** A sign on the ceiling directs you toward droid and baggage claim. **>108** Episode I concept art appears in a glass case above the photo station. **>109** A few pages of the Episode I script is in the same case, as well as on the wall to the right of the photo station. You can flip through the second one, which details the scene in which Qui-Gon, Padmé and Jar Jar arrive in Mos Espa. **Tatooine Traders: >110** The gift shop resembles the buildings of spaceport Mos Espa. **>111** Tags label many items on its upper shelves as props for Tatooine sets. Some walls and boxes are labeled "Mos Espa." **>112** The abstract face of Goofy is formed by a streetlamp on the side of the shop—at least according to fans of Goofy. Disney says it's a coincidence.

▶ Hidden Mickeys

>113 Outside the building, the three-circle shape appears as greenish-white moss on a tree trunk under the Ewok village platform, facing the building entrance. **>114** It appears in the first queue room, as dials on C-3PO's upper monitor. **>115** In the silhouette window, an R2 droid adjusts two satellite dishes on its head to make it appear to have Mickey ears. **>116** Three planets occasionally align to form the shape on the passenger scanning screen behind droid G2-4T. They come together on the lower left of the screen. The ears the planets form are small. **>117** City spotlights form the shape in the Coruscant segment of the ride, in the lower-right corner of your view. **>118** It shows up again at the end of that segment, as a row of door hatches along a back wall. **>119** Finally, Mickey hides in the Tatooine Traders gift shop, in the Build Your Own Lightsaber station. He's on a panel on the lower right, his ears formed from lightsaber blast marks.

Hollywood**Studios**

76

26

12

```
         CREW STATUS ROSTER     SHIP: NOSTROMO      LINK 2.56.99805-343

   SECTOR LOCATION # 00294                           PERSONNEL CODE

   ERIC JACOBSON..........SYSTEM ALTERATION SUPERVISOR          4Q7
   BOB JOSLIN.............UNEXPLAINABLE PHENOMENON EXPERT        96K3
   ERIC SWAPP.............** M I S S I N G **
   GLENN KOCH.............INTERGALACTIC GOO ANALYST             0I2
   BOB WEIS...............SPACESHIP DRIVER                      83JY
   KATHY ROGERS...........COORDINATION COORDINATOR             5X5
   BROCK THOMAN...........OUTER SPACE PLANNER                  3-5609
   ROBIN REARDON..........** M I S S I N G **
   DOUG ESSELSTROM........SHIRT SUPERVISING OFFICER            8P4
   CORY SEWELSON..........** M I S S I N G **
   GEOFF PUCKETT..........VIDEO EYEWASH DESIGNATOR             77L9
   JACK GILLETT...........RE-WIRING SPECIALIST                 9U2
   WALT STEEL.............TECHNICAL SYSTEM UNTANGLER           6-44M9
   DOUG GRIFFITH..........STILL PROGRAMMING THE WITCH          5W3
   CRAIG RUSSELL..........EVERYWHERE AT ONCE                   2B4
   RON BEUMER.............** M I S S I N G **
   JOHN SULLIVAN..........LOOKING FOR RON BEUMER               34L6
   TIM KIRK...............INTERIOR DETAIL EXPERT               3PV
   PAUL OSTERHAUT.........** M I S S I N G **
   MIKE VALE..............EAR DAMAGE OFFICER                   6M4
   MICHAEL SPROUT.........OPERATION MANUAL RE-WRITER           7-20X4
   CAROL ROTUNDO..........STAR SEARCH ASTROPHYSICIST           1K5

                                                              19
```

Also at Hollywood Studios

Hollywood Boulevard

Grounds: >**1** Offices above Keystone Clothiers include those of tailor Justin Stitches and >**2** Allen Smythee Productions. When the park was built, the pseudonym "Allen Smythee" was used by directors when they hated how a project turned out but were still required to be listed in its credits. **The Great Movie Ride:** >**3** More than 100 Hollywood celebrities have visited the attraction and left their handprints and signatures in its concrete courtyard. Easy to find are those of Warren Beatty, >**4** George Burns, >**5** Bob Denver, >**6** Audrey Hepburn, >**7** Bob Hope >**8** and George Lucas. >**9** Dustin Hoffman and >**10** Robin Williams included their children's prints. >**11** Kermit the frog's tiny prints appear next to Jim Henson's. >**12** Charlton Heston misspelled his name. During his 1995 ceremony, a photographer called to the then-72-year-old star just as he was drawing the "R" in his first name, causing him to look up. When he got back to work, he forgot about the "L." >**13** In the preshow, the trailer for "Singin' in the Rain" contains a glimpse of the actual Chinese Theatre. >**14** In the boarding area, a profile of Minnie Mouse hides in the mural. Tucked under some palm fronds, she faces left, just above and to the right of a tile roof. >**15** On the ride, an argument takes place in a Gangster Alley flat, above Patrick J. Ryan's Bar. >**16** In the Western town, a sheriff's office sign swings when hit by an illusionary bullet. >**17** In the Nostromo spaceship (from the 1979 movie "Alien"), a few inside jokes appear on monitors along the left floor. The first screen tracks the ride's "estimated time till next special effects failure" and extends a >**18** "welcome to all aliens visiting from the Glendale galaxy" (a suburb of Los Angeles, Glendale is the home of Walt Disney Imagineering). >**19** A "Crew Status Roster," the third screen lists Disney imagineers who worked on the ride, including one who is "still programming the witch." >**20** In the Well of Souls scene (from 1981's "Raiders of the Lost Ark") a pharaoh holds Star Wars character R2-D2 while C-3PO repairs him with a screwdriver. The trio appear in a center carving on the Well's left wall, two blocks up from the floor. As many "Raiders" and "Star Wars" fans know, the carving also appears in the movie, on the same wall. >**21** Once it captures its victim, the statue of Anubis expresses its content by having its eyes glow red. >**22** Along the left wall of the skeleton room, a snake squirms out of the eye of a sarcophagus while >**23** a pharaoh pets a mummified cat. >**24** A Munchkin pops out of a yellow-brick-road manhole at the beginning of the song "Ding Dong the Witch is Dead"— just like he does in the 1939 movie "The Wizard of Oz."

HollywoodStudios

25

Sunset Boulevard

Grounds: >**25** Real 1940s vehicles often sit on the street and its side alleys. >**26** "Buy War Bonds & Stamps" urges a painted mailbox. >**27** "We're standing behind you" is the slogan of the International Brotherhood of Second Assistant Directors (say it slowly: IB-SAD), which has an office above the Villains in Vogue shop. During the Great Depression "Second Assistant Director" was a Hollywood mercy title given to gofers, who were often told to "get coffee and stand behind me." **Beauty and the Beast Live on Stage:** >**28** Thirty television stars have left handprints around a fountain in an entrance plaza to the Theater of the Stars amphitheater. James Doohon (Scotty on "Star Trek") added "Beam Me Up" to his prints; >**29** "Jeopardy" host Alex

Trebek included "Who is Alex Trebek?" >**30** The musical begins with a pun: a ringing bell. >**31** Gaston admires himself in any reflection he can find during the first two songs, "Belle" and "Gaston." >**32** The show's "Mob Song" steals a quote from Shakespeare. "Screw your courage to the sticking place" Gaston commands, rallying the villagers to kill the Beast with the phrase Lady Macbeth uses to urge her husband to kill Duncan. >**33** Gaston stays in character even after his final bows, often flexing his biceps as he winks or flashes the "call me" sign at females in the audience. **Rock 'n' Roller Coaster Starring Aerosmith:** >**34** Mounted on a headstock of a huge electric guitar, an upside-down 1950s Cadillac convertible tops off the entrance gate.

> **35** G Force Records is the name of the mythical Hollywood music company headquartered at the grounds. The building holds its offices and studios. > **36** Guitar necks form the columns of the studio's circular foyer. > **37** A 1958 Gibson Les Paul Standard guitar is among the authentic vintage musical items displayed in glass cases. > **38** Other items include a disc cutter, a device that "cut records" by etching sounds from a mixing console onto a master disc; and > **39** record players that range from a 1904 external-horn Edison Fireside to a 1970s Disc-O-Kid. > **40** The sounds of Aerosmith rehearsing can be heard behind doors marked "Studio A" and "Studio B." > **41** A poster from Aerosmith's first national tour, a night in 1973 when it opened for the New York Dolls, is among many that line a poster gallery. > **42** A poster for a show by the band MC5 includes a marijuana leaf that Disney has not-quite-covered with a small American flag. > **43** Sam Andreas and Sons Structural Restoration has done some repair work on the building, according to a sign in a back alley that serves as the ride's boarding area. Other signs indicate that > **44** Lock 'n' Roll Parking Systems runs the alley's parking garage and > **45** Rock 'n' Rollaway Disposal Co. takes care of its trash. > **46** Wash This Way Auto Detail promotes its rates in a glass case. > **47** 2FAST4U and H8TRFFC are among the vanity license plates on the ride's limos. > **48** "Rock 'n' Roller Coaster!!!" screams singer Steven Tyler at the Aerosmith concert you supposedly rushed to, on a video screen after the ride just before the gift shop. **Twilight Zone Tower of Terror:** > **49** A real plaque from the American Automobile Association honors the "13-diamond" status of the attraction's Hollywood Tower Hotel. It's in the lobby, near the reception desk. The group gave the award to Disney when the ride opened. > **50** Alligator-skin luggage has been abandoned at the reception desk, > **51** as have a fedora, topcoat and folded newspaper. > **52** Still sporting its porcelain handset, an elegant French telephone sits on the concierge and check-in counter. > **53** Nearby is the hotel's open registration book, mail-slot mail and guest messages. > **54** A bag, cane and white fedora lean against the counter. > **55** A poster promotes a show in the hotel by Anthony Fremont—the name of a 6-year-old boy in a 1961 episode of the television series "The Twilight Zone" ("It's a Good Life") who used telepathic powers to terrorize neighbors. > **56** A diamond ring, white glove and two glasses rest on a table to the left of the poster. Next to it is a champagne bucket. > **57** A mahjong game has been abandoned on a nearby table. Tea has just been served to the players; a cart holds cups ready for pouring, roses and a newspaper. > **58** Another teacup rests on the end table in front of a fireplace; a goblet and small plate sit on a table to the right. > **59** In

Hollywood**Studios**

the library, bookcases hold props from the TV show. They include the Mystic Seer (a devil-headed fortune-telling machine that invites users to "Ask Me a Yes or No Question") seen in the 1960 episode "Nick of Time," a story of a man unable to make decisions for himself; and >**60** a tiny silver robot from the 1961 episode "The Invaders," a tale of a farm woman who kills what appear to be small invading aliens, but are actually full-size human astronauts, as she is an alien giant. >**61** On the library television, vintage footage of Rod Serling—the host of "The Twilight Zone"—has been altered to remove a cigarette from his right hand. >**62** A little girl in the video sings *"It's raining, it's pouring…"*—the nursery rhyme she'll still be singing when you see her again on the hotel's fourth floor. >**63** In the boiler room, the dials of the service elevators go only to floor 12, though once you board you'll go floor 13. >**64** In the elevator, a small inspection certificate on the wall is signed by "Cadwallader," a jovial character who secretly is the devil in "Escape Clause," a 1959 episode of the show. Dated Oct. 31, 1939, the certificate has the number 10259, a reference to the date the series premiered, Oct. 2, 1959. >**65** As you take your seat, a hint at your 13th-floor destination appears in front of you—a "1" on the open left door and a "3" on the right. When the doors close the number becomes a "B" as you're in the hotel basement. >**66** As the ride ends and the elevator stops, it's next to a storage area that includes the slot machine (marked "Special Jackpot $10,000") from "The Fever," a 1960 episode of "The Twilight Zone" in which a talking slot drives a tightwad crazy; and >**67** two ventriloquist dummies seen in both 1962's "The Dummy," in which a dummy switches places with its human owner, and in 1964's "Caesar and Me," in which a ventriloquist uses his dummy to commit crimes. >**68** A clock in a basement office is still stopped at 8:05, the time lightning struck the hotel on Halloween night, 1939. >**69** A small silver spaceship in the top left corner of that office comes from the episode "The Invaders," in which it was the home to the robot that today hides in this attraction's library. >**70** "Pocket watch, sentimental value, broken crystal" reads a note from someone who has lost that item on a bulletin board to the right of the basement office—a reference to the 1963 episode "A Kind of Stopwatch" in which a bank robber stops time forever when he breaks an unusual timepiece. >**71** Seen from outside the building, the windows of the hotel's gift shop—the ride's gift shop—are still decorated for the Halloween of 1939.

Echo Lake

Grounds: >**72** "We've Finished Some of Hollywood's Finest" proclaims the slogan of acting-and-voice studio Sights and Sounds. Located in the Keystone Clothiers building, it's run by master thespian Ewell M. Pressum, voice coach Singer B. Flatt and account

Hollywood**Studios**

81

85

84

80

77

WARNING!
DO NOT
PULL ROPE

SHIP TO:
GEORGE BAILEY
320 SYCAMORE
BEDFORD FALLS, NEW YORK

MAROON STUDIOS
BABY HERMAN   Roger Rabbit   Jessica Rabbit

executive Bill Moore. **>73** Nearby is Holly-Vermont Realty, the name of a real Hollywood business that in 1923 rented its back room to Walt and Roy Disney to use as their first office. **>74** Dentists C. Howie Pullum, Ruth Canal and Les Payne have an office on the second floor, according to a building directory. **>75** The office of Eddie Valiant—the grumpy gumshoe of the 1988 movie "Who Framed Roger Rabbit"—sits above the Hollywood & Vine restaurant. It has two windows, one of which his client Roger Rabbit has crashed through. **>76** The office next door is available to rent, for 75 cents a day or $5 a week. **>77** A billboard for Roger's employer Maroon Studios tops Keystone Clothiers. **>78** Shipping crates to the left of Min & Bill's Dockside Diner reference three classic movies. One headed to "Scarlett O'Hara, Tara Plantation, 121539 Mitchell Lane, Jonesboro County, Georgia" from "Fleming Fashions Ltd., Atlanta" alludes to the director, premiere city, lead character, main setting, premiere date, novelist and inspiration (Jonesboro, Ga.) of the 1939 film "Gone With the Wind." **>79** On its way to "Rick Blaine" from the "Curtiz Wine & Spirits Ltd." a second crate refers to the director (Michael Curtiz) and main character (Rick Blaine) of 1942's "Casablanca." **>80** Addressed to "George Bailey" of "Bedford Falls," a crate from "Wainwright Enterprises" honors the main character, location and key secondary character (Sam Wainwright, the boyfriend of George's eventual wife) of the 1946 classic "It's a Wonderful Life." **>81** Having left her huge footprints in the walkway behind her, Gertie the Dinosaur stands along the shore of Echo Lake, converted into an ice-cream stand. In 1914 the childlike dinosaur starred in the earliest cartoon to be widely seen, the aptly named "Gertie the Dinosaur." **Indiana Jones Epic Stunt Spectacular:** **>82** "I have a bad feeling about this," Indy says during the show's Cairo street scene—repeating a line that's appeared in nearly every George Lucas movie. **>83** Jeeps and trucks used in 1989's "Indiana Jones and the Last Crusade" serve as gift stands in front of the theater. **>84** Its side gun barrel still exploded from being stuffed with a rock, that film's "Steel Beast" tank sits alongside the show's left exit-way, behind the Outpost gift shop. **>85** "Warning! Do Not Pull Rope!" a sign reads to the left of the show entrance, next to a hole a British archeologist has lowered himself into. Pull the rope and he'll yell back a series of complaints, including "I say! Stop mucking about up there!" **Backlot Express:** **>86** Call sheets from the 1980s television series "Cheers" and the 1989 movie "Star Trek V" are taped on an indoor window of a paint department office in this supposed former prop warehouse, a fast-food spot. **>87** The Bennie the Cab stunt vehicle from "Who Framed Roger Rabbit" sits in a back corner; **>88** that film's Toon Patrol truck is on the outdoor patio.

Hollywood**Studios**

89

Streets of America

Grounds: >**89** On New York Street, service bullets W and D on a subway entrance allude to—of course—the words "Walt" and "Disney." >**90** Sound effects include honking horns, playing children, screeching buses, murmuring crowds and whistling police. >**91** In a nod to the 1952 movie "Singin' in the Rain," standing under an umbrella that hangs off a lamppost will mist you with rain. It's just off New York Street, near the entrance to the Lights, Motors, Action stunt show. To trigger the spray, stand on a metal plate. **Jim Henson's MuppetVision 3-D:** >**92** Above the building, a grayscale Gonzo hangs off the clock of a tower in the same way Harold Lloyd hung off the clock of a skyscraper in the 1923 black-and-white silent film "Safety

Last!" >**93** A hanging Acme anvil is a nod to classic Roadrunner cartoons from rival studio Warner Bros. >**94** On the building, an outdoor staircase leads to the theater's projection room, the door of which indicates is used by the Swedish Chef to run a combination editing and catering business. Its slogan: "Frøöm Qüick Cüts tø Cöld Cüts." >**95** To the side of the building, large planters on a brick wall hold giant ice cream sundaes. One is half-eaten. >**96** Painted by Jim Henson and other Muppet artists, colorful pipes and walls in the outdoor queue are their homage to a closet. In 1963, when the Muppets were booked on NBC's "The Jack Paar Program," Jim Henson and his associates mistakenly arrived six hours early. To kill time, they defaced a utility closet with their puppet paint, covering the walls and pipes with loopy designs and faces. >97 Queue posters promote faux Muppet films such as "Beach Blanket Beaker." >98 Queue placards demonstrate how to use the show's 3-D glasses, >99 stick out your tongue and touch your ear >100 and get from "here" to "there." >101 "This door is alarmed! And genuinely concerned!" reads a sign on a backstage door. >102 At the building entrance, a sign at its security office reads "Key Under Mat." Flip up the mat beneath it and you'll find the key. >103 A wanted poster seeks Fozzie Bear "for impersonating a comic" inside the office; >104 a pinup calendar features Miss Piggy. >105 "You must be shorter than this to enter" reads a sign above the building's entranceway, about eight feet off the ground. It's chipped. >106 In the building's entrance hall, a directory case lists offices for Statler and Waldorf's Institute of Heckling and Browbeating and the Muppet's Gonzo-run MuppetLabs Department of Poultry and Mold Cultivation. >107 "This is not a door," reads a door to the Department of Artificial Reality. >108 A net full of Jell-O hangs inside the theater's storage-room lobby, a coy reference to Annette Funicello, a 1950s Disney Mouseketeer. >109 Next to it, an empty bird cage has a perch—not a rod, a fish. >110 Nearby, a crate shipped to the Swedish Chef holds "Der Noodle Frooper"; >111 a box

of "2-D Fruities" holds flat cutouts of a banana, cherry and lemon; and >112 a box of Gonzo's helmets includes some covered with "fungus and mold" and others covered with "mold—no fungus." >113 Along the walls are parodies of classic paintings by Henri Rousseau and Hans Holbein. Rousseau's "Sleeping Gypsy" has become "The Sleepy Zootsy." >114 Holbein's "Portrait of Henry VIII" has become "Jester at the Court of Henry VIII," a portrait of Fozzie holding a banana up to his ear. Underneath him, the Latin phrase *Bananum In Avre Habeo* translates to "I'm holding a banana in my ear." >115 On catwalks above the room, actual Muppet props include The SwineTrek spaceship used in the "Pigs in Space" skits of the 1970s television series "The Muppet Show," and >116 the toy soldiers and frontiersmen seen in the finale of the MuppetVision movie. >117 In the movie, live chickens wander behind host Kermit the Frog as he welcomes you to MuppetLabs. >118 The show's 3-D glasses appear in the film on a bust of Beethoven (on its head) >119 and on a brass bald eagle. >120 The orchestra penguins cackle at Statler and Waldorf's barbs from the balcony, especially the one about them— that they "probably took the job for the halibut." >121 They cough when squirted by Fozzie's boutonniere. >122 In Dr. Honeydew's lab, two goldfish eventually appear in a beaker above some Chinese takeout boxes. >123 In a production error

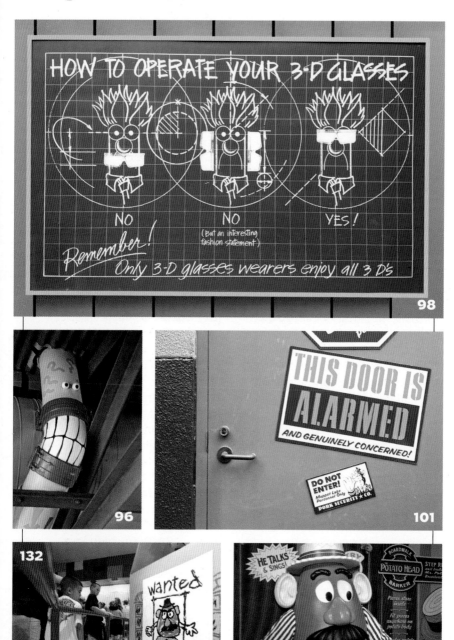

at the end of Miss Piggy's performance of "Dream a Little Dream of Me," her head falls off her body as she's yanked forward by a water-ski boat. **>124** Statler and Waldorf gape at the MuppetVision machine, nod as Waldo bounces off people's heads, and duck for cover from the VacuuMuppet and the Chef's payback cannon. **>125** "Large formalwear for the hard-to-fit. Small formalwear for the hard-to-find" reads a poster for penguin outfitter Frankie alongside the theater exitway. **>126** "Absolutely no point beyond this point" reads one of many silly signs in the store. **Honey I Shrunk the Kids Playground:** **>127** On a back wall, the nose of a huge dog sniffs you then sneezes.

Animation Courtyard

The Magic of Disney Animation: **>128** Handprints of some legendary Disney animators appear in a small outdoor plaza—those of Ken Anderson, Marc Davis, Ollie Johnston, Ward Kimball, Ken O'Connor and Frank Thomas. **Voyage of the Little Mermaid:** **>129** A replica of P.T. Barnum's FeJee Mermaid—a grotesque body of a monkey stitched to the tail of a fish—hangs in the lobby over the right door to the theater. Promoting it as a real mermaid that had been caught off the Fiji Islands, Barnum toured with the thing in 1842.

Pixar Place

Toy Story Mania: >130 A handwritten note from Andy is taped to the back door of the Pixar Place security gate. It diagrams how his toys (his Barrel of Monkeys, Mr. Spell and Green Army Men) are sending secret messages to passersby which hint how to get a top score in the game. (For a complete list of cheats see our other book, "The Complete Guide to Walt Disney World.") **>131** In the Standby queue, a huge pink crayon in Andy's room is the only one that he hasn't used. **>132** Andy's hand-drawn wanted poster of One-Eyed Bart (a closeup of it opens the 1995 movie "Toy Story") sits along the queue. **>133** A robotic Mr. Potato Head carnival barker interacts one-on-one with guests in the Standby line, thanks to a wealth of phrases pre-recorded by the voice of the character, comedian Don Rickles. He often sings a song; sometimes he takes off his ear. **>134** Near the end of the line Andy's little sister Molly has painted Nemo, the star of 2003's "Finding Nemo." **>135** On the ride, practice rounds show portraits of "Toy Story 3" characters Bookworm, Chunk and Stretch. **>136** As your vehicle heads to the next game, a carnival in a wall mural includes Toy Story Mania. **>137** At Woody's Rootin' Tootin' Shootin' Gallery, on some screens Bo Peep kisses Woody as the curtain closes. **>138** As you leave the attraction, two toy blocks facing you show the letters "C" and "U." **>139** Nearby, a "Tin Toy" Little Golden Book has jammed Andy's bedroom door closed, so the toys can play with his new arcade game indefinitely.

HollywoodStudios

Hidden Mickeys

Hollywood Blvd. grounds: >**140** Mickey's three-circle shape appears on the front of the Cover Story shop, as a repeating pattern in the molding under its second-floor windows. **The Great Movie Ride:** >**141** A silhouetted Mickey profile appears on your left in the ride's Gangster Alley, in the second-story windows of the Western Chemical building. >**142** Just past that, a period-correct Mickey cartoon poster has been covered up by a newer one for the movie "A Public Enemy"; Mickey's shoe and tail are still visible. >**143** The mouse appears twice in the Well of Souls—first on your right below the Ark of the Covenant, as a light profile on a dark stone (easy to see); >**144** then on your left, etched into the stone wall as a full-figure Mickey Mouse pharaoh, being served cheese by an Egyptian Donald Duck (tough to see unless you catch it on first glance). **Citizens of Hollywood:** >**145** Mickey's three-circle shape appears as dark smudges on the chin of Sparky Sparks, a Hollywood Public Works electrician. **Sunset Blvd. grounds:** >**146** Curb stamps read "Mortimer & Co. Contractors 1928," a reference to Walt Disney's working name for Mickey Mouse and the year he created him, 1928. **Rock 'n' Roller Coaster Starring Aerosmith:** >**147** Mouse ears top the little boy on the poster for the ride on the building. >**148** The three circles appear as a pattern on Steven Tyler's shirt in that poster;

>**149** as floor tiles in the foyer; >**150** as carpet patterns in the first queue room; >**151** as cables on the floor of the recording studio; >**152** as registration stickers on the limos' rear license plates; and >**153** as the "O" in a "Box #15" stamp on a trunk in the exit. **The Twilight Zone Tower of Terror:** >**154** A pair of folded wire-rim glasses form the circles on the concierge desk in the lobby; the temple wires Mickey's face; the lens rims his ears. >**155** The little girl in the library video holds a period-correct Mickey Mouse doll. >**156** Sheet music for 1932's "What! No Mickey Mouse? (What Kind of a Party is This?)" hides in the left library. >**157** The three-circle shape appears in the boiler room as round ash doors beneath a fire box on a furnace and >**158** as water stains to the left of a fuse box on the left wall, just after the queue splits into two lines; >**159** on the ride's 13th floor, in the center of a star field as it becomes a pinpoint; >**160** after the ride in a basement office, as gauges in an open drawer to the far left. **Sunset Ranch Market:** >**161** It's formed by gauges on a welding torch behind the counter at Rosie's All-American Cafe. **Fantasmic:** >**162** The shape appears in water-screen bubbles, one of which holds Pinocchio. **'50s Prime Time Cafe:** >**163** The shape appears in the restaurant's napkin and utensil holders and >**164** as washers that secure table tops at the adjacent Tune-In Lounge. **Jim**

165

145

Henson's MuppetVision 3-D: >**165** Mickey appears in the fountain out front as a ring float; >**166** along the outdoor queue as a small sketch of a DNA model in a "5 Reasons" poster; and >**166** in the early moments of the preshow video, as a test pattern. **Stage 1 Company Store:** >**167** As drips of purple paint on a recessed light outside the store, under a bronze lion head. **Lights Motors Action:** >**168** A vintage full-figure Mickey is in the window of the Antiquites Brocante shop. >**169** A gear and two circular belts form the three circles in the window of the motorcycle shop, in the top right corner. **Mama Melrose's Ristorante Italiano:** >**170** As spots on a vine leaf at the bottom right of a lattice fence to the right of the check-in desk and >**171** as a spot on the right shoulder of a nearby dalmatian statue. **Toy Story Pizza Planet:** >**172** As star clusters in a mural above the cash registers, near a pizza-slice constellation left of a spaceship; >**173** and as moon craters in a mural above the arcade (a three-quarter profile). **Toy Story Mania:** >**174** The three circles are formed by an upside-down paint splotch under the tail of a clownfish near the end of the standby queue; >**175** in the boarding area by frames on a Toy Story Midway Games Playset box in a large wall mural; and >**176** on the ride just after the final game, by the dot in the exclamation point of the phrase "Circus Fun!" that appears on a mural on your right.

Disney's
Animal
Kingdom

3

The Oasis

>**1** A swaying footbridge crosses a creek off the left walkway. >**2** The back of a waterfall can be touched from a grotto. >**3** Disguised as leaves and vines, performance artist DiVine conceals herself in foliage.

Discovery Island

Grounds: >**4** Mushroom shades cap walkway lights. >**5** The digestive tracts of alligators, birds and turtles appear as gaps in backrests of plastic benches. >**6** A Wilderness Explorers Club House (a covered stand to meet characters from the 2009 Disney-Pixar movie "Up") includes Bark-O-Later machines that translate your speech into dog language. >**7** Regardless of what you say, a common translation is "I think that I will never see, a thing as lovely as a… SQUIRREL!" **Tree of Life:** >**8** The front viewing area is framed by animals emerging from roots, including an armadillo, >**9** big-horned sheep, >**10** buffalo, >**11** crocodile, >**12** deer, >**13** elephant, >**14** Komodo dragon >**15** and otter. >**16** The side of the tree facing the park entrance includes a bald eagle, >**17** buffalo, >**18** deer, >**19** rhino, >**20** roadrunner, >**21** songbird taking flight, >**22** seahorse and >**23** tiger. >**24** From the kangaroo trail, the left side of the tree hides an ant, >**25** cheetah, >**26** duck-billed platypus, >**27** egret, >**28** gorilla, >**29** moose, >**30** sable antelope, >**31** squid, >**32** tortoise >**33** walrus, and >**34** some flying ducks. >**35** From the Discovery Trail you can see a beaver, >**36** beetle, >**37** bittern, >**38** camel, >**39** chimp, >**40** climbing elephant, >**41** fish, >**42** fox, >**43** giraffe, >**44** orca, >**45** peacock, >**46** porcupine, >**47** rabbit, >**48** shrew, >**49** snapping turtle, >**50** tapir and >**51** a wolf. >**52** The back side of the tree, visible from a path along the Discovery River as well as the walkway between Africa and Asia, includes a barn owl, >**53** bat with wings outstretched, >**54** bear, >**55** gibbon, >**56** hippo, >**57** rearing horse >**58** humpback whale, >**59** meerkat >**60** octopus >**61** scorpion, >**62** snail >**63** and a herd of wildebeest running up the trunk. **It's Tough To Be A Bug:** >**64** The Termite-ator is one of the stars of the 4-D movie promoted on posters outside its Tree of Life Repertory Theater. >**65** A wall plaque just outside the lobby honors Dr. Jane Goodall's work with chimpanzees. It's next to a carving of chimp David Graybeard, one of her favorites. >**66** "A Stinkbug Named Desire," "Barefoot in the Bark," "Beauty and the Bees," "Little Shop of Hoppers" and "Web Side Story" are among previous theater shows commemorated in lobby posters. >**67** Nearby is a giant dung ball from its presentation of "The Dung and I." >**68** Ambient music in the lobby comes from those shows. >**69** The auditorium itself is inside an anthill; >**70** the projection booth a wasp nest. >**71** "The stinkbug will be played by Claire DeRoom" reports a preshow announcer. >**72** After Claire

Animal**Kingdom**

39

64

6

5

85

performs Flik asks her to "lay off the churros!" >**73** As the show ends, fireflies swarm to exit signs. **Pizzafari:** >**74** Each of the four rooms of the restaurant are lined with murals that portray a different kind of animal—those that carry their homes, >**75** camouflage themselves, >**76** hang upside down >**77** and are nocturnal. >**78** Bugs rule the porch out back. >**79** In the camouflage room, animals hiding in the murals include two bitterns standing in the reeds under an orange fox, >**80** a frog resting on the tree trunk under a brown leopard and a >**81** stickbug, posing on a leaf at the top of a plant left of an orange tiger. >**82** In the upside-down room only one animal is right-side up: a small blue bug under a purple bird toward the back, painted on the header that frames the rearmost seating area. >**83** On the opposite side of that header, an opossum tail without a body appears between the second and third opossums from the right. >**84** Dozens of carved wooden bats hang from the ceiling. >**85** In the nocturnal room, red mice scurry to escape a green spraying skunk on a back mural. They're joined by nine white stars. **Flame Tree Barbecue:** >**86** Predator & Prey is the theme of the restaurant's outdoor seating pavilion. Hungry owls watch a bevy of skittish rabbits at the first pavilion; a windsock shows a bunny descending into a hole being chased by a swooping owl. >**87** Spiders hunt butterflies in a second pavilion; >**88** snakes scurry

from eagles in a third; >**89** the snakes are in control in a fourth, as they hunt mice; >**90** in a fifth pavilion crocodiles munch on fish; >**91** anteaters collect ants; and >**92** eels hunt crabs. **Stands and stores:** >**93** The carvings and paintings on many Discovery Island snack stands relate to the product they sell. Safari Coffee is adorned with hyper critters such as kangaroo rats; >**94** Safari Popcorn's creatures snack on popcorn-like clusters of flies, mice and minnows; and >**95** Safari Pretzel is decorated with eels, octopus and other animals that contort themselves into strange shapes. >**96** Migrating and working animals embellish Island Mercantile. >**97** At Disney Outfitters, ground animals decorate the right room; those of the air the left room.

Africa

Grounds: >**98** Foundations of former buildings appear in streets. >**99** Lampposts bear the phrase "Harambe 1961," honoring year the village gained independence from Great Britain. >**100** Makeshift wires carry electricity throughout Africa (and Asia). >**101** Though notices strictly forbid advertising posters, they're plastered on walls everywhere. >**102** "Ivory poachers beware!" warns a notice. **Kilimanjaro Safaris:** >**103** Elephants featured in the ride's original poacher-focused storyline, Big Red and Little Red still show up in a poster in the queue just past the safari office. >**104** On the savannah, "prehistoric" drawings

Animal**Kingdom**

101

99

102

appear on a gate past the flamingos and **>105** on rocks to the right as you pass the lions. **Pangani Forest Exploration Trail: >106** "Beware of Buffalo!" a stone warns along the walkway, just past the okapis. There are no buffalo. **>107** Past the aviary, cabinet drawers in a research station hold collections of preserved insects, claws, feathers,

seashells, small skulls and tarantulas. **Festival of the Lion King: >108** "Slow down! I'm supposed to be center stage!" urges meerkat Timon to a dancer holding the remote control to his float as it enters the theater and heads to a corner. **>109** During the show, he cracks up watching the Tumble Monkeys, **>110** trembles during an

106

ominous "Be Prepared" and >**111** swoons throughout the romantic "Can You Feel the Love Tonight?" >**112** The giraffe on a parade float often mouths the words to songs. >**113** On another float, Pumbaa sometimes waves his tiny front legs at Timon or at guests. Puppeteers hide inside all four floats and can see out; their animals can respond to guests. >**114** Tumble Monkey acrobats pick bugs off guests and each other. >**115** They perform to a zippy medley of instrumentals that combines swing standards (Benny Goodman's "Sing Sing Sing," Duke Ellington's "Caravan," Kay Kyser's "Playmates") with snippets of 1895's "The Streets of Cairo" (AKA "They Don't Wear Pants in the Southern Part of France") and the 1923 ditty "Yes! We Have No Bananas." >**116** Acrobat cues include a Tarzan yell,

>**117** a cow moo and >**118** a train whistle. >**119** As Timon protests that he can't do his "Songs of the South Seas Medley," he scats a few bars of the "Hawaiian War Chant," an ancient love song made famous by big-band leader Tommy Dorsey as well as Walt Disney (in his Enchanted Tiki Room). >**120** After the show Timon's live microphone picks up his aside, "Could somebody hose down those tumble monkeys? They're starting to smell a little gamey." **Tusker House:** >**121** Murmuring voices, clanking pots and pans and a radio are among the sounds of hotel residents heard from a kitchen behind a back door. >**122** Sometimes a landlady knocks, trying to collect back rent. >**123** The Safari Orientation Centre of Harambe, the dining area is lined with real African artifacts, faux

Animal**Kingdom**

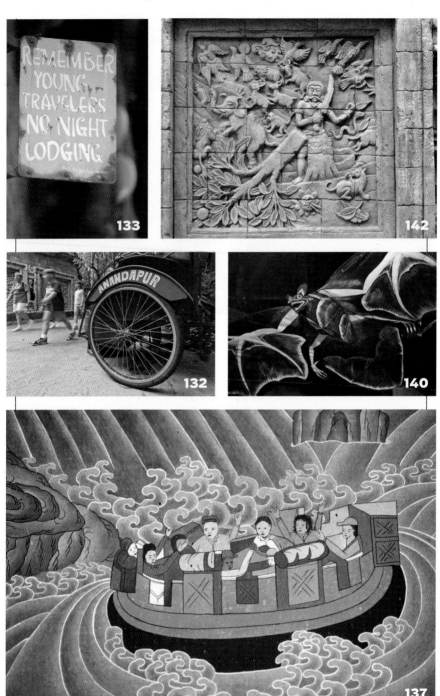

133

142

132

140

137

maps and notices. **>124** Its Jorodi Masks & Beads shop is an homage to Disney Imagineer Joe Rohde, the park's chief design executive. It's on the second floor of the open-air market (the serving area). **>125** A sign at the shop promotes its earrings, a reference to Rohde's distinctive lobal adornments. **>126** Rohde also appears as Cap'n Bob in a Harambe poster for Cap'n Bob's Super Safaris.

Conservation Station

Grounds: >127 Along the walkway, impressions of animals and the Tree of Life eventually form a Circle of Life. **Building: >128** Restroom placards offer The Scoop on Poop and a Whiz Quiz.

Asia

Grounds: >129 Bicycle tracks and footprints are embedded in "dried mud" pathways. **>130** Walls and drain covers shoot water at a small play area just past the entrance to Kali River Rapids. **>131** Each business in Disney's mythical kingdom of Anandapur displays a tax license displaying its king and queen. The bigger the license, the more taxes the business has paid. **>132** Authentic rickshaws sit alongside some walkways. **>133** "Remember young travelers, no night lodging," reads a sign at the Drinkwallah snack stand near Yak & Yeti. **>134** Asian Coca-Cola signs surround the stand. **>135** Bells celebrate answered prayers on a crumbling Indian tiger shrine decked with scarves and garlands. It's near the gibbons exhibit. **Kali River Rapids: >136** "Antiks Made to Order" reads a sign in Mr. Panika's Shop, a building in the queue. **>137** In the last room, King of Pop Michael Jackson is among the raft riders in a mural created in Nepal by a Jackson fan. He's at the top right of the raft with his hands raised. **>138** Raft names include "Khatman-Doozi," "Papa-Do Ran-Rani," "Sherpa Surfer" and "So Sari." **>139** On the exitway, buttons on a footbridge shoot sprays of water on unsuspecting rafters. **Maharajah Jungle Trek: >140** Giant painted bat kites hang over the entrance to the bat house. **>141** In the second tiger viewing area, a family of wild great horned owls often sit in the trees. **>142** Just before the aviary, an environmental history of mankind is shown in a sequence of carvings on a stone wall—man emerges out of the water; comes to a paradise rich with wildlife; chops down its tree; faces floods, death and chaos; and finally gains happiness when he learns to respect nature. **>143** An actual fertility urn sits in the aviary entrance building, which in Disney's story is the tomb of Anantah, the first ruler of Anandapur. Anantah's ashes are said to be in the urn, which shows an abstract couple engaging in, um, fertility activity. **Expedition Everest: >144** Posters and other warnings from Serka Zong villagers urge you to cancel your trip. **>145** The ride's height-minimum bar is a vertical Yeti footprint. A bar above it reads

Animal**Kingdom**

138

139

145

148

YETI

GUARDIAN OF THE REALM OF THE SNOWS

RESPECT TRADITION

BEWARE

FORBIDDEN MOUNTAIN

FOR MORE THAN 1,000 YEARS, THESES MOUNTAINS HAVE BEEN
PROTECTED FROM INTRUDERS BY THE YETI. DO NOT IGNORE THE LESSONS OF THE PAST.

"You must be one Yeti foot tall to ride." >**146** In the queue, ringable bells hang from the red structure (a mandir) just past the first building. >**147** Each train pulls out with a "toot-toot!" >**148** On the lift hill, a small temple is filled with eerie music. >**149** As the track comes to an end, prayer flags stretch across the broken tracks, and >**150** Yeti claw marks and footprints appear in the snow to your right. >**151** When you stop in the cave, watch the track in front of you. It flips over. >**152** Steam escapes from each train's boiler after it pulls back into the boarding area. >**153** The gift shop appears to be made from a common Himalayan building material—dried yak dung.

Animal**Kingdom**

189

163

198

154

170

168

161

192

DinoLand U.S.A.

Grounds: >**154** A road sign identifies the main walkway as U.S. 498, a reference to the park's opening in April, 1998. >**155** "Lost—My Tail" reads a note on the bulletin board across from the Boneyard entrance. It's from the nearby apatosaurus cast, which has a disconnected tailbone. >**156** The land's original layout, which included a real fossil preparation area and cast display room on the site of today's Dino-Rama, is shown on a map on the board. >**157** Three fictional grad students and their professors have posted work schedules and notes on a whiteboard along the top back wall. >**158** The students' notes to each other and personal possessions are scattered about the playground, >**159** on that bulletin board and >**160** in the converted fishing lodge Restaurantosaurus, where they live in the rafters. >**161** A folk-art dinosaur sculpture stands across from the Dino-Rama entrance.
>**162** Two baby dinosaurs hide underneath it. One is hatching.
>**163** Some mischievous graffiti on the side of an adjacent snack-stand cooler shows the folk-art dino stealing a sip of Coca-Cola from a 1960s teenager. **The Boneyard:** >**164** Notes sound when children bang a "xylobone" embedded in a wall near a Jeep. >**165** Nearby, dino tracks trigger loud roars when kids step on them. >**166** Heard on pirate radio station "W-DINO," the playground's ambient music includes 1970's "Brontosaurus" by The Move (the British band that would become the Electric Light Orchestra) >**167** and the 1977 hit "Godzilla" by Blue Oyster Cult. **Dinosaur:** >**168** A cast of the largest and most complete T-Rex fossil ever found (Sue, South Dakota, 1990) stands in front of the ride. >**169** Trees that appear to be behind the building are actually on its roof. They create the illusion that the structure is much smaller than it is; just a small museum, not a huge indoor ride. >**170** A statue of Aladar from Disney's year-2000 film "Dinosaur" smiles at you as you approach the building. >**171** At the entrance door, a dedication plaque is dated April 22, 1978, exactly 20 years before the attraction opened.
>**172** A parody of 1970s museum displays, a cheap lobby diorama features an obvious plastic rat glued to an obvious plastic tree, beneath which swim obvious plastic fish in an obvious plastic pond. >**173** In a preshow video, Dr. Seeker claims flash photography "interferes with the homing signal and that's not good." >**174** Actually part of an above-ground warehouse, the "underground research facility" where the ride begins creates the illusion of being subterranean. It's cooler than the earlier rooms, and its lights flicker. >**175** Red, yellow and white pipes are marked with the chemical makeups of ketchup, mustard and mayonnaise — a nod to McDonald's, the ride's original sponsor. >**176** The lights of its time-machine transporter resemble heating coils of a toaster. >**177** After the ride, gift shop monitors show its iguanodon wandering the building.

AnimalKingdom

>**178** A cast of an ancient giant sea turtle hangs from the shop's ceiling. **Primeval Whirl:** >**179** Hubcaps and >**180** egg beaters decorate the queue's time portal. >**181** An egg timer, >**182** A.M. radio and >**183** an alarm clock front its 1950s-styled "Time Machine" ride vehicles.

Finding Nemo—The Musical: >**184** Before the show begins, Nemo swims back and forth through oversized bubbles on the sides of the stage. >**185** In the show, as he longs to explore "the big blue world," Marlin warns "Sharks are not our friends, Nemo. Haven't you seen 'Jaws'?" **Restaurantosaurus:** >**186** Dino ditties in the ambient music include the 1988 Was Not Was hit "Walk the Dinosaur," proto-punk icon Jonathan Richman's "I'm a Little Dinosaur" and "Ugga Bugga," a Springsteen-like tune by Barnes and Barnes, a band led by one-time child television star Bill Mumy.

>**187** Greasy hand prints form dinosaur shapes on the walls of the restaurant's Quonset hut garage, as do >**188** the cans of Sinclair Litholine Multi-Purpose Grease and Dynoil ("keep your old dinosaur running") on the shelves of that room. >**189** A hangout of those grad students, the restaurant's Hip Joint rec room includes posters for rock bands Dinosaur Jr. and T Rex; >**190** and a juke box filled with songs such as "Dust in the Wind." >**191** Dino-Rama entrepreneurs Chester and wife Hester appear on a poster in the main dining hall. >**192** Outside the rec room, the students have rearranged the letters in the word AIRSTREAM on the back of its converted travel trailer to read I ARE SMART. >**193** Four sketches for "The Rite of Spring" sequence in Disney's 1930s film project "Concert Feature" that became the 1940 film "Fantasia" hang by the restrooms.

Dinosaur Treasures gift shop: >**194** "DAK 1998"— a reference to the year Disney's Animal Kingdom opened—reads the license plate on a truck in front of the shop for S. McKayla's Wildlife Endeavors. >**195** The price of gas is 29.9 cents a gallon on rusty gas pumps in front of the converted gas station as well as >**196** on a painted-over sign on its rear roof. >**197** "Rough scaly skin... Making you groan?... Don't despair... Use Fossil Foam" read four sequential signs hanging above the shop entrance from one direction; >**198** "When in Florida... Be sure to... Visit... Epcot" from the other. >**199** In the garage, boxes above the doors include "Chester's dig '47," "Chester's pet rocks 1966" and "Train Parts." >**200** Items turned into dinosaurs on the walls include an oil funnel and >**201** a gas-pump nozzle. >**202** Above the main room, tiny plastic dinos ride trains, snow ski and flee lava flows. >**203** Station owners Chester and Hester appear in a photo in a corner of the room. >**204** The ambient music in the shop and its restrooms includes The Hoosier Hot Shots' 1935 ditty "I Like Bananas Because They Have No Bones" *("I don't like your peaches; they are full of stones. I like bananas because they have no bones.")*

Hidden Mickeys

Tree of Life: >**205** As grayish-green moss facing the front of the park, just to the left of a buffalo's face. **It's Tough To Be A Bug:** >**206** As a tiny dark splotch on a tree in the queue, near the handicapped entrance doors, just to the right of a door that reads "Cast Members Only." **Pizzafari:** >**207** As orange spots on the lower left side of a spotted shell of a painted turtle in the room with murals of animals carrying their homes on their backs. >**208** As black spots on a leopard (and gray spots underneath it) in the camouflage room. **Adventurers Outpost:** >**209** As the center of radiating rays of orange and brown, in the bottom left corner of the giant-postcard photo backdrop. **Harambe village:** >**210** As a drain cover and two round pebble groupings in front of the Tamu Tamu snack stand, facing Discovery Island. >**211** As a similar grouping just left of Mombasa Marketplace. >**212** As gray pavement behind the fruit market. **Kilimanjaro Safaris:** >**213** As puffy spots between a split branch, just beyond the clay pits past a baobab tree, opposite a large elephant habitat; >**214** as a flamingo island; and >**215** just past that island but before the next gate, as indentations in a boulder on the right. **Pangani Forest Exploration Trail:** >**216** As tiny beads on the tile counter of a cash-register cart near the trail. The head is a white and blue bead; the ears black. >**217**

In the research station, as a mark on a backpack to the left of the naked mole rats, and >**218** on a box of soap on a small ledge behind the desk lamp, as the "O" in the word "Asepco" and two paper-reinforcement rings. **Wildlife Express station:** >**219** As blue circles in the rafters' cross beams. **Conservation Station:** >**220** Mickey hides in multiple places in the entrance mural. On the left wall his three circles appear as a squirrel's pupil; >**221** wrinkles on a hippo chin (a profile); >**222** a scale behind the eye of a crocodile; >**223** a shadow on a walrus neck; >**224** an owl's pupils; >**225** a spot on a yellow fish (obscured by an octopus); >**226** and black spots on a butterfly's left wing, above a bat. >**227** On the middle wall as an ostrich pupil; >**228** green snake scales; >**229** a sucker on a starfish (a Mickey profile); >**230** on the top of a butterfly body (a detailed, smiling Mickey face); >**231** as spots on butterfly wings under a monkey; >**232** and as a silver frog's left pupil (another profile). >**233** On the right wall as a pink spot on a spider abdomen, above a white owl chick; >**234** in an opossum's pupil; and >**235** as black spots on the yellow wings of a butterfly, above the arm of a praying mantis. >**236** Near the Song of the Rainforest as yellow flower petals; >**237** as a white spot on a fly, above a flower; >**238** a tree shadow in front of the rainforest doors (a profile); >**239** a white spot on a tree to

Animal**Kingdom**

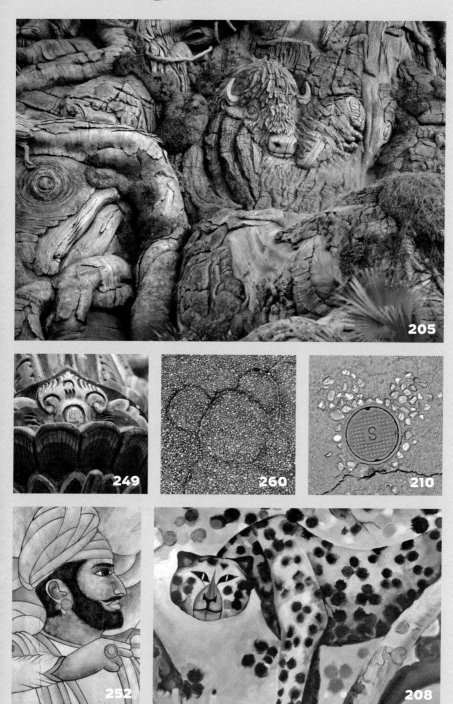

205

249

260

210

252

208

the left of The Accidental Florist sign; and >**240** a spot on tree bark about 4 feet off the ground, across from a fly. >**241** As a bark impression in the Song of the Rainforest sign to the lower right of Grandmother Willow's face (a profile). >**242** As a nearby painted hole in a leaf; >**243** spots on a wooden cockroach inside a tree in the front of the area; >**244** and dark green spots on a chameleon above a Giant Cockroach sign.

>**245** In the reptile display room as petri dishes in a far left window.

>**246** In the Affection Section petting zoo as a pattern on a sheared sheep (often); and >**247** orange spots on the wall of the nearby stage, to the right of a lizard door.

>**248** As overlapping circles in tree grates in the Conservation Station lobby and in Affection Section. **Asia grounds:** >**249** As a small golden crown on a carved cermonial mask on an inside wall of the Drinkwallah snack bar. **Maharajah Jungle Trek:** >**250** As leaves under an archer's wrist in a mural just past the first tiger viewing area, in a mural on the left, inside the first arch. >**251** At the second tiger viewing area, as painted swirls of water under a painted tiger, in the first mural on the right and >**252** a maharajah's earring in the first mural on the left. >**253** After the windowed tiger area as painted green leaves on the left, on the left side of a decaying mural that faces backward. **Expedition Everest:** >**254** In the queue, as a hat on a Yeti doll in Tashi's Trek and Tongba Shop.

>**255** As light switches in a nearby display of patches. >**256** In the queue's Yeti Museum, as a dent and holes in a tea kettle; >**257** a tiny black mark mixed in with animal tracks in a Documenting Bio-Diversity cabinet display, under a Small Mammal Tracks sign near the top of the third paper from the left; and >**258** with a sorcerer's hat as stains in a photo of a woman with a walkie-talkie on the left wall. >**259** In the gift shop, as carved yellow spheres at the bottom of both sides of a merchandise display across from a photo-pickup area.

DinoLand U.S.A. grounds: >**260** As cracks in the asphalt next to the Cementosaurus, near the Dinosaur Treasures gift shop. >**261** On the back of the statue, on a Steamboat Willie cast-member pin on the right of its fourth hump. >**262** As a half-dollar sized orange rock embedded in the concrete, to the right of the leftmost post in front of Dinosaur Treasures, near the restrooms.

>**263** As small black scales on the back of a red and green hadrosaurus on the Cretaceous Trail. **The Boneyard:** >**264** As a large water stain under a drinking fountain near the entrance. >**265** As a quarter and two pennies on a table behind a fenced area, on the second level by slides in the back. >**266** As a fan and hardhats in a fenced area at the back of the mammoth excavation. **Dinosaur:** >**267** As marks on a tree trunk in a lobby mural. **Finding Nemo—The Musical:** >**268** As blue bubbles, two lit and one drawn, at the bottom left of the stage wall.

Water
Parks

WaterParks

11

12

30

7

Blizzard Beach

Grounds: **>1** The park's eclectic soundtrack mixes summertime tunes with Christmas ditties. It includes "Day-O" (Harry Belafonte, 1956), "Joy to the World" (Three Dog Night, 1975), "Hot Dog Buddy Buddy" (Bill Haley & His Comets, 1956), as well as "Frosty the Snowman" (the Beach Boys version, 1964). **>2** Alternating cutouts of a palm tree and a Christmas-tree-like evergreen decorate fences and railings. **>3** "Snowman's Land" read signs leading to cast-member-only areas. **Entrance:** **>4** "Lift and Drift Tickets" read signs above the ticket booths. **>5** A soft-drink machine displays a silhouette of a snowman drinking a Coke and a St. Bernard with one attached to its collar. **>6** "We'd Love Toboggan With You!" reads a sign in front of a Sonny's Sleds display, just before the Beach Haus gift shop. **>7** "High Prices Low Snow" reads a tag on one of the sleds. Others read **>8** "Sno Down Payment," **>9** "Sliding Prices" and **>10** "Price Freeze." **Alpine Village:** **>11** "Caution: Low Flying Gator" reads a sign behind the women's dressing room, the

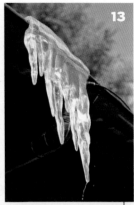

Julie Neal

roof of which has ski tracks from Ice Gator, the park mascot, on its roof. **>12** Apparently he flew over the sign and into the Beach Haus shop, which has a hole in its wall in the shape of his silhouette. **>13** Water drips from plastic icicles that hang from the buildings. **>14** "Sleighbelles" reads the sign for the ladies' room; the men's room is marked "Snowmen." **>15** Ice Gator changes into trunks on a metal sign in front of the dressing rooms. **Beach Haus: >16** Ice Gator's silhouette tops the weathervane. **>17** "No Skis Inside Please" reads a sign on the outside wall. **>18** Apparel and other merchandise displays look like sleighs. **Chairlift: >19** The wait time sign is an old temperature indicator. **>20** Skis extend underneath your feet when you sit in a seat, creating the visual illusion you're actually wearing them. **>21** "Instant Snow—Just Add Water!" read barrels at the exit. **Cross Country Creek: >22** "Ancient" drawings on the walls of the cave include a beach chair with an umbrella, a Yeti, people in tubes and a skier with his leg in a cast. **>23** Colorful Northern Lights shine through the cave ceiling. >**24** "B-r-r-r-occoli," "Chilly Peppers" and "Sleet Corn" are planted in Ice Gator's garden along the creek, just past Manatee Landing. >**25** "Anybody got a hanky?" he asks from within his hut in the middle of the creek. >**26** "I gotta code in by dose," he sometimes adds. >**27** After he sneezes, water spurts out of the chimney and onto unsuspecting floaters. >**28** His dripping gloves and socks hang on a clothes line over the creek. **Melt-Away Bay:** >**29** "Frosty the Joe Man was a Java-happy soul" reads the front of a Joffrey's coffee stand near the pool. The words wrap around a snowman holding a cup of coffee, his arm melting. **Slides:** >**30** Sunshine State Snow Making Co. machines sit alongside Cross Country Creek as well as the queue for the Toboggan Racers mat slide. >**31** Across from the entrance to the Downhill Double Dipper tube slide, melting snow drips off a roof of a shack marked "Safe to Approach Unless Melting." >**32** "Avalanche Above: Look Out Below!" reads a nearby sign, above crates labeled "Dynamite! Explosives! Danger!" >**33** Cowbells announce the start of each Downhill Double Dipper race, replicating those heard at slalom races. >**34** Snowmaking equipment from the Joe Blow Snow Co.— which has the slogan "When You Think of Snow… Think Joe Blow!"—lines the walkways to the Slush Gusher, Summit Plummet and Teamboat Springs slides. >**35**

Its "storm generators" have "Slush," "Cold," "Water" and "Blast" compartments. >**36** Crates of "Polar Island Ice Cubes" have been shipped to the company. **Tikes Peak:** >**37** A snowman (snowperson?) has buried another one in the snow along the left walkway, so only his head and feet stick out. >**38** Other snowpeople are having a snowball fight. One is sticking his tongue out, taunting the others. >**39** A little girl gator perches on skis on the roof of the ice house. **Snack stands:** >**40** "Brrr-everages" are sold at snack carts throughout the park.

Typhoon Lagoon

Entrance road: >**41** "A furious storm once roared cross the sea" >**42** "catching ships in its path, helpless to flee," >**43** "instead of a certain and watery doom," >**44** "the wind swept them here to Typhoon Lagoon" read four separate signs along the entrance road, hinting at the park's backstory. **Entrance:** >**45** Nautical flags atop the park's entrance gate spell out WELCOME TO TYPHOON LAGOON. >**46** Those just to the right read PIRANHA IN POOL. >**47** A key to the flags stands nearby. **Grounds:** >**48** Ramshackle snack stands are patched together from planks and crates salvaged from debris left by a hurricane that has supposedly devasted the area. >**49** Actual boat salvage decorates the roofs and walls of the park's stands and shops. >**50** Old license plates do too. >**51** Lashed ropes create

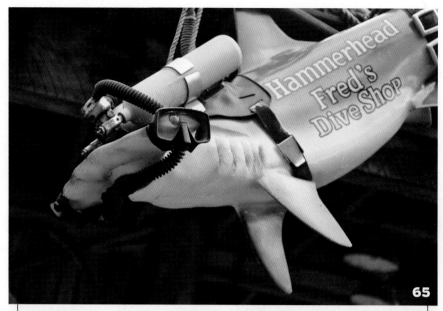

65

66

76

60

96

makeshift railings. **>52** A rocking chair lashed to two barrels has a sign that reads "In Case of Typhoon Cut Rope." It's on the walkway to the Leaning Palms food stand. **>53** The park's ambient music differs by area. Recalling its mythical days as the Placid Palms resort, the grounds that surround the Leaning Palms restaurant feature 1940s big-band tunes, including "Between The Devil and the Deep Blue Sea" (Cab Calloway, 1931) and "Rum and Coca-Cola" (The Andrews Sisters, 1945), the latter one famous in music publishing circles for being "stolen" by actor Morey Amsterdam, who copy-writed it even though actual song-writer Lord Invader had already gained fame with it in Trinidad. **>54** A cappella sea shanties from the 1800s play in the area around the park's saltwater Shark Reef pools. They include "Homeward Bound"*("Oh fare you well my bonnie young lassies. Hurray, my boys, we're homeward bound…")* and the bonnie-young similar "Rio Grande" *("Singin' fare you well, my bonnie young gal. 'Cause your bound to the Rio Grande…")* **>55** "Margaritaville" (Jimmy Buffett, 1977), "Catch a Wave" (The Beach Boys, 1963) and the profound "Surfin' Bird" (The Trashmen, 1963) are among the beach tunes that play throughout the rest of the park. **Castaway Creek: >56** A boat from the Happy Days Cruise Lines has beached itself on the bank of the creek, just past its Starfish Landing. **>57** Sparky, a small fire boat, sprays its hose at you past Snail Landing. **Crush 'n' Gusher: >58** The ride's signs are painted-over salvage from the Tropical Amity (say it slowly) fruit company, which once used these spillways to wash its fruit. **>59** A bent pipe forms the ride's height-minimum bar. **>60** At the bottom of the metal tower, the hurricane embedded a coconut into a sign. **>61** It also snapped several steel beams, drove a tractor's harrower into the structure, crashed another one through its roof and tossed its machinery throughout the area. **>62** "Wash flumes are not to be used for recreational purposes. No horseplay!" scolds a sign listing Tropical Amity's Produce Wash Guidelines. **Ketchakiddee Creek: >63** C-Worthy is the name of an overhanging boat that drips water onto a splash zone. **Shark Reef: >64** Stuck in a shark's jaws, a broken piece of driftwood serves as the sign for the snorkeling pool. **>65** Wearing a dive mask over each of its eyes and a scuba tank on its back, a stuffed hammerhead shark is the sign for "Hammerhead Fred's Dive Shop," the stand that hands out masks and snorkels. **>66** Above the building, the saw (and fins) of a sawfish stick out of a crate labeled Acme Taxidermy. **>67** Cartons of Gatlin Gun ammunition sit nearby. **>68** The building is a bait shop and its dock, left high and dry after the hurricane. **>69** "Shark-proof" cages sit along the queue area. **>70** Impressions of seashells and starfish hide in the

WaterParks

concrete floor of the upside-down tanker, the pools' underwater viewing room. **Surf pool: >71** Water spits out between planks of the pool's "wooden" back wall, as if it's a levee ready to burst. **The Board Room: >72** An alligator totem stands next to this shack, the home of park mascot Lagoona Gator. **>73** A small surfboard forms the flag of the shack's pink mailbox. **>74** Hurricane flags hang above the shack. **>75** Oars form the hands of a damaged clock tower nearby. **>76** Inside the shack is a copy of the Omar Blondahl album "Down to the Sea Again: A Selection of Folk Songs of Newfoundland." Also known as "Sagebrush Sam," Blondahl gained fame in Canada during the 1950s singing long-lost songs of the island. **>77** "How to Get a Golden Tan Without Being Turned into a Suitcase" is the name of an article in an issue of Surfin' Reptile magazine, which rests behind the record. **>78** "So cold blooded, they're hot!" proclaims a poster inside the shack that promotes Lagoona Gator's singing group, The Beach Gators. **>79** The movie "Bikini Beach Blanket Muscle Party Bingo" starred "Lagoona Gator as Freddie and Annette Crocochello as Bee Bee" according to another poster—nods to 1960s beach movies that starred Frankie Avalon and, as Dee-Dee, once-time Disney Mouseketeer Annette Funicello. **>80** Disney imagineers who worked on the shack are honored in the movie's credits: Cayman Lafferty (Kevin Rafferty), **>81** Croc Buzoo (Chuck Ballew) and **>82** Ron Scaly (Ron Chesley). **>83** The Beach Gators appear in the film courtesy of Swampywood Records, a nod to Disney label Hollywood Records. **Mt. Mayday Trail: >84** A lashed-together suspension bridge spans Castaway Creek. **>85** Wedged atop a volcano, shrimp boat Miss Tilly (the park's icon) spouts water at the top of each hour. **>86** Its nautical flags spell out HELP. **Food stands and bars: >87** A boat wedges through the tin roof of the Happy Landings ice cream stand. **>88** Controlled by anyone who walks to them, outboard motors squirt water through their props at helpless floaters on Castaway Creek. The motors hang off a railing in front of the ice cream stand. **>89** Around the surf pool, "Soul Food for Surfers" reads a surfboard-based sign for the hot-dog stand Surf Doggies, a converted three-wheeled scooter. **>90** A baseball tops its gear shift. **>91** Its bell is a tangled wind chime. **>92** Nearby, a faded yellow and red surfboard is lodged completely through a tree. **>93** A surfboard painted like a smiling whale forms the sign of the Let's Go Slurpin' beach bar; painted corrugated tin creates the whale's fins and tail. **>94** License plates from Hawaii, California and Florida line the bar's interior. **>95** A mobile made from a tin coffeemaker hangs from the rafters of a Joffrey's Coffee stand. **>96** Over a dozen tin spoons hang from a tin coffee pot.

▶ Hidden Mickeys

Blizzard Beach: ▶**97** The three-circle shape appears inside the Beach Haus gift ship, as rocks in a painted scene on a light fixture near the changing rooms. ▶**98** The shape also is formed by three rocks on Mt. Gushmore, on a ledge under the chairlift; ▶**99** as three stones on a bridge that spans Cross Country Creek, at the back of the park near the splash pool of Runoff Rapids, topped by a fourth stone that forms Mickey's triangular Sorcerer's hat; and ▶**100** as a large upright raft and two attached small tubes at the exit to Teamboat Springs. ▶**101** Button, the toddler in a snowman family, wears Mickey ears in a photo spot just past the gift shop as you enter the park.
Typhoon Lagoon: ▶**102** The three-circle shape appears on a bridge that crosses Castaway Creek near its Shark Landing entrance, on the bottom of a railing strut; ▶**103** as a hole in the wall of the cave at the kiddie playground

Ketchakiddee Creek, about a foot off the ground, to the left of a drain; and ▶**104** about halfway up the the walkway to the Storm Slides body slides, as an extension of a wooden step across from a lantern, just before an anchor on the right.

99

101

100

Index

50's Prime Time Cafe 224

A
Adventurers Club 56, 58
Adventurers Outpost...................................241
Adventureland 135, 136, 180, 181
Affection Section 243
Africa 230-23
Agent P's World Showcase Adventure............78
American Adventure 18, 124, 191, 193, 195
Animation Courtyard...................................223
Ariel's Grotto 152, 184
Asia..234, 243
Astro Orbiter..175

B
Backlot Express..219
Barnstormer, The..........................158-164, 185
Be Our Guest...152, 185
Beach Haus..247, 253
Beauty and the Beast Live on Stage.............214
Big Thunder Mountain RR.........18, 82-103, 143
Big Top Souvenirs.................154, 155, 172, 173
Blizzard Beach 246-248, 253
Board Room, The..252
Boneyard, The..239, 243
Buzz Lightyear's Space Ranger Spin.....175, 185

C
Canada pavilion 193, 195
Carousel of Progress ..12, 40, 71, 175, 185, 186
Casey Jr. Splash 'n' Soak Station..168-171, 185
Casey's Corner..113, 114
Castaway Creek 251, 252, 253
Chamber of Commerce.................................107
Chapeau, The.......................................107, 108
Chester and Hester's Dinosaur Treasures.....240
China pavilion 193
Cinderella Castle....................................39, 144
Citizens of Hollywood 224
Citizens of Main Street 112
City Hall 107
Columbia Harbour House.............................181
Conservation Station 233, 241, 243
Country Bear Jamboree 18, 19, 36, 70, 140, 141
Cover Story...222
Cretaceous Trail 243
Cross Country Creek 247-248, 253
Crush 'n' Gusher 251
Crystal Arts 112

D
DinoLand U.S.A. 239-240, 243
Dinosaur 239, 243

Discovery Island.....................................228, 230
Disney Outfitters 230
DiVine 231
Downhill Double Dipper...............................248
Drinkwallah..234, 243
Dumbo the Flying Elephant...155, 157, 158, 185

E
Echo Lake 217-219
Electric Umbrella...190
Ellen's Energy Adventure.............................193
Emporium, The 110, 112, 114, 134
Enchanted Tales with Belle..................151, 183
Enchanted Tiki Room........19, 97, 136, 137, 181
Expedition Everest 234, 243

F
Fantasmic 224
Fantasyland..144-185
Fantasyland railroad station 171, 172
Festival of Fantasy Parade..................176, 186
Festival of the Lion King 233
Finding Nemo — The Musical..............240, 243
Flame Tree Barbecue...................................230
France pavilion 195
Frontierland 139-143, 181-182
Frontierland Shootin' Arcade 139, 140

G
Gaston's Tavern 152, 185
Germany pavilion 193, 195
Great Movie Ride, The 62, 213, 224

H
Hall of Presidents, The 76, 137, 139, 181
Harambe village........................ 230-233, 2419
Harmony Barber Shop 107, 114
Haunted Mansion, The.................. 10-51, 60, 72
Hollywood Boulevard...........................213, 224
Honey, I Shrunk the Kids' Playground 223

I
Indiana Jones Epic Stunt Spectacular 219
Innoventions 190, 194
Island Mercantile...230
It's a Small World 12, 71, 119, 120, 147, 183
It's Tough to Be a Bug 228, 230, 241

J
Japan pavilion...195
Jim Henson's MuppetVision 3-D ..220-223, 225
Jingle Cruise...66
Journey into Imagination..............193, 194, 210
Jungle Cruise...52-67

K

Kali River Rapids.............................234
Ketchakiddee Creek..................251, 253
Kilimanjaro Safaris 55, 231, 241

L

Le Cellier 195
Liberty Square 137-139, 181
Liberty Square Riverboat 139, 143
Lights, Motors, Action Stunt Show 225
Living with the Land....................62, 192, 194

M

Mad Tea Party..................................151
Magic Carpets of Aladdin.............135, 136, 180
Magic of Disney Animation, The..............223
Maharajah Jungle Trek...................234, 243
Main Street Bakery 112
Main Street Electrical Parade.............176
Main Street Vehicles.....................108, 178
Main Street windows 116-133
Main Street U.S.A. 104-133, 178-180
Mama Melrose's Ristorante Italiano 225
Many Adv of Winnie the Pooh..48, 149, 151, 183
Memento Mori shop........................50, 51
Mickey's Not-So-Scary Hallown Party....27, 180
Mickey's PhilharMagic.................147, 148, 183
Mission Space............................193, 194
Monsters Inc. Laugh Floor 175
Morocco pavilion 193, 195
Mutoscopes 110

N

New York Street...............................220
Norway pavilion 193

O

Oasis, The 228

P

Pangani Forest Exploration Trail ..231, 233, 241
Pecos Bill Tall Tale Inn and Cafe 98, 141, 142
PeopleMover.................................186
Pete's Silly Sideshow......93, 156, 164-168, 185
Peter Pan's Flight 148, 149, 183
Pirate's Adventure, A 71, 77, 78
Pirate's Bazaar..............................76
Pirates League................................77
Pirates of the Caribbean...............36, 68-81
Pixar Place...................................223
Pizzafari....................................230, 241
Primeval Whirl 239, 240
Prince Charming Regal Carrousel.........144, 146
Princess Fairytale Hall 146, 147

R

Restaurantosaurus...............239, 240
Rock 'n' Roller Coaster 214, 215, 224

S

Seas with Nemo & Friends....190, 192, 194, 210
Seven Dwarfs Mine Train................151, 183
Shark Reef 251
Soarin' 192, 193, 194
Souk-Al-Magreb..............................195
Space Mountain......................175, 176
Spaceship Earth....................190, 191, 194
Splash Mountain 142, 181, 183
Sportsman's Shoppe......................195
Stage 1 Company Store 225
Star Tours...............................200-211
Starbucks...................................112
Storybook Circus 154-173, 185
Streets of America.....................220-223
Sunset Boulevard.................214-217, 224
Sunset Ranch Market......................224
Swiss Family Treehouse..66, 129, 135, 180, 181

T

Tamu Tamu.................................241
Tangled restroom 152, 153
Tatooine Traders 211
Teamboat Springs.........................253
Test Track 194
Tikes Peak 248
Tom Sawyer Island..................143, 143
Tomorrowland 175, 176, 185, 186
Tony's Town Square Restaurant 178
Tortuga Tavern 71, 78, 80
Town Square.......................107-108
Town Square Theater 108-109, 178
Toy Story Mania.................223, 225
Toy Story Pizza Planet Arcade 225
Tree of Life 228, 241
Tune-In Lounge 224
Tusker House.............................233
Twilight Zone Tower of Terror......215, 217, 224
Typhoon Lagoon 248-253

U

Under the Sea.................151, 152, 183, 184
United Kingdom pavilion 193, 195

V

Voyage of the Little Mermaid 223

W

Walt Disney World RR..........109-110, 178, 183
Wishes 176

About the authors

A FORMER WALT DISNEY WORLD concierge supervisor, Julie Neal is the author of "The Complete Walt Disney World" series of travel guides. As such she's spent over 2,500 days at Disney World not counting her time behind the desk. For the production of this "Fun Finds & Hidden Mickeys" book she traveled to Disney nearly every single day for seven months—if there's one thing Julie's an expert on it's how to get around the place. A roller coaster freak and a wildlife enthusiast, she lists Expedition Everest and the Pangani Forest Exploration Trail as her favorite Disney attractions. Her passions outside the world of theme parks include animal rights, reading and old movies.

Julie's husband and coauthor Mike designed the book and took most of the photos for it. As it's been since he first rode it in high school, his favorite Disney attraction is Space Mountain, from the front seat. Outside of work his interests include cheeses, filmmaking and palm trees.

Julie and Mike live in Orlando with their daughter Micaela, who helps out in the family business when she's not scuba diving in the Caribbean or going to school at Florida State. Spending most of her recent summer and winter breaks at Disney, she researched this book's largest sections, including the mega one on The Haunted Mansion. Her favorite Disney attraction: Big Thunder Mountain Railroad.

The Neals share their home with the most important member of their family: Oliver, the world's most cuddly 85-pound rescue dog.